The Scandinavian Option

NORWEGIAN FOREIGN POLICY STUDIES NO. 15

BARBARA G. HASKEL

The Scandinavian Option

Opportunities and Opportunity Costs
in Postwar Scandinavian Foreign Policies

Universitetsforlaget
Oslo - Bergen - Tromsø

B.48.44-003T

ISBN 82-00-01561-0

Cover design by Bjørn Roggenbihl

Printed in Norway by
Universitetsforlagets trykningssentral, Oslo

FOREWORD

The perspective of the informed outsider is frequently needed in order to discern the main features of processes and events in any given country or area. It is only in recent years that Scandinavian scholars have turned to their recent history, not for purposes of writing final or lasting history, but rather with the aim of generating hypotheses about the nature of decision problems which remain on the agenda. However, much of the Scandinavian writing on foreign policy has been normative and prescriptive rather than exploratory and descriptive. Social science discipline has typically been brought to bear on more limited and less dependent processes than those of foreign policy behavior.

It is most valuable therefore that Barbara Haskel has contributed the present study of regional policy interaction on the Nordic level using a systematic social science approach. Her conceptual tools are not too elaborate. They remain tools for analysis rather than linguistic smokescreens for trivial insights. They help her in answering relevant questions rather than substituting for such answers. Her major concepts are derived from economics and decision theory. Cost-benefit calculations constitute, in the view of the author, critical ingredients in foreign policy decision making. But such calculations can be properly understood only in their real situational, historical and perceptual context. Calculations may be less than perfect. Perfect information will never prevail. But there is an inexorable necessity for choice. Non-action is also a choice. Decision-makers try to act rationally in the sense of relating means to ends, risks to costs. "Irrationalities" may enter the picture, but decision-makers seldom if ever succumb to making decisions which are unrelated to considerations of cost, broadly understood.

The logic of high-policy decisions in post-war Scandinavia has militated against common undertakings in the security or market policy areas.
Dr. Haskel explains the calculations which have determined the outcomes at critical junctures in the 1940's and '50's. Interdependence as a state of affairs did not translate into imperatives for joint solutions or integration. The Nordic framework was for a variety of reasons too limited. The Nordic area is part of a larger framework of inter-state relationships. The area performs important functions of delimitation and transition with respect to the East-West division in Europe. In other contexts there is a discernible tension between European and Atlantic perspectives, particularly in the policy making of Norway - - the maritime country of Northern Europe.

Against the background of failures, or abortive attempts, on the level of high policy, Dr. Haskel provides an insightful study of successful low-level integration capitalizing on the cultural and social homogeneity and affinity of the people in Northern Europe.

Hers is a collection of three case-studies drawn together by a conceptual framework. A broader history would have revealed the dialectical relationship between broader participation in a European or Atlantic framework and an intensification of compensatory initiatives on the Nordic level.

If we attempt to gauge the future, and the author does not transcend the safe bounds of empirical investigation for purposes of flimsy prediction, it may be interesting to raise some of the following questions: How heavily will historical memories weigh in the calculations at future junctures? When will memories of the second World War fade in the shadows of more recent events? How will perspectives on different cleavages and functional dimensions in international society other than those which are directly related to the East-West conflict affec priorities and outlooks? Under what circumstances would Scandinavian options become compatible with the logic of the political order in Europe? What will be the long-term dialectical interaction between the configuration of the external environment of which the Nordic States are a part and the indigenous perceptions and propensities which prevail in the Nordic area at any one time? What may be the long-term interaction between sentimental outlooks and realpolitik calculations? Answers to such questions are unavailable, but it is often useful to project such inquiry as a corrective to the assumption that particular decision patterns form immutable iron-laws. The element of human will, and indeed human folly, cannot be ignored.

The Nordic region has remained a stable area in spite of the different roads chosen by the countries therein with respect to high policy. In fact, it may be that the differentiated pattern has provided a more stable situation than would have prevailed in the event that the three core countries had succeeded in implementing joint solutions. Such solutions might have had a disruptive impact on the policies of the peripheral Nordic States, and, particularly, on the policies of the great powers vis-à-vis the peripheral states of Northern Europe. A system of checks and balances, of commitments and constraints, was perhaps more consistent with the "Euro-Atlantic logic" than a Scandinavian community option.

Johan Jørgen Holst

TABLE OF CONTENTS

Chapter THREE:

Chapter FOUR:

Chapter FIVE:

ACKNOWLEDGEMENTS

It is with gratitude and pleasure that I thank the numerous people on both sides of the Atlantic who over the years have spared time and thought to answer questions and provide insights into politics in the Scandinavian countries. Scandinavian politicians in Governments and legislatures, senior civil servants, and others active in public life were extremely generous with their time for interviews. They are listed in the bibliography but I would like to give special thanks to them here. Officials in government, the Nordic Council secretariats, business and labor, were prompt and helpful in replying to requests for information.

My interest in one of the cases, that of the defense pact, was first aroused in a seminar conducted by Professor Nils Andrén of The University of Stockholm. The study expanded into an investigation of the three cases presented here when I wrote a doctoral dissertation at Harvard University in 1972. Professor Stanley Hoffmann has put up with various versions of this subject over a long time; he has influenced this study in ways which he most likely will not recognize. Professor Joseph S. Nye, Jr. gave me encouragement and stimulation. I am indebted to both of them.

Many people, some professional colleagues, others who were sources of information or even occasionally objects of this research took time and patient effort to read and painstakingly comment on previous drafts of part or occasionally all of this book; I am enormously grateful. These include: Nils Andrén, Erik Brofoss, Gustav Cederwall, Mary Dau, Antal Deutsch, Ingemar Dörfer, Knut Getz-Wold, Johan Holst, Donald Horowitz, Christian Lange, Geir Lundestad, Olav Riste, John Sanness, Arne Skaug, and Nils Morten Udgaard. Hans Skoie must be specially mentioned because on his own initiative he sent invaluable collections of newspaper clippings over a long period of time; the discussion of the Nordek proposals of the 1960s owes much to that material. Per-Olav Jonsson was generous in sending me his doctoral dissertation, which provided valuable information on the common market negotiations, as well as detailed letters of commentary. Archivist Erik Norman of the Norwegian Foreign Office was helpful in responding to many queries. It goes without saying that whatever the efforts of these friends and colleagues, errors of fact or interpretation which remain are my responsibility alone.

I am very much indebted to several organizations and institutions which have contributed with great generosity to the undertaking and completing of this study. The Fulbright Program of the United States Government made possible my year's study at The University of Stockholm in 1962-63; Mrs. Catherine Djurklou of the Fulbright Office in Stockholm helped make the year a fruitful one. At various times the Institute for English-Speaking Students and the Swedish Institute of International Affairs, both in Stockholm, as well as the Norwegian Institute of International Affairs in Oslo, provided me with office space and help. Two grants from the Faculty of Graduate Studies and Research of McGill University in Montreal helped in travel and revision expenses. A generous Travel Grant from the Norwegian Foreign Ministry and Information Service made possible a visit to Scandinavia in the summer of 1974. Finally, the Norwegian Council for Applied Research has aided the publication of this book by Universitetsforlaget (Norwegian Universities' Press).

Finally, I own thanks to Mrs. Margaret Blevins and Mrs. Lucy Felicissimo, both of Montreal, for their patience and care in typing the manuscript, and for their kindness to its author.

CHAPTER ONE

THE SCANDINAVIAN OPTION

Is Scandinavia One or Many?

Scandinavia has long been thought of as a distinctive area of the world. Whether talking of the "Scandinavian welfare states" or "Scandinavian design", foreign observers are rarely altogether clear about which country in particular they mean; they usually have a composite picture in mind. Not only do the three Scandinavian countries seem to be characterized by many important cultural, economic, social, and political similarities, and acknowledge a Scandinavian identity, but they also act together to some degree on the world scene in such a forum as the United Nations.

Why is it that they have never formed strong joint organizations as did their neighbors in the European communities? In the post World War II era, the formation of joint institutions among nation-states seemed in the air. Why, given the seemingly propitious wealth of shared characteristics, did these three countries form so few and so weak joint arrangements? Why did several proposals for stronger ones fail to win agreement? This study is addressed to these questions.

In this introductory chapter we shall set the stage both historically and analytically. In what ways do the Scandinavian countries seem similar? What experience have they had in common, and where have their experiences significantly diverged? Have these countries themselves thought of the lack of unified institutions as a problem? What kinds of questions or what analytic perspective might help us examine this failure to create joint institutions? In the following chapters three case studies illustrate the usefulness of the analytical perspective which we shall propose in this introduction.

Contemporary Scandinavia

Before describing the characteristics of the Scandinavian area, it is necessary to pause to explain why the Nordic area - the Scandinavian three plus Iceland and Finland - has not been chosen instead as the potentially integrative area. Iceland and Finland have been excluded from consideration on different grounds. Iceland is omitted for a geographical reason; Reykjavik, the capital of this isolated island-state of 200,000 inhabitants, is 1095 miles from Oslo, the nearest Nordic neighbor. This plus its varied economy -- 80-90% of its exports are fish -- make its security and economic considerations substantially different from those of the other Nordic countries. Finland, on the other hand, is much closer geographically, but excluded here because for the period under consideration - 1945 to about 1960 – it was much more severely restricted in its foreign policy choices, including those choices bearing on relationships with the other Nordic countries, by its special relationship with the Soviet Union, formalized in the 1948 Treaty of Friendship, Cooperation, and Mutual Aid.[1] Therefore, although these two countries share many features of the core three, Denmark, Norway and Sweden, it will be only of those three that we ask the questions, "what drew them together?", "what kept them apart?"

The shared features are both subjective and objective. Such ideas as a "Nordic culture" or "Nordic democracy" or a "Nordic way of life" are used, and have both substantive and emotional meaning in the Scandinavian (and other Nordic) countries.[2] This self-perception seems based on ethnic, linguistic and/or historical ties as well as similarities of contemporary culture in general, and political culture in particular.

The racial and religious homogeneity of the Scandinavian countries is well known. Until recently, there were no large minority groups except perhaps for the Lapps, a nomadic people who range across northern Norway, Sweden, and Finland.[3] Approximately 95% of the populations of each of the three are Lutheran; Lutheran Protestantism is in all three the state religion. Religious divisions have occurred and sometimes have been politically significant, but they have taken the form of fundamentalism and lay movements within Protestantism.

Educated people in the three countries have a relatively easy time understanding the languages, especially the written languages, of the other two countries. Despite differences in construction and in the most common words, they are not much farther from each other than what elsewhere would be called dialects of a common language. Newspapers of one Scandinavian country, for example, are easy for people from the other two to read with some practice. Outside the social group which used to be termed akademiker (those with a university degree), however, people wish to have books and also radio programs in the other languages translated for them.[4]

There are two politically significant language splits, both of which coincide with social divisions. The linguistic division of Finland which has a Swedish speaking minority, is very important but outside our domain. The other politically salient language difference, that between predominantly urban, Eastern Norway and predominantly rural, Western Norway, has been formalized into two distinct and officially recognized variants of Norwegian.[5] Its political organization, and its effects have been intra-national and intra-state.

This is not to say that national language differences do not matter; the objections to several attempts to standardize Nordic terminology show that they do.[6] It is simply that communication for elites should be - considering language alone - easier than among national elites elsewhere in the world.

Collectivist States: Parties and Interest Groups

If one then turns from attributes such as ethnicity or language to elements of political structure and values, there are also major commonalities. The Scandinavian countries are "collectivist" societies, legitimizing disciplined parties and concentrated interest groups. They share as well a political culture emphasizing responsibility and competence.

In contrast with Britain to which the term "collectivist" was first applied, the political scene in the Scandinavian countries is not dominated by two great parties; on one side in each of them has been the Social Democratic party, with from 35 to 50% of the votes, and on the other side until recently Conservative, Liberal, and Agrarian parties, sometimes a religious

Christian party, or other small parties.[7] The major line of division since the 1930s has been the socialist-non-socialist one. However, the post World War I compromises which instituted proportional representation had the effect of "freezing" party formations; the splits among the non-socialist parties of the time persisted. "That great carnivore", the British Conservative Party, has no equivalent in Scandinavia; urban-rural cleavages remained.[8]

Rivaling the enduring and stable political parties is the other normal channel of social representation, organized groups. The Scandinavians call themselves "gjennomorganiserte", literally, "organized through and through", or thoroughly organized. The folkrörelser or "popular movements" of the nineteenth century showed this capacity to organize for such purposes as temperance, adult education, producer and consumer cooperatives, the lay church, or recognition of rural language forms. These movements were closely intertwined with the developing parties, and the use of the term "popular movements" (instead of "pressure groups") carries with it the associations with the growth of democracy.[9] Thus the massive twentieth century economic organizations of workers, employers, and farmers, benefit from a favorable tradition.

It has been argued that the variety of organized groups is no greater than in other industrialized countries.[10] However, distinctive to Scandinavia is the combination of the following characteristics: the legitimacy, density, and centralization of groups, and their systematic incorporation into the legislative and administrative process. Their long standing legitimacy is illustrated by the fact that in Sweden, for example, the legal climate raised few obstacles to association. Unincorporated associations were held to have juridical personalities provided that they had some enduring internal organization. The underlying attitudes have been described as follows:

> The fundamental principle of freedom of association is not based upon the idea that the activities of collective bodies are superior to individual efforts; its underlying rationale would rather seem to be that each individual should be free to choose his allegiance and give his contributions to other individuals.[11]

This combination of the assertion of the supreme worth of the individual with the desirability of collectivities has resulted in a very powerful social norm: that "every man should have his group".

The norm of group representation is reflected in the high "density" of organizations, that is the large percentage of the potentially organizable who, in fact, join. The most striking statistics are those of trade union membership (about 90% of wage earners), in the absence of requirements such as the union or closed shop. Among white collar workers and professionals, elsewhere considered difficult to organize, 70% have joined unions.[12]

Another characteristic of the Scandinavian organizations is their high degree of centralization. While the managed economy encourages (indeed, requires) a large degree of centralization, in Scandinavia the small population of the countries, their unitary structures, and their relatively scarce resources were probably stimuli to organizational centralization in even earlier eras. Almost every type of organization has a national "peak" organization. In the labor market the negotiations between the labor and industrial federations result in "framework agreements" which regulate the settlements for most organized labor; the settlements are, therefore, not merely industry-wide but economy-wide.[13]

In addition to the advisory and quasi-administrative roles which interest groups play in Scandinavia as well as other modern societies, in Scandinavia there is an institutionalized method of consulting such groups, the <u>remiss-yttraden</u>. Relevant ministries and agencies of government as well as interested groups are sent preparatory drafts of proposed legislation for comment. The practice varies somewhat among the countries. In Sweden the comments are published with the legislation; in Norway the sending agency has more discretion in deciding whether or not to publish them.[14] Thus at an early stage interested parties are encouraged to make their views known.

It is the presence of many, varied "dense" centralized interest organizations with regularized and legitimized access to policy makers and administrators, which is characteristic for Scandinavia. The formal "two-tier system of decision-making" has been described by Stein Rokkan, that is first, the electoral-parliamentary-Cabinet line of authority, and second, the quadrangular bargaining among Government, Employers, Employees, and Agriculture over wages, prices, and subsidies.[15] It is supplemented by informal practices such as what for a time came to be called <u>Harpsunds-demokrati</u> -- Harpsund is the Swedish Prime Minister's summer residence where many top level, although unofficial, meetings among government, business, and other organizations have been held.[16] Thus both formally and informally complex norms of consultation are adhered to.

Political Culture: Responsibility and Competence

One may say of the Scandinavian countries what has been said of Holland: there "politics is business".[17] That is to say, it is considered a serious affair. Political leaders talk often of their tasks (oppgave). Representatives or leaders are noted for their "capacity for work" (arbejdsevne) and are praised for being "conscious of their responsibility" (ansvarsbevisst). The favored political style requires that individuals subordinate themselves to their tasks; modesty (beskedenhet) is prized. To be accused of strebermentalitet (the mentality of a striver or status-seeker), or karriärjakt (the chase after a career) is politically pernicious.[18]

If politics is business, it is nevertheless not businesslike in a narrow sense. Scandinavian political thinking is what might be called "sociological thinking": in social and political thought intent and effect are never divorced; society must be responsible for the unintended, as well as intended consequences of its arrangements, for what it neglects as well as what it encourages.[19] "Nondecisions" are understood as also having consequences. The result is to widen the scope of conscious or deliberate decision-making or, in a sense, of politics. Choice of some sort is seen as inevitable. Yet choice must not be arbitrary; it must be made in a context of carefully defined responsibility.

This widened political scope is bounded not only by responsibility, but also by the sphere of the technical, by expertise. Because politics is serious business, effectiveness is valued above expressiveness. For effectiveness one needs practicality and competence (saklighet).[20] Flamboyance is not the Scandinavian style; politics is not "theater".[21]

More so than elsewhere, I believe, politics has been political education. This is still another aspect of what is here called sociological thinking, thinking which emphasizes the interconnectedness of phenomena; the links between policies for the parts and policies for the whole society, for example, have been clearly explained to the public. In the 1930s a kohandel (horse trading, literally cattle trading) or political deal between the Agrarians and Social Democrats enhanced the power of the newly elected Social Democrats in Sweden. The quid pro quo of support for agriculture in exchange for a public works program, was tied together with Keynesian countercyclical theory which made it something more than a bargain at the public's expense. The leading Social Democratic theoretician Ernst Wigforss, "lectured" the Riksdag on the multiplier effect as early as 1932.[22] Likewise, in the 1960s, the "active labor policy" for continuous retraining of workers, was based not only on openly and explicitly argued interconnections between aid to one sector of the community, and benefits to the whole, between job retraining, and effects on the vital balance of payments, but also between social justice and economic development. The successful implementation of the program was due, therefore, not just to sophisticated analysis or expertise, but also to successful political education.[23]

Politics as a serious enterprise, of broad scope, bounded on the one hand by an ethos of political responsibility and on the other by the requirement of competence, and always entailing sustained effort at political education - this characterizes the approach common to the Scandinavian countries.[24]

Nordic Cooperation: The "Web" of Relations

In addition to sharing specific features in political life and political values, the Scandinavian countries have established numerous cooperative arrangements among themselves. The variety of forms of this cooperation, together with the types of measures taken, create a rather distinctive gestalt which one Scandinavian analyst, Nils Andrén, has characterized as a "web" of relationships.[25]

The forms of such relationships are both official and unofficial. Contacts are distinguished by their frequency, regularity, scope, and "density". For example, on the ministerial level, the Foreign Ministers meet twice a year (since 1947) as do the Defense Ministers (since 1956); the following Ministers meet once a year: Justice (since 1955), Communications (since 1960), Finance (since 1963 in connection with the Nordic Council sessions), while Social Affairs Ministers and Education Ministers meet once every other year since 1945 and 1946 respectively, and the Fisheries Ministers once every year or two. If one takes the Norwegian ministries as a rough guide, then in 1955 six out of fifteen met regularly with their Nordic counterparts, in 1960, eight ministries, and in 1965, nine.[26] Regular contact in many functional areas then, is usual. Moreover such contacts are usually "dense", that is, backed up by contacts on several levels, administrative, parliamentary, and (private) organizational, as well as intergovernmental. There are, for example, Nordic administrative committees on agriculture (1961), fishing (1962), atomic energy (1957), social policy (1946), and so on. On the parliamentary level there is a joint Nordic consultative organization called The Nordic Council, composed of members of parliament from each country (mirroring the proportions of the party alignments in the domestic legislatures), as well as members of the governments. The Council, established in 1953, meets annually, but its five permanent committees may now meet between sessions as well. Nearly all aspects of Nordic life and relations sooner or later leave their trace in the Council's records.[27]

Unofficially too, almost every organization of significance (and some without) has ties with its Nordic counterparts. Political parties are included here, especially the Social Democratic parties whose Nordic connections go back to the birth of the Scandinavian labor movement.[28] Foreningen Norden, the Norden Association, established in 1919, includes not only five hundred local branches with individual members in the five countries, but also nationwide organizations (many of them unions or professional or youth groups) as members. This organization (structured, significantly, nationally, and then federated) encourages in all possible ways "closer cooperation among the Nordic countries".[29]

Nordic cooperation falls roughly into three groups, described in 1965 by Christian Lange.[30] In the first category are measures to make Norden one unit in legal and social matters. This includes parallel and reciprocal legislation standardizing certain rights and giving citizens of other Nordic countries many of the same rights as their own. The elimination of customs and passport barriers, the creation of a common labor market, the harmonization of the laws, and the reciprocating of social benefits, all fall within this group.[31] The second group is the development of common projects or coordination of national activities with a view toward specialization or division of labor. The Scandinavian Airlines System is the model here. Some coordination in research and occasional joint research institutions also fall under this heading.[32] The third category is coordination and cooperation concerning Norden's interests vis-à-vis the external world. The Scandinavian caucusing in the United Nations and their cooperation in peacekeeping forces are cases in point. Occasional joint projects abroad such as a hospital in Korea or an education-health complex in Tanzania combine elements of the second and third groups. In later years the coordination of trade positions under one negotiator in the Kennedy Round was extremely successful and led to a demand that other foreign policy matters be treated the same way. When UNCTAD was formed the Scandinavians developed joint position papers in that forum.[33]

The problem of integrative ties in the Scandinavian area might be summed up as the difference between "contacts" which are plentiful, and "commitments" which are few. Against the background of substantial homogeneity, and significant contacts of many kinds and at many levels, why have commitments to joint arrangements been so few? The major Nordic body of the postwar years, the Nordic Council, has only consultative status. The two major diplomatic proposals of the period did not succeed. In 1948 Sweden offered Denmark and Norway the possibility of a joint Scandinavian non-aligned defense pact; the proposal was ultimately rejected. In the second case, a more diffuse one, there were a dozen years of negotiations for what ranged from a common Scandinavian economic market to a free trade area; no version succeeded. By contrast however, a proposal originating at the parliamentary level, for the elimination of personal customs and passport barriers within the Nordic area, a step which was unusual in the early 1950s when it was proposed, did succeed. The remainder of this monograph will be devoted to finding out what sort of explanation one needs to answer the question "why did the first two fail, while the third (and others like it) succeed?"

History, The Ambiguous Legacy

In seeking explanations, some readers will balk at the assumption of substantial similarity. They will argue that the historical experiences of the countries were sufficiently different to explain their hesitations in joining forces with each other.

Indeed, history in Scandinavia _is_ an ambiguous legacy. First, various relatively enduring configurations of states have existed. For a period in the middle ages, Norway, and Sweden-Finland and their possessions, were under Danish rule (with considerable local autonomy) in what was known as the Union of Kalmar (1397-1520), actually a defense union against the German Hanseatic towns. This was the only time the five countries were ever under one sovereign. For the next three centuries the area was split by a Swedish revolt, into an eastern (Swedish-Finnish) state, and a western (Danish-Norwegian) state. Norway was ruled by civil servants from Copenhagen; not until 1811 did it have even its own university. Many differences of governmental organization, administrative practice, and law, in eastern and western Scandinavia, stem from this enduring division.[34]

The Napoleonic era introduced great changes. Denmark, having entered the European wars on the wrong side, lost Norway to Sweden to compensate the latter for having had to cede Finland to Russia. Thus the configuration was at this time: Denmark (left with Norway's old possessions, the Faeroe Islands, Iceland, and Greenland), Sweden-Norway in a joint dynasty, and Finland now administered as a Grand Duchy of the Russian Empire. In the twentieth century further fragmentation ensued: Norway dissolved the union with Sweden in 1905; Finland became independent of Russia in the aftermath of the Russian Revolution and World War I; Iceland, having been separated _de facto_ from occupied Denmark during World War II, became independent in 1944.

The variety of political experiences was compounded by the uneven development of the three core countries. Denmark, in the aftermath of the Thirty Years' War (in which it lost Skåne, the rich agricultural provinces now forming the southernmost provinces of Sweden), reorganized its government as an absolute monarchy with centralized bureaucracy and a new aristocracy. Denmark was the only Nordic country to have a form of serfdom, retained until well into the eighteenth century. The absolute monarchy endured until 1849 when liberal ideas and the demonstration of the 1848 revolutions elsewhere in Europe, and concomitant romantic nationalism, led to the interesting combination in Denmark of a kind of irredentism over Slesvig with a liberal reform constitutional movement. A new Constitution created a co-equal, bicameral legislature, one chamber resting on male suffrage over the age of thirty, the other chamber indirectly elected, with suffrage qualified by property restrictions. Denmark went directly from an absolute monarchy to a relatively modern system based on individual representation.[35]

However, the attempt to incorporate Slesvig, and the ensuing wars with Prussia and Austria, led to the loss of what was, at that time, a third of Denmark's territory and two-fifths of its population.[36] In the reaction which followed, the Constitution was revised restrictively, and the last third of the century was marked by disputes between the King and the lower house where an Agrarian Party was backed by the newly formed Social Democratic Party. Only in 1901 was parliamentarism adopted, and in the period before World War I, proportional representation reforms were enacted. The nineteenth and early twentieth century had been a time of rather extreme political changes in Denmark.

Swedish and Norwegian political developments differed not only from those of Denmark, but from each other as well. The era of absolute monarchy had been brief in Sweden, and the system of estates (<u>four</u> traditional estates including the peasantry, unlike estate systems elsewhere in Europe), had deep roots. Cultural and political influences from the Continent were weaker than in Denmark. In the 1809 constitution a system of checks and balances was instituted but also one of estate representation, which persisted, unreformed, through the eras of both the French Revolution and the 1848 Revolutions until finally in 1867 individual representation and a bicameral parliament was established. Not until after the first World War was parliamentarism finally acknowledged, and then only in exchange for proportional representation, intended to preserve the legislative strength of the Conservatives.[37]

In Norway, on the other hand, the settlement of the Napoleonic wars had been taken as occasion to declare that the Danish king had not been entitled to alienate the Norwegian domain (ceding it to Sweden), and that consequently Norway was now independent and would be governed under a liberal Constitution.[38] This was courageous but only partially successful; after brief fighting, agreement was reached uniting Norway to Sweden in a joint dynasty with a joint foreign policy, but retaining most of the provisions of the new Norwegian Constitution - in effect, a high degree of local autonomy. Perhaps the new King of Sweden, a Bernadotte, was amenable to this because "influenced by the Revolutionary doctrine of natural frontiers", his chief interest in acquiring Norway had been the desire for "one strategic unit which would be easy to defend".[39] The main point here is that in the following years there was a significant disparity in the political conceptions and experiences of Norway and Sweden even within the dynastic Union.

Within Norway itself, over the next ninety years, domestic social and political positions became linked with attitudes toward the Union with Sweden. Conservatives supported the King and Union as a bulwark against the new democratic forces in politics. The Venstre (Left) or Liberal Party fought for parliamentarism and hence against the (Swedish) King and his right of veto. As royal prerogatives became anathema, their foreign policy concomitants became the objects of dispute as well. Parliamentarism was achieved in Norway by 1884.[40] The next twenty years were preoccupied with Liberal opposition to the joint diplomatic and consular services; Union itself was becoming a party-creating cleavage. The Swedish Foreign Minister, banking on the political growth of the Norwegian Conservatives, pursued a wait and see policy.[41] The strategy failed, however, when Christian Michelsen, a member of the more conservative wing within the Norwegian Liberals, decided that the Union issue itself was serving as a distraction from what he conceived to be the real coming need, a joint Liberal-Conservative front against the rising socialists. The sooner the issue was off the agenda the better; he fostered a coalition on the Union issue, bringing the Conservatives around to an anti-Union stand which resulted in the split of Norway from Sweden in 1905.[42]

The ambiguity of Scandinavian historical tradition is indicated by the minor theme which emerged, that of Scandinavian unity. From the 1840s to the 1860s "Scandinavian" movements existed. However, they drew on quite different sources in the different countries. In Sweden Scandinavianism was related to the old imperial dream especially with regard to Finland; its adherents, therefore, tended to be inflexible in Union disputes with Norway.[43] In Denmark, "Scandinavians" hoped for aid in the border dispute with the Germans.[44] "Student-scandinavianism" flourished until 1864, when political Scandinavianism died because neither Norway nor Sweden were able to aid Denmark against Prussia.

The events of 1864 set off a reaction against what came to be seen as <u>punschskandinavism</u> (the rhetorical flourishes common in toasting with <u>punsch</u>). New efforts (often undertaken by those from the older movement) turned toward less spectacular arenas, now considered more practical. Some of the old "students" became involved in legal cooperation. A currency union was established among the three countries, and, for a dozen years, also a customs union between Norway and Sweden.[45] The "folk high school" movement and the cooperative movements also kept feelings of Nordic brotherhood alive. The Scandinavians lowered their sights. The ideal which developed is expressed in the following quotation, actually from the nineteen-thirties but equally representative of the dominant attitudes in the nineteen-fifties:

> We have never been subject to any illusions about a fusion (among the Scandinavian states) which eliminates all reasons for friction; we have not dreamed of new unions which would make Scandinavia into a Great Power in the usual sense; we do not speculate about defense pacts and such things. What we strove for and are striving for, is nothing other than a trusting and practical cooperation without any encroachment on the various countries' independence.[46]

In general, this was what one might call "Scandinavianism without illusions".

While World War I did not lead to a joint defense or foreign policy, the three Scandinavian countries did issue a joint declaration of neutrality. Since all three remained territorially intact (although economically scathed), the issue of solidarity among them never became acute. In the 1930s however, as storm signals from the Continent became ominous, there were feelers from Denmark. Stauning, the Danish Social Democratic Prime Minister noted publically in 1933 that Denmark's southern border was also "the boundary of Norden (the Nordic area)", a hint which met strong opposition from Norway, a cold shoulder from Sweden (and, it should be added, opposition within Danish pacifist circles as well). Overtures from Denmark to Britain were clearly rejected. By 1937 there were no more expectations by the Danes. Stauning, responding in a public address in Lund (Sweden) to Swedish press criticism of Denmark's (non-existent) defense capability, asked rhetorically whether Denmark had been given the task of being a "watchdog" for Norden, and answered that other considerations besides Norden must be weighed in Denmark's defense policy decisions.[47]

To those who emphasize the divisiveness of Scandinavian history, the experience of World War II is central; only Sweden of the three countries, all of which had attempted to stay neutral, managed to remain outside the conflict. The effects of the war will be a central issue in the next chapter. It may be noted here, however, that some of the most visionary ideas of Nordic unity emerged precisely during the war,[48] although they mostly developed in Sweden and Denmark, where the frustrations of being unable to fight back were immense, rather than in Norway, whose Government was in exile and one of the Allies.

The conclusions one can draw from this brief survey begin with the observation that historical development in Scandinavia has meant growing away from each other. History has long since come to mean the "record of the national past",[49] as the national historiographies have shown. Secondly, even in periods when some or all of the countries have been jointly ruled, what looks like "common history" _sub specie aeternitatis_ has rarely been common experience.

However, this having been said, and the conclusion having been drawn that the legacy of history in Scandinavia has been more divisive than unifying, does this vitiate the argument that the countries are substantially similar, or does it preclude their unification? The undifferentiated concept of historical differences is difficult to use analytically. No two countries have identical histories. (Frequently, as we have seen, even parts of the same country do not share the "same" history.) If no two histories are alike, we will always have an explanation for non-cooperation or be left with the uniqueness of each case. What we need to know is what elements in the historical experience are important for which particular behavior in the present; in what way will these elements become relevant when choices are posed? Unless such connections are specified, it is legitimate to consider the problem unsolved, or to hope to incorporate historical factors into a more precise explanation.

Why So Few and Weak Joint Institutions?

Two Possible Approaches

Community Formation

Two approaches to the problem of institution formation have been common in the literature. The first, a theory of the social environment favorable to institution building, has been described by its originator, Karl Deutsch, as "market research for regional or international government".[50] The favorable environment, "community", is described in his seminal work on the formation of national communities, Nationalism and Social Communication, as shared values, preferences, memories, aspirations, loyalties, and is indicated by characteristic patterns of quantitatively intense and qualitatively varied and rich communications.[51] International or regional community formation is modeled, then, on national community formation. Deutsch is careful to explain that he is interested not solely in numbers of "transactions" (although they indicate the salience of the relationship to the parties), but also in their "covariance", the degree to which rewards vary jointly. (This is intended to exclude clearly exploitative relationships where interchange brings benefits to one party as a function of losses to the other.) Deutsch argues that "...the acceptability of a particular institution will not depend primarily upon the intrinsic merits of this institution itself but rather upon the context of community perception based on previous transaction flows and the previous experience of reward".[52] This addition of the requirement of favorable "perception" is a major modification. The relationship between previous transaction flows and the inferences which will be drawn from them is disrupted. More precisely, it is made to depend upon previous "experience", which combines the actual fact of joint reward (or deprivation) with the subjective appreciation of it. The relationship between a sense of community and numerous transactions is still, then, a contingent one.

Donald Puchala, whose work is largely in this same tradition, emphasizes, however, that "saying that the presence of community implies the presence of intense communications is not the same as saying that the presence of intense communications implies the presence of community",[53] and warns that "community formation" and "regional integration" are "neither semantically synonymous, conceptually congruent, nor empirically inseparable"; while the theory of community formation is modeled on (Deutsch's) theory of nationalism, the theory of joint institution building should be modeled on a theory of federalism,[54] (implying deliberate decisions).

We would argue here that what Deutsch should be saying is not "perception" but appreciation, or evaluation or assessment. Is this just a matter of semantics? The distinction is that these terms, all in the language of (intended) rational choice, all imply comparison, comparison not only of the past with the present, which is what Deutsch discusses, but also of one set of rewards, current or potential, with rewards from other opportunities current or imagined, the fruits of one possible course of action with those of other possible courses of action.

There is one set of circumstances where this modification would be relatively unimportant: where a community has been long established and stable, and where there has been a process of "institutionalization",[55] the attachment of value to an arrangement itself, comparisons with alternatives may be inhibited or counteracted. But this is highly unlikely at the point of initial decisions. To the extent that Deutsch is interested in "market research" for institutions, then his hypothesis is incomplete. Perhaps what may one day tie together the concepts of community formation and regional integration is a concept of decision which includes comparison. In any event, for our current understanding of how organizations are established, the assumption of constant comparison of alternatives must be made.

"Neofunctionalism"

The "neofunctionalists", Ernst Haas and others, are nearer to our concerns. They are interested in two questions: why joint institutions giving significant powers to a common organ were able to be formed among some countries at a particular time, and not among others at other times; and what the likely or possible consequences of such institutions are for the relationships among the constituent members. The major part of their theory - and the part which has stimulated the most interest - has been the latter. The establishment of organizations which have an institutionalized spokesman for the common interest and which are given specified power, has been used as a benchmark for the investigation of change, change in the authority of the organization, and change in the relationship of the members to the organization. Haas' original work on the European Coal and Steel Community centered on the unique powers given to its joint organs and to the process this seemed to generate, a dynamic of "unintended consequences", stimulating new group expectations, and leading to the "spillover" of authority into functional areas beyond those originally included, thus strengthening the organization.[56]

Haas linked the establishment and development of strong joint institutions to a "background condition" he considered important: "pluralism". Pluralist societies were modern industrialized societies with functionally specific, universalistic, and achievement oriented groups. It was these groups, as well as the governments themselves, which might have interests which could be allied across borders. Networks of converging interests below governmental level could affect governmental bargains as well.[57]

Since the organization which <u>has</u> been established in Scandinavia, the Nordic Council, is solely consultative and thus would not meet any of the criteria of the neofunctionalists, this aspect of the theory is of little help. (The one case which seemed to bear some resemblance to Haas' spillover conception, the strategy for the elimination of customs and passport barriers among the Scandinavian countries, will be investigated in chapter IV.)

Haas did address himself directly to the <u>formation</u> of joint organizations although this was a relatively minor theme in his work. He analyzed the calculations of the parties and suggested that one could distinguish two kinds of formative agreement; <u>identity of aims</u> (identical demands based on identical reasoning patterns), and <u>convergent expectations</u> (expectations based on reasoning patterns peculiar to each of the groups but resulting in sufficiently similar aims to support an agreement).[58] It was argued, for example, that the European Coal and Steel Community was the result of converging interests and expectations (between France's wish to control

Germany and Germany's wish for equal status), rather than identical ones. This was not solely an observation on this particular case. The conceptual distinction between identical and converging aims was made in order to counteract the tendency to argue, almost tautologically, that fundamental, implicit agreement is what creates negotiated agreement. Compared to traditional arguments in foreign policy analysis, Haas' argument, while concerned with deliberate governmental decisions, de-emphasized the "initial degree of commitment" required.[59] The "unintended consequences" of initial commitments might enlarge the parties' commitments at a later stage.

It is this aspect of Haas' work, the focus on the initial calculations, which needs elaboration. Haas and his coworkers devoted much effort to exploring the background conditions which facilitate the establishment and more especially the growth of joint organizations. They have investigated, for example, the question of whether in non-pluralist societies, other attributes may take the place of pluralism.[60] We shall focus on the other element, the initial aims of the parties and the calculations which lead to them. We shall examine the interaction of the parties' strategies of negotiation in an effort to explain the outcome, in the Scandinavian cases, negative, of negotiations for common organizations.

To explain this approach we must make a more general argument. Mancur Olson has suggested that it is useful to distinguish two questions: "why do states (or individuals, or groups) want what they want?" <u>and</u> "given what they want, how do they strive to achieve it?" This sounds like the traditional distinction between goals and means. But Olson is interested in emphasizing something else. He argues that our intellectual tools for answering the first question stem primarily from the tradition of sociology, which seeks the "determinants" of behavior. (We might add that the tradition of psychology is similar.) Our tools for answering the latter question stem chiefly from economics, which is a theory not of determinants but of choice, or, as Olson puts it, "the analysis of advantage".[61] It is the burden of this study that <u>both</u> questions must be asked to account for decision outcomes which are strategies or negotiating positions: it is the interaction of these strategies which in turn will account for the outcome of negotiations. The formation, or lack of formation of joint institutions may be analyzed in this way. In our study we shall treat decisions to establish (or not to establish) joint institutions, to act jointly (or not to act jointly) all as instances of foreign policy decisions in general. Within this our focus will be primarily on what might be called the "logic" of the decision situation, that is, the dilemmas confronting decision makers. This is in contrast to focussing primarily on the "perceptions" of the decision "environment"; it is just as well to explain this choice at this point.

The Rejection of a "Perceptual" Framework

Recent studies of foreign policy have leaned heavily on the concept of "perception".[62] Let us see why this would be unsatisfactory for our purposes. To perceive is defined in two ways in the dictionary: to obtain knowledge through the sense, to see, hear, etc.; and to apprehend with the mind, to understand. The literature on the psychology of perception has dealt with perception in the first of these meanings, and it is this literature which has stimulated political scientists.

The basic problem with the concept of perception in the analysis of policy can be illustrated by an example: an historian has contrasted the ideas and styles of behavior of two leaders, a Prime Minister and a Leader of the Opposition. Both, he says, "advanced the heterogeneity of the...people as a major justification of his special form of leadership".[63] Yet those conceptions of leadership were quite opposed, one a consensus style, emphasizing what was shared, and expecting changes to be slow, the other seeing leadership as above the divisions of the nation, pursuing the national interest on its behalf. The main point is that the inferences each drew from the same "perception" of the national population were quite different; in fact these inferences were, we would argue, really different strategies for dealing with the same "fact", heterogeneity. In studying decisions or policies and their explanations one must be aware that perceptions and the inferences from them are rarely well distinguished. In addition, statements of "perceptions" are frequently used strategically.[64]

The example illustrates still another way in which the concept of perception is inappropriate. Although the language of perception and image encourages us to think in terms of the "objects of perception", what are frequently referred to and what are often of most consequence, are relationships, often contingent relationships (such as those in this example, between a leader and his followers). In general, conceptions (such as a desirable role in the world for one's state, or the possibilities for effective leadership of that state) do not "flow from" perceptions as some have suggested.[65]

It is not that the important work on perceptual problems, or for that matter other psychological regularities in the decision process, should be ignored. They should not, especially since they uncover patterns of behavior which would be hidden from the perspective of deliberation or purposiveness. It is rather that these perceptual problems should be treated as deviations from or qualifications of deliberate decisionmaking, not as substitutes for it.[66]

Perceptual data, as well as the analysis of attributes (historical, sociological, geographic, economic), help one to answer the first of Mancur Olson's questions: "why do nations want what they want?" or "why do they believe what they believe?" However, his second question - "given what they want, how do they strive to achieve it?" - uses the information thus derived, plus an analysis of the decision situation. The focus of this study shall be on the latter question, and will introduce material from the former - what the countries "were like" or what they had experienced - only as it bears on that question.

The "Costing" Perspective

The focus of this study, then, shall be what might be called the "logic" of the decision situation. By decision situation is meant the circumstances in which national decisionmakers find themselves insofar as they are acting in their official roles, insofar as they are trying to decide what the "national interest" requires. This approach asks what questions they would have had to have asked (in such a role), if they had proceeded rationally. It begins, then, by the "analysis of advantage" from their situation, if not (yet) from their perspective.[67]

Next it attempts to ascertain, from the best evidence available, what answers to these questions the actual decisionmakers seem to have given (explicitly or implicitly). Thirdly, it asks: why did they answer this way? One works, therefore, from situation to perspective on it.

Raymond Bauer suggests that "...policy formation is a social process in which an intellectual process is embedded".[68] Much current literature or decision making has emphasized the social process. It has been argued persuasively, for example, that bureaucratic bargaining or the quasi-automatic processes or organizations often have more to do with the decision outcome than do (imputed) rational calculations.[69] Such alternative approaches have been extremely useful checks on and correctives to the more or less rational "unitary actor" decision-making model which tended to dominate the field. They caution us not to attribute intention too quickly and casually to all behavior, to avoid misreading ambiguous incidents as tactical choices, or every detail as if it were the calculated decision of an omniscient and Machiavellian strategic intelligence. Conversely, they help alert us to the systematic nature of what from the viewpoint of the decision-maker appears simply to be "accidental". Ultimately, however, these approaches are supplements to, not alternatives to, the traditional rational model, in that the major questions of political or strategic choice still seem most completely answered by reproducing calculations appropriate to that model.

This study returns to the traditional model, attempts to use it self-consciously instead of implicitly, and reverses the emphasis in Bauer's view: <u>the intellectual process of decision-making is viewed as the core, and the social process is examined as, and only as, it seems to have affected that intellectual process</u>. From this it should be clear that all the traditional sources of data can be and are usable. One goes to history, geography, political institutions, convention, or behavior whenever necessary. It is not <u>what</u> is used but <u>how</u> it is used, which is different. One does not, then, choose in advance which 'factor' to trace, but rather looks for indications of what has been selected in answer to which questions, how it has been used, by whom, and at what point in the process.

Attributes, whether similarities or differences, do not, in and of themselves, determine a relationship. No characteristics of individual countries, or of the relationship among them, can determine by themselves decision outcomes. Two classic theoretical paradigms, polar models of "integration", illustrate this point as Mancur Olson points out. The economic model, based on a division of labor, implies the meshing of complementary differences:

good ground for integration would be disparities; "opposites attract". The sociological model, based on the idea of socialization to identical wants, implies the ease of assimilation of the familiar; good ground for integration would be similarities; "birds of a feather flock together". The problems which both of these models have faced can be explained by the omission of costing.[70]

Just specifying attributes omits "costing", that is, decision-making in which alternative opportunities are considered. Such opportunities are in part, a function of the individual units or of the set of units under consideration. They are also a function of the decision situation and the alternatives available in it. Alternatives must, of course, be 'seen' and appreciated. Conversely, 'unrealistic' alternatives can be constructed. It is clear that the subjective understanding is a crucial intervening factor. But the assumption of this investigation is that there is usually a reasonably strong relationship--although not one to one--between the decision situation and the decision-maker's discerning of it. This is not to say that they choose correctly but that it makes more sense to begin by assuming a strong relationship of perception or discrimination to reality--and then noting any distortions and accounting for these--than by assuming the opposite.

Therefore we shall begin with the decision situation of the Scandinavian countries and with their "costing" of those situations. We shall, of course, make use of their attributes. From this point of view, for example, their major historical experiences may be considered as resulting in important attributes (political configurations, alliances, allegiances, expectations and fears,[71] memories of rewards and punishments, and so on). Clearly such attributes will affect costing in a given situation. The question is, then, how far can we get without resort to history for an explanation? When, and for what purposes must it be brought into the explanation? The point is not to ignore history, but to bring it into the explanation self-consciously, not globally but specifically to explain particular pieces of the puzzle.

To take an example from our own cases: many conventional explanations of Norway's choice of Nato in preference to a proposed Scandinavian defense pact "explain" the decision by Norway's experience of "the war". As we view it, the first questions to be posed should be: 'how much - or what aspects - of the decision can be accounted for according to the logic of decision-making for Norwegian national leaders given the decision situation in 1948-1949? If the second world war was crucial to this decision, in exactly which way or ways? Which aspects of the wartime experience? In answering what questions? 'How much can be accounted for' signals that this is not a description of "what actually happened". Nor is it stated in terms which would <u>necessarily</u> be those participants would have used at the time. (Since most decision-makers at least intended to be rational, however, there will be some, perhaps frequent, coincidence.)

Choice and Cost

Either "decision" or, more broadly, "policy" (in the sense of a commitment to or intention to sustain some degree of predictable behavior) are useful concepts only where there is the possibility of choice; without choice there can be acceptance but not decision and not policy. The idea of choice is the heart of the economic paradigm of behavior. The "necessity of choice" (to cite the title of a well known book about foreign policy) is a logical deduction from (1) the fact of scarcity and (2) the assumption that the chooser wants 'more rather than less of whatever good or combination of goods he prefers. Scarcity--less than unlimited supply in relation to wants (or needs, or what economists call preferences)--may pertain to any resource: time, energy, expertise, skill, attention, for example, as well as to material resources. If one assumes scarcity, and if those wants can be ranked in order of preference, then alternative 'packages' or combinations of satisfactions, can be specified. Different courses of action to produce these different packages can then be imagined. The problem of choosing becomes one of assigning net values or payoffs (expected gains minus expected costs), calculating the probabilities associated with each alternative course, and choosing that with the highest combined value and probability.

This <u>logic</u> remains the same in principle, even when the values cannot be specified quantitatively. It is a general method of analysis. Having said this, it is just as well to acknowledge that where the common measuring rod of money (or comparable units) is lacking, while the logic does not change, the ability to predict unique outcomes does. It has been argued by critics that this makes such an analytical perspective merely "metaphorical".[72] It does, except not "merely". The claim, here, is that before we have exhausted the metaphor we have gained considerable insight into the decision dilemmas we are investigating.

The mental stance described here is worth emphasizing. It is one of anticipation, conjecture, of mental rehearsal of the possible outcomes of alternative courses of action, their payoffs (positive and negative) and their likelihood (risk, uncertainty, or certainty).[73] The time is always "before", the calculations always in advance of expected outcomes. What are being compared are probable futures.

Everyone knows that choosing involves assessing the benefits and costs of various alternatives. But it needs to be emphasized that costs are not separate from, but rather the reverse side of, benefits. To understand why, let us note the change in the very concept of cost in the history of economic theory.[74] In Adam Smith's writings, costs were "resource-outlays", what was expended in the attaining of one's object. Costs were what one "spent". But modern economic theory underlines that the reason that 'spending' or 'paying' has such a central place is that once spent, resources cannot be used for other things. Using up resources really means that the individual must foreclose other lines of action, other choices. The true meaning of 'cost' is thus taken to be the best alternative which has been foreclosed by the fact of choice.

This concept, which is termed the _opportunity cost_ of a decision, is defined as "the decision-maker's own evaluation of the enjoyment or utility that he anticipates having to forego as a result of selection among alternative courses of action".[75] The point is that alternatives are not some sort of entities with costs and benefits "attached" to them, but are rather alternative _courses of action_, the choice of any one of which forecloses others. Another way of saying that is that _the opportunity cost of following one course of action is the anticipated net benefit of the next best, foregone, alternative course of action_.

It is for this reason that this economic perspective has been termed (by Olson) "the analysis of _advantage_" (emphasis added): it is always _com-_

parative. Comparison suggests, in turn, a relatively refined question: from those courses of action available, which is likely to result in the best package of desired goods? It does not ask, for example, the frequently asked and usually oversimplified questions: will this help me or hurt me, is this for me or against me, is this a "tool" (to gain what I want) or a "threat" to me.[76] All of these questions structure the choice in advance as polar extremes. They exclude in advance the possibility that one may be comparing "good" with "better" (or "bad" with "worse" for that matter). The calculation may be, instead, that one course is good (not a threat but a promise) but not so good as another course when their expected outcomes are compared. In the chapters which follow the logic of decision-making in particular decision situations, and especially the self-conscious use of the concept of opportunity costs, will be shown to be useful in accounting for foreign policy decisions, which were rarely questions of good and bad but, since politics is the art of the possible, of better and worse.

Before proceeding to our cases, however, it is useful to be clear about some of the most general reasons for the significance, in the analysis of social decisions, of the concept of opportunity costs. First, if one is interested in the interplay between the intellectual and social processes involved in decision-making, attention to (opportunity) costs and benefits helps focus on the former and relate it to the latter. The imputed intellectual process is costing but the content of the expected benefits, costs, risks, uncertainties, is "social" in the broad sense, i.e. influenced by history, geography, social and political customs and forms, by institutions, reference groups, group psychology, and also by the psychology of individuals. Deviations from the imputed logic as well, will be affected by these factors.[77] Thus the concept of opportunity costs ties together the intellectual and social processes.

Secondly, the concept is important because it helps the analyst to take the environment into account in a systematic, rather than an ad hoc way. It has the virtue of requiring a scanning of the environment in terms of alternative possibilities for action. This compares for example with scanning in terms of a priori distinctions which may or may not be useful. One such distinction is the distinction between internal (domestic) and external (foreign) environment, categories which actually may be misleading since it is often the conjoined impact of domestic and foreign "factors" which is significant. In the view proposed here we would ask instead: what will be the potential responses of elements in the environment or of combinations of them (e.g. foreign powers, domestic clientèles, _or_ the reactions of domestic groups _to_ the reactions of foreign powers) _if_ a certain course of action is undertaken, _compared to_ their potential responses _if_ other courses are taken. A variety of _contingent relationships_ is, therefore, explored.

Thirdly, the concept of opportunity costs alerts us to the possible connections between what have come to be called "issue areas". The process of decision-making on any single issue is _not self-contained_. In foreign affairs the relations among nations are not like "a game" but like many simultaneous games, some with the same sets of players, and others with different players. (Domestic politics can also be seen as a set of different games.) Geoffrey Vickers makes the most general statement of this point when he writes:

> Each solution...is appraised not merely as a solution to the problem which evoked it, but also for its impact on other problems which it may make easier or harder of solution. Thus _the criteria by which one solution is preferred to another cannot be derived merely from the problem set_. (Emphasis added.)[78]

If the "problem set" does not contain all the criteria for decision, one needs some concept that will help take into account _the environment "external" not only to the state, but to the particular game or issue under consideration_.[79] Opportunity costs is such a concept because it involves comparing courses of action in terms of their net benefit which in turn may reflect their impact on other issues or concerns. One must select from the (objective) environment that subjective environment which one believes to have been relevant to the decision-makers. (This selection is, of course, open to challenge.) There are no _a priori_ criteria of relevance to help in the selection of environmental influences or of decision-makers' concerns, _but_ there are some restrictions: the analyst must be able to argue convincingly for the relationship of those elements he selects _to the costs_ of the various possible alternative courses open to the decision-makers. It is this latter requirement which makes this analysis systematic.

Fourthly, the concept may be helpful in narrowing the intellectual gap between the scholar and the policy maker, without reducing the scholarliness of the former. Charles Frankel has put the dilemma of the psychological distance between insiders and outsiders this way: "The difference (between the scholar and the policy maker) is between being able to focus undistractedly on the essence of an issue and having to pay attention to all the accidents that surround it."[80] The concept of opportunity costs gives the scholar a handle for including those "accidents" in his analysis.

Finally, the costing perspective as a whole, although focussing on subjective evaluations of future possibilities, can be connected to changes in objective conditions. John Harsanyi's discussion of social change as the result of choice processes is relevant here: "...social values change basically for the same reasons that human behavior in general does: they change because there is a shift, real or apparent, in the balance of the advantages associated with alternative forms of behavior."[81] The "real" or "apparent" changes in the balance are, thus, the incentives for change in behavior, including choice-behavior. Those incentives are reflected in the changing opportunity costs associated with a course of action.

To apply this more specifically to politics, we might formulate the point this way: changes in the relevant aspects of the environment beyond a certain point make it probable that some of the decision-makers (<u>or</u> their advisers, <u>or</u> their political opponents) will perceive the change and assess the potential significance of those changes with respect to the alternatives open to them. This might be thought of as the 'mounting casualty rate' model: at some point the accumulated casualties in a war are likely to shift the benefit-cost calculations. However, that point may differ among decision-makers, among members of the public, or between decision-makers and their publics. Appraisals and reappraisals may well be subject to time lags for cultural, motivational, or organizational reasons. The main point, however, is that changes in the objective environment are likely to 'induce' a series of subjective recalculations.

The following chapters will reconstruct three cases in postwar Scandinavian relations in which opportunities arose and decisions had to be made as to whether or not to join together for common purposes. They will show the usefulness of the costing perspective in explaining the decisions made, and the advantages of the concept of opportunity costs in taking into account the domestic and especially external environments. The first, the case of the attempt at a Scandinavian defense pact, defines a country's "fall-back position" as the appropriate measure of opportunity cost, and argues that it helps us to explain, for example, Norway's decision not to join such a pact, and hence the failure of the pact to materialize. The second, the case of extended negotiations for a Scandinavian common economic market, argues that the negotiating strategies of the countries were related to major disparities of strength among them. However, an account of such strategies alone, without reference to their opportunity costs, would not permit explanation of either the phases of the negotiations or their ultimate outcome. Finally, the case of the successful reduction of personal customs, passport regulations, and other restrictions in the communication among the Nordic countries, was one in which reformers managed deliberately, gradually, and successfully to reduce the opportunity costs to the Governments, of their proposed reforms, in comparison with the _status quo_, thus creating incentives for agreement among them. The most striking achievement, that of a _de jure_ common labor market was the result of its cheapening - or changing marginal utility - relative to other issues in Scandinavian diplomacy.

CHAPTER TWO

A CRITICAL COMMITMENT: THE CASE OF THE PROPOSED SCANDINAVIAN DEFENSE PACT

A nation's foreign policy is seen both by those creating it and by those observing it as entailing commitments. This may be a commitment to some country in particular, as in an alliance or alignment, or it may be a commitment only to a particular stance, as in non-alignment, but it is always a commitment to some degree of predictability of behavior. Such commitments are critical in the sense that they are "character-defining"; one differentiates them from routine decisions by their effects on subsequent behavior.[1]

Once a critical commitment has been made, other decisions are evaluated among other ways in terms of their effect on it, and conformity with it is highly valued. That is why the credibility of a commitment or policy, which is really a question of its predictability for others, is so frequently treated by policy makers as a question of consistency. The commitment or policy comes to have an almost "constitutional" status; it becomes the yardstick against which other policies are measured. As with a constitutional principle, interpretive decisions and precedents as well as formal declarations define its meaning; it develops as well as is created.

Part of establishing a policy is distinguishing it from other models; the varieties of alignment and of non-alignment, for example, testify to this. Again, as with a constitution, the locus of interpretation becomes important; in defending the credibility of the policy, one method will be a fight for autonomy in interpretation, both vis-à-vis other nations, and vis-à-vis domestic opposition.[2] The Foreign Office especially will come to see itself as the guardian of credibility.

The very fact that two countries have different basic policies makes a relationship or a set of negotiations to some extent competitive. There need not be "goals" in conflict. Even if neither state is proselytizing for its policy, even if each renounces all intention of converting the other state and even if its spokesmen come close to saying that the other state's policies may be best for it, the situation is inherently competitive whenever it is the case that what enhances the credibility of one state's policy diminishes the credibility of the other's.

The sense in which a critical commitment sets limits to future decisions is not absolute. Credibility is, after all, only one among several considerations. There is leeway for creative invention and skillful diplomacy in interpretation of the meaning, circumstances, and limits of a commitment.[3] Nevertheless, the fundamental policy creates a strain in a certain direction, a tendency which must be outweighed by strong counter-reasons. The major consequence of the critical commitment is that the policy itself becomes an element in the costing process in subsequent decisions.

This chapter will examine the establishment of critical commitments, the choice of Denmark and Norway to ally with the West, and the reaffirmation of Sweden's hundred and fifty year old neutral stance. In the period of late 1947 to early 1949 several security options developed for the three countries. A Swedish proposal of a defense pact to the other two in May of 1948 exposed the choices for each. Why did Sweden offer the pact? Why did Denmark prefer to accept? Why did Norway choose NATO rather than the Scandinavian pact? We shall split the question of why each country came to the decision it did, into two parts. First, what were the common issues each of them had to address? Second, on what premises were their divergent judgments based? Our argument will be that their differing assessments of three crucial issues resulted in differing subjective opportunity costs and caused the failure of the defense pact negotiations.

First, however, we need to describe briefly the policies, events, and negotiations of the period, and to examine the explanations offered by other writers. It should be underlined here that it is not the intention either in this brief description or in the analysis which follows to rewrite a history of this time, but rather to draw on the historical accounts now available[4] and using our own method of analysis to deal with the question of why a joint Scandinavian defense organization failed to come into being. Our account should not conflict with what is known historically, but will be deliberately selective.

A Brief Chronology

Points of Departure: Not United but Parallel

The major events of the early postwar years and their cumulative impact - what came to be called "bipolarization" - are too well known to need description here. The end of 1947 had seen stalemate over Germany, the Truman Doctrine, the Marshall Plan in which Eastern Europe had refused to participate, the growth of sizable domestic Communist parties in France and Italy - in general, increasing tension between East and West.

Despite the fact that until this point Denmark, Norway, and Sweden all had pursued policies of refusing to "choose sides",[5] the reactions of the three to Bevin's famous speech of 22 January 1948 hinting at a Western European grouping, revealed differences of nuance among them. These differences were to be indicative of future political attitudes and assessments. Swedish Foreign Minister Östen Undén's was the first formal reaction; in an important foreign policy speech to the Riksdag he said, "...We do not want, through prior commitments, to deprive ourself of the right and possibility of remaining outside a new war."[6] Danish Prime Minister Hans Hedtoft was quoted as rejecting involvement in blocs, although, he added, he doubted that any Scandinavian country would reject Bevin's "thoughts" in advance.[7] But Norwegian Foreign Minister Halvard Lange, addressing the Storting on 12 February underlined that Scandinavian cooperation was not such that one automatically spoke for all. Norway's assumption was that world antagonisms could be overcome. If this proved wrong, Norway would have to reconsider seriously its present position.[8]

Thus the three countries started from parallel "no-participation-in-blocs" policies. Only Sweden, in this period, took specific cognizance of the existence of blocs both inside and outside the United Nations, and declared that this had not undermined the conditions for its non-alignment policy. Norway hinted that should the situation worsen, it might be forced to reconsider the "working hypothesis"[9] on which it had based its "bridge-building" policy - that the world was not irretrievably split. (Sweden was asserting that in just such an antagonistic world it would maintain its neutral policy.) Permanence was the keystone for Sweden's posture, conditonality for Norway's. Denmark said little publicly, maintained its current non-alignment policy in what it did say, but also gave the impression that it would not rule out of consideration ties with the West. The Bevin speech had opened up the possibility for choice; the choice revealed the defferences in premises in what, judged strictly as behavior, had seemed to be identical policy.

This divergence was only confirmed after the coup in Czechoslovakia and the Soviet note to Finland in February. In an important speech on 19 April, Lange indicated that the Czech coup increased world tensions; the establishment of Cominform was undermining "bridge-building"; the case of Finland indicated that the Soviet Union was thinking of its northern flank. What he predicted was "a war of nerves" but he did not exclude the possibility that a power vacuum might tempt occupation in a "strategically important area". Norway would not shut itself off from closer cooperation with the West. He hoped that there could be a united Scandinavian policy, but stressed that the problems of the three countries were not identical.[10]

An earlier Norwegian emphasis on doing one's part in maintaining world peace by not exacerbating existing - or developing - tensions, and by attempting to bridge the conflicts, had changed now to an emphasis on the danger of being insufficiently protected and defended. This "straw in the wind" was noticed in many quarters. Swedish newspapers clamored for a Swedish answer while on May Day, Danish Prime Minister Hedtoft noted that he was glad that the Norwegian Foreign Minister also thought that it was extremely important "to preserve a common Scandinavian foreign policy attitude".[11] It is indicative of the difference in the standpoints of Norway and Denmark that the Norwegian Foreign Minister spoke of the need "to reach" (finne fram til) a common Nordic policy, while the Danish Prime Minister spoke of the need "to seek to preserve" (søge bevaret) the same.

The Developing Options

It was against this backgound that on May 1 Sweden made a private proposal to Norway and Denmark for an independent Scandinavian defense pact, intended, as the Swedish Foreign Minister later explained, to prevent the foreign policies of the three from diverging. As Undén carefully informed the Danes, there was no possibility of a Swedish-Danish pact, unless the Norwegians joined.[12] (The effect of this dependent position on the negotiating behavior of the Danes, will be examined later.)

There were no immediate results. In mid-May there were allusions to possibilities of defense cooperation as well as a clear statement from Undén that no connections with the West, direct or indirect, could be contemplated by Sweden.[13] In June, Lange emphasized quite explicitly that there was no common Nordic policy. He explained the different attitudes of the three countries - the different assessments of current risks, and the different proposals to meet them - by calling attention to their different strategic situations and their different wartime experiences. He was to repeat this explanation several times over the next year.[14] By contrast, the Danes continued to express their interest.[15] Undén on his part stressed the "conscious common interest" which a defense pact might serve, took up a Norwegian hint of possible "partial solutions", and proposed as well the formula which was ultimately to serve publicly as the umbrella for joint investigations: "...the assumption that we strive to keep ourselves outside a conflict".[16]

Western defense efforts were beginning to develop, but were as yet unformulated. The Vandenberg resolution for cooperation was passed at the end of June, and negotiations between the United States and the Brussels Pact countries began early in July. The labile nature of the situation was underlined by, for example, the Arbeiderbladet commentators in Norway; the implication drawn by this Government organ was that no actions likely to foreclose a Western option should be taken now.[17] Even so, efforts continued during the summer to reach agreement on a joint Scandinavian defense investigation, and a compromise was reached finally in September.

Documents released by the Danes in 1968 support the appraisal made by Lennart Hirschfeldt as early as 1949 that the Norwegians had agreed to investigations of an alliance-free pact in exchange for which the Swedes did not insist that the neutrality condition be made public.[18] The compromise found was Undén's June formula (cited above) which intimated an alliance-free policy, although strictly interpreted it could cover remaining out of a future war through preventing it via alliances _or_ through obtaining unilateral guarantees. This battle over words should be seen as a defense of present and future credibility. Sweden, of course, did not want to participate in anything which might cast doubt on the permanence of its foreign policy stance. Norway, on the other hand, did not want to create the impression that its possible future commitments to a Western pact might be half-hearted.[19]

That fall, both Denmark and Norway were informed that, if they wished, they would receive an invitation to join the developing Atlantic alliance. The Danish Foreign Minister told Bevin that an invitation would be inopportune while the intra-Scandinavian investigations were still continuing; to Marshall he stressed the importance of Sweden, the only armed power in Scandinavia, in defense arrangements.[20] Norway "ventilated" the Scandinavian pact idea with Great Britain and the United States early in the fall, and asked about the possibilities of aid to an independent pact.[21]

Denmark also continued its emphasis on mediation between the other two.[22] On Danish initiative the three Prime Ministers met at a town ceremony in Uddevalla in December; there had been no prior preparations for a negotiating session[23] but according to the official Danish account released in 1968, "During the discussions here there was agreement to seek to strive for (_enighed om at søge at tilstraebe_) a Scandinavian defense alliance as a regional pact within the framework of the United Nations".[24] That was hardly binding but it was optimistic.

The Scandinavian Defense Committee's Secret Report and the Final Negotiations

The Scandinavian Defense Committee (_Skandinavisk Forsvarskomité_, hereafter SFK) which had been established to carry out the joint investigations-negotiations, was to report by 1 February 1949, but by New Year's Day the main lines of their report were known to the governments. Denmark and Norway were privately asked soon after whether they wished to receive invitations to be among the original NATO signatories, and about the "form and timing" of such an invitation. This provoked Norway to ask for the high level Scandinavian political discussions to be pushed ahead. In an "interview" in Arbeiderbladet, Lange commented pessimistically about the sufficiency of purely Scandinavian cooperation in such an insecure world. Cooperation "with people we feel related to, also outside the borders of the North (Norden)", he concluded seemed increasingly necessary.[25]

Just two days later the three nation negotiations among the Prime Ministers, Foreign Ministers, and Defense Ministers began at Karlstad, Sweden, in secret. The documents published by the Danes in 1968 reveal what actually was decided there. The resumé states that there was a preliminary agreement, which was to be reported to and discussed by the responsible authorities within each country, about the "possibility" of a binding Scandinavian defense pact within the UN framework, implying "coordination of defense plans, military forces, and military production". Its provisions excluded outlying possessions.[26] The Swedes agreed only if no country joined NATO.

> It is the wish in all the three Scandinavian countries to reach a common standpoint in security questions. The three governments have therefore agreed on undertaking a common investigation in Washington and London of the following:
>
> 1. Are the American and the British governments interested in the establishment of a defense pact such as described above?
> 2. Are the American and British governments willing to support such a defense pact with matériel with the necessary time priority and on reasonable conditions?[27]

In mid-January the SFK reported to the governments. The full text of their report has never been published but their summary concluding remarks were released in 1968 among the Danish documents.[28] The report assumed that Denmark and Norway would have to build up their armed forces substantially, and that Sweden would have to maintain and modernize its, and also assumed joint planning and coordination of efforts. It assessed three factors: the deterrent capabilities of the pact, the need for matériel from outside the pact, and the need for aid in event of attack. On the question of deterrence the committee concluded that an independent Scandinavian pact "could be expected to a certain degree to have a preventive effect and to form something of a guarantee against particular actions", but could not in itself suffice to prevent "an isolated attack or one accomplished through a coup".[29] At least in the published summary the SFK seems not to have dealt with the question of involvement in a general war. The notion of "a certain degree" of deterrent effect seems to imply but not state a comparison. Presumably the only comparison permitted officially to the committee was a comparison with the status quo, each of three countries in isolation. Of course, the Danish and Norwegian Foreign Offices at least had an additional option to compare.

The committee "strongly underlines" that the pact could not under any conditions eliminate the necessity of outside help in two respects: first, all three countries needed some matériel. In general "a significant part" would have to come from outside, and because of the great need in Denmark and Norway, would have to be on favorable economic terms. Secondly, in the event of attack the SFK agreed that aid would be needed "already in the initial phase".[30] The committee estimated that without preparations in advance, such aid could take "several months" to obtain and put to full use.[31]

The Danish and Norwegian members on one side, and the Swedish members on the other, separately underlined different possible implications. The Danish and Norwegian members accepted the theory that a joint pact would have a deterrent effect because of the increased probability that an attack on the larger unit would loose a reaction from outside powers. They stressed again the necessity for their countries to rearm rapidly and the need for outside help both with matériel and in case of attack. "Quick and effective help will only be possible, if prearranged (forberedt) in peacetime."[32] The pact must not be formulated in such a way as to cut off such help.

The Swedish members intimated that Denmark was a strategic liability, but concluded for several reasons, among which were supply (food provisions?), politics, and psychology (feeling of Scandinavian identity?), that the pact should encompass the three countries.[33] They also argued that in the event that delivery of matériel could not be assured, it should be remembered that "the existence of a pact, which makes serious efforts to use its own means to increase its resistance capacity, can stimulate matériel help from outside".[34] Outside powers will help those who help themselves.

One should note that the SFK conclusions were not in the nature of comparison of possible alternatives, or, therefore, in the form of recommendations. The report could not be an exercise in joint costing because it could

bäck in using the newly available minutes of the Labour Movement's Nordic Cooperation Committee, has found that in 1946 Halvard Lange remarked to his Scandinavian colleagues: [If the world divides into blocs] then "Finland will go towards Russia, Iceland towards the West, and *Denmark*, *Norway*, and *Sweden* will lie on the dividing line like a louse between two finger nails".[52] (My italics.)

For Denmark too, the spheres of influence perspective was inconclusive. Their Ambassador in Washington, Henrik Kauffmann, made clear in a dispatch just after the breakdown of the Scandinavian negotiations his assessment that the United States, if not bound by treaty, would be unlikely to intervene if Denmark were attacked. It was more likely that Denmark would be "written off" (*afskrevet*) both by the American government and by the public. Kauffmann noted that U.S. military experts calculated that it might be impossible (*det evt. bliver ugørligt*) to hold Denmark; in and of itself, it was a military deficit.[53] That Denmark was wanted as a pact member even so, was because of its possession of Greenland. Not only the United States, but also Canada, England, and others wanted assurances that Greenland would be within the NATO system. But Denmark itself was not clearly demarcated as being within any particular sphere.

For none of the three countries, in fact, was perception of possible spheres of influence decisive. The Swedes knew of Soviet interest in eastern Scandinavia, and of Communist opposition to any significant Scandinavian cooperation, yet chose to offer the others a common defense pact. The Danes knew that their traditionally difficult southern flank was not an immediate problem, but it was unclear what forces would rush in to fill the gap left by Germany's defeat. Would Germany be defended at the Rhine or the Elbe as the question was later put? They could hardly consider the question to have been settled by geography. The most recent evidence for the Norwegians pointed to shifting and unsettled boundaries of influence by the great powers. Thus the concept of a sphere of influence -- and of a "core area" as well -- turns out often to be decided after the fact, to specify that country to which another country has, in fact, turned. That is to say, it is used tautologically.

"The War"

The most popular explanation of the differences which led to the failure of the defense negotiations centers on domestic determinants, namely the impact of the divergent historical experiences in World War II on attitudes in the three countries. Norway had been among the Allies, and had established an exile Government in London and a Resistance movement at home. Denmark had also been occupied, but had had no government in exile, and a Resistance movement only from the middle of the war. Sweden had been able to maintain its independence and neutrality. It is commonly argued that these differences determined the courses chosen in 1949.

Since the problem of the 1949 decisions is most often posed as "why did the Scandinavian pact negotiations fail", the paradox seems to be Norway's refusal. To allude to the war-time experiences has fitted in quite naturally with the semi-official views of Norwegian foreign policy which have emphasized the continuity of policy after a major reappraisal in 1940.[54] A scholarly account of the negotiations, whose implicit thesis is similar, contrasts the "image" of the international system held by Norwegian decisionmakers before and after 1940, and argues that the new image was decisive for the Norwegian refusal of the Scandinavian pact.[55] Or as the Swedish Prime Minister commented sadly after the break-down of the Scandinavian negotiations, "One learns from one's own experiences but not from those of others."[56]

The argument of the following pages is that neither from wartime nor immediate postwar evidence could one have concluded that the Norwegian choice of NATO over a Scandinavian pact was to be taken for granted. Although "the idea of solidarity in one form or another"[57] was accepted by most people in Norway after 1940, the question remained, "in which form" or, more pointedly, "solidarity with whom?"[58] There was a significant reorientation of Norwegian foreign policy from neutral to committed ally in 1940. This stance, however, was subsequently modified. Differences in orientation between the London Government and the Resistance leadership, as well as shifts in the position taken by the London Government itself, moderated the policy during the war years. Moreover, "bridgebuilding," the policy of the 1945-48 period, as a role was not so far from the role of a neutral.[59] Clearly, the decision for NATO and against the Scandinavian pact in 1949 did not flow directly from the 1940 reorientation.

The major change in orientation had been symbolized by the November 1940 replacement of Halvdan Koht as Foreign Minister by Trygve Lie. Koht, who had held the position since 1935, had so focussed on the possibility of being provoked into war by the British that he had been unresponsive to signals of imminent German attack.[60] He did not believe in the value of wartime political agreements with Britain for the postwar period, and tried to keep such agreements to matters of practical cooperation.[61] Lie broke with neutrality and those attendant attitudes of aloofness both in public statements and in the "Main Lines in Norwegian Foreign Policy" sent from the London Government to the Home Front organization in May 1942. This document argued for "organized cooperation" by Norway with other countries, both in a world-wide organization and in regional agreements. Norway should be part of a "North Atlantic" defense.[62] This was, and was perceived as, a radical change for Norway.

The new line, however, was never undisputed. Although the Home Front leadership agreed that "at the beginning" it could be necessary to obtain military and economic security through regional arrangements, they warned against binding Norway in advance of liberation and of consultation with representatives at home. They argued that Norway must avoid being the only small power in any Atlantic organization; such an organization should include Sweden, the Low Countries, and, in some way also, the Soviet Union. "We ought to strive to avoid coming into any opposition whatsoever to Sweden, which would make future cooperation more difficult."[63]

The Home Front reply, the product of consultation among eight of the leaders, was drafted by Halvard Lange, who in 1946 replaced Trygve Lie as Foreign Minister. The cosmopolitan upbringing and international experience of Lange have been stressed in later years, making his choice of Atlantic political associations seem "natural".[64] But Arne Ording, who was one of the main foreign affairs advisers for the London Government after Lie took over, and who remained as adviser to Lange, wrote that Lange had "adhered to his Scandinavian outlook" during the war, and that "There was no disagreement about the position of the Soviet Union (in postwar plans), but it was clear that Lange attached greater importance to Scandinavian cooperation than did the Government in London."[65]

Thus the admittedly important change in 1940 was never a uniform and unanimous change throughout the elite; some, like Lange, who were crucial in postwar foreign policy, were associated with essential qualifications to it. Two lines of thought emerged. Like a court decision with a dissent, both were part of the heritage of the war.

Secondly, it has been argued convincingly by Udgaard that the London Government itself changed its emphasis from a vocal policy of Atlantic regional cooperation to a more reserved policy during the course of the war. This was due to the impact of several converging factors: the rise in the prestige of the Soviet Union with the course of the war, and the increasingly reserved reception by the United States and Great Britain of any "Atlantic" policy as they--particularly the United States--began to concentrate on a universal organization (the future United Nations). In addition, the increasing doubt as to where Norway would fit in "spheres of influence" which might emerge, and the overriding need to preserve unity with the Home Front, contributed to moderating the original Atlantic orientation.[66]

Thus the change in orientation in 1940 was never undisputed among the elite, and the policy of the exile Government itself shifted over time. Therefore one should be wary of exaggerating the elements of continuity in explaining the 1948-49 defense pact decision.

Finally, there is a host of contextual details from the postwar period which suggest that Norway's choice in 1949 was not foreclosed. Labor Party leaders were neither so "westward leaning" (vestvent) as they later came to be, nor was the role of "bridge-builder" between East and West so far from the prewar role of neutral mediator.

One such suggestive detail is the following. In choosing Halvard Lange to replace Trygve Lie as Foreign Minister in February 1946, Prime Minister Gerhardsen consulted, among others, Johan Nygaardsvold, who had been Prime Minister both of the prewar Labor Government and of the wartime national Government-in-exile. Nygaardsvold, who had certainly shared the traditional prewar foreign policy outlook, approved the choice.[67] Less than a year before this, Lange himself, anticipating the war's end, had warned against Norway's coming into a position where she would be "bound one-sidedly to the high-capitalist Atlantic powers."[68]

There are also other signs, as Arbeiderbladet, the Labor Party's organ in Oslo, reveals. Its tone changed greatly from the summer and fall of 1947 to the spring and summer of 1948. In the first period leading columnists reflected suspicion of the United States as a capitalist great power, fear of American interference with planned economies, and concern about the organization of a "Western bloc."[69] On September 23 the foreign affairs commentator wrote, "The British cannot break with the Americans. But neither do they wish to be chained to an American triumphal chariot." Even in February 1948, when the Oslo Labor Party resolution on the Bevin plan was passed (and was interpreted in Britain, among other places, as extremely significant, and as distinguishing the Norwegian from the Swedish response), Arbeiderbladet's editorial interpreted the resolution as if it applied only to economic cooperation within the Marshall Plan. That is, it reflected the division in internal Labor Party opinion by giving the resolution a minimalist interpretation.[70] The events of early 1948 changed this tone radically. By May and June the same foreign affairs analyst was warning against doing anything to foreclose prematurely a possible future Western option.[71]

Another significant index was Norway's quite reserved policy with respect to the Marshall Plan which, as Udgaard points out, was really the first operational test of the bridgebuilding policy. For example, Norway sent "experts" (fagmenn) rather than politically responsible Ministers to the Marshall Plan Meetings in the summer of 1947.[72] Norway and Sweden did not take part in the September study group although Denmark did; both Norway and Sweden strove to have the United Nations Economic Council for Europe rather than a separate agency chosen as the Marshall Plan organization. In Norway this policy was still being carried on as late as February 1948. How central this orientation was is suggested by Magne Skodvin's comment: "When one studies the antecedents of NATO one must be very aware that for a long time the Marshall Plan was incomparably more important a subject within the Norwegian Government than was security policy."[73]

For the moment the point to underline is that seen from the period 1945-1947, the future choice of NATO in preference to a Scandinavian plan could by no means have been taken for granted. We shall return to the problem of the differential rates of "learning" between leadership and followership and to the problems of maintaining domestic cohesion and cohesion within the Labor Party.

What then, did the war "teach" Norway, its policy makers and its people? There is evidence of a loss of faith in the efficacy of neutrality as a legal concept, involving reliance on international rules and the fulfilling of legal obligations.[74] It was no longer politically feasible to argue openly for neutrality. Even non-alignment for a single state was now open to the charge of "isolation." The belief in the opposition of interests between Big and Small Powers, and the identity of interests among Small Powers was no longer so widely held.

Strategically, Norway was now considered more exposed because the Nazi attack in 1940 had taught that not just expansion but also preemption may be sufficient motive for attack. Norway was now seen as more central because the latter half of the war had taught that Norway was at the point where the various spheres of interest overlapped. Udgaard maintains, moreover, that the war had taught that, in contrast to the interwar years, there had to be a systematic relationship between foreign policy and defense policy; they now had to be constructed and debated together.[75] And Skodvin argues that a lasting effect of the war, and the <u>inefficacy</u> of British help in 1940, was the conviction that aid must be "prepared in advance".[76]

The wartime alliance had left both the habit of close consultation with the British, and the networks of such consultation. In the Foreign Office itself Lange had inherited one of Lie's important advisers from London Government days, Arne Ording. British Ambassador Collier was, in turn, a friend of Ording from that time. Magne Skodvin calls this period one of "functional ties to the West" and exphasizes the British equipment, supplies and even organizational forms in the defense apparatus, which remained to the Norwegians after their wartime collaboration. In this earliest period, he argues, the connections were material, institutional and also personal.[77] Military people had channels in London; this was especially true of Minister of Defense Hauge, who during the recent war had led the Home Front's military operations.[78] While Skodvin stresses that "Norwegian-British exchange of <u>opinions</u> about Norway's defense policy" was frequent and easy, former Foreign Minister Lange mentioned in addition that the Norwegians continued to have excellent access to British <u>sources</u> <u>of</u> <u>information</u>.[79]

Britain played a vital role for reasons quite different from the wartime ties. (Despite such ties, in the "bridgebuilding era" the Norwegian Government had delayed a visit from Churchill to avoid associating itself with his Fulton, Missouri "iron curtain" speech of March 1946).[80] That the British Labor Party was in power in 1948 was to be important first through Bevin's influence on Lange, and second, through the impact of an important country with a ruling socialist party. These two factors helped to make the Atlantic Alliance palatable to those within the Norwegian Labor Party who felt politically alienated from the United States.

To conclude: as a role in the world, "bridgebuilding" seemed close to Norway's prewar role of neutral mediator and conciliator. And judged strictly behaviorally, the foreign policies of the three Scandinavian countries seemed identical. But as subsequent events would reveal, the premises of prewar and postwar policy were different, even when actions or positions seemed similar. What were Norway's premises?

Udgaard has argued that there was continuity between Norway's prewar and postwar foreign policies in that Norway still relied on the international system as a producer of security, although this time they relied on the international political, not the international legal, system.[81] In that respect, there was indeed continuity. But to this writer the significant new characteristic is contingency; the impact of the experience of war was both to thaw the old premises and to leave the new ones subject to revision. If the assumptions of the bridgebuilding policy were correct, then the international system could be "relied on"; but those assumptions themselves were subject to scrutiny. In February 1948 Lange referred to the premises of his policy as "a working hypothesis"; they were not absolute, but conditional.[82] This was no longer geographically conditioned 'real-politik'; it left room for politics.

Norway as a "New Nation"

The recent independence of Norway from Sweden is sometimes adduced to explain political divergencies. In 1948 it had been only forty-three years since Norway's independence (1905) and, of course, there were still people for whom the feelings generated by the political struggles before, and by the climate of just won autonomy after, were still vivid. One such person was the Norwegian Ambassador in Washington, Wilhelm Morgenstierne, for whom national independence had been the formative experience of his youth. Morgenstierne was opposed to the connection with Sweden and decided early on the NATO option.[83]

In general, this factor is one whose weight is extremely difficult to judge. In the Labor movement, clearly much tradition pointed in the other direction. The trade unions especially had Nordic ties from their days of infancy--the union movement had spread from Denmark to the others-- and annual joint meetings of trade unions and party representatives from the Nordic countries--The Nordic Labor Movement's Cooperation Committee--had been continuous from 1934.[84] This, of course, is consistent with the eventual divisions within the Labor Party over the NATO versus Scandinavia choice. But one should be sceptical of this argument even with respect to the non-socialists, who aligned early and solidly for a connection with Western defense plans.[85] From two later cases, the proposed Scandinavian economic market (late 1940's to early 1960's), and the proposed entry of Norway into the European Community (1960's , early 1970's), we know that groups which had opposed closer economic ties with Scandinavia (especially with Sweden) in the first instance, suddenly became advocates of such plans once they were faced with the prospect of closer ties with Europe.[86] This writer feels justified in concluding that in this respect too, "history" in Scandinavia is ambiguous.

The "Cheaper Solution"

It is sometimes argued that Norway chose NATO in preference to the Scandinavian pact as the "cheaper solution".[87] Norway had suffered extensive damage during the war, and it was the poorest of the three in any case. It had now embarked on an ambitious reconstruction program in which it was investing annually more than a third of its gross national product. The first postwar defense plan, written in 1946, had defined the defense goal as: "...Norwegian defense must (be able to) hold out alone until we get effective help from those who must be our allies"; even for this task Norway was clearly unequipped.[88] Especially after the events in Czechoslovakia and Finland heightened the sense of danger, the decision of the United States to sell weapons on a priority basis and favorable conditions to NATO members was decisive, so the argument goes.

There are several important objections to this line of reasoning. First, this is not really an explanation of why, under the _given_ conditions, the

Norwegians made their choice. Instead, it alters the conditions of choice, the decision situation itself. To put it another way, the "cheaper solution" argument is really an attempt to answer a reasonable, but different, question: what condition or conditions in the situation would have had to be altered to obtain a different outcome of decision making in Norway? Secondly, a choice is paradoxical only by comparison with differing choices by others under the same conditions, or by comparison to some standard of rational or proper choice. (The latter argument is usually implicit, but is difficult to establish, and is therefore rarely made explicit.) To look at the available comparisons: both Denmark and Norway were military vacuums after World War II (in contrast, for example, to Sweden) yet Denmark did not seem moved by economic difficulties to give priority to NATO. Even if we allow that Denmark's domestic economic policy was not so ambitious as Norway's it does not suffice to explain Denmark's relative lack of interest in the presumed "cheaper solution".

Finally, what the "cheaper solution" thesis does not explain, as this writer has argued previously,[89] is why Norway did not put the matter to a test by participating in a joint Scandinavian démarche to the United States for military aid to an independent Scandinavian pact.

Fall Back Positions and Opportunity Costs: A Refinement

No joint defense pact was created; why? The argument here is that rather than beginning by seeking explanatory factors, one should begin by locating <u>the questions</u> that any decision makers would have had to answer whether explicitly or implicitly. Next, one should look for evidence of the assessments and judgments which were involved in the answers to these questions. Only then should one begin to ask what factors seem to have influenced the particular judgments. One begins with the intellectual process and shows how the social process impinges on it.

In this case, the argument is that differences among the national leaders on three important and unavoidable questions prevented agreement on a joint pact. Each country's leadership had to come to a judgment on:

1) the likely United States response to the establishment of a joint pact; 2) the deterrent effect of such a pact; 3) their individual domestic political environment as it might affect not only their first preferences, but also their fall-back possibilities. All these contained significant elements of risk for such a decision.

Of course not only the risks of the proposed options but also the risks of the status quo needed to be evaluated. The first differences lay here. One of the questions frequently asked is "what were the expectations for the immediate future?", "what did they think might happen?". There is more information on Sweden and Norway than on Denmark and for those two countries, the polar ones in this analysis, we might draw up the following schematic description of their order of expectations. Sweden: first, peace in the foreseeable future. Peace might mean tension, but specific political pressures on Sweden were not a major concern. Second, a general war whose technical means and theater of operations could not be predicted in advance, and which therefore did not warrant the assumption that Scandinavia automatically would be drawn in. Third, an isolated attack.[90]

For Norway, a similar list could be constructed. First, peace is likely, but, and this is important, accompanied by "political pressures", a "war of nerves" which might lead to self-imposed restrictions limiting Norway's de facto sovereignty. Models here would be the Soviet note to Finland requesting a treaty of friendship--possible also the Nazi invitation to Denmark in 1939 to sign a non-aggression pact. (There had been rumors of an imminent invitation to Norway for such a pact shortly after the note to Finland in early 1949. In February 1949 an invitation to join a non-aggression pact was proferred by the Soviet Union in reaction to Norway's contemplated membership in NATO). Second would be a general war; if so, it must be assumed that Norway was strategically sufficiently important to tempt preemption. Third would be an isolated attack.

In the opinion of this writer, then, it was not a difference about the likelihood of peace or of war per se which distinguished the two positions but primarily a difference on the possible dangers short of outright war, and second, a difference about the possibility of keeping out should war come.

Assessments of the Likely American Response

For Norway, the judgment of the probable American response to a Scandinavian pact was the culmination of a process which had started even before Undén's proposal. It is worth stressing the notion of process. There were a variety of ideas in the air in those years, little was certain, and foreign policies of nearly all countries were being reappraised, although this only slowly became clear to outsiders. Given this context, the significance of isolated incidents, even diplomatic forays, should not be exaggerated. A political leader might try out an idea, judge its resonance, elicit the views of others, estimate which aspects guided their actions, make adaptations to that. Given the uncertainties of those years between 1947-49, what is striking is the degree of mutual adaptation; neither the Europeans nor the Americans allowed the best to be the enemy of the good.

Within the Norwegian political leadership there was a variety of responses. Prime Minister Gerhardsen, together with Haakon Lie, the secretary of the Labor Party, initiated the important Oslo Labor Party resolution welcoming Bevin's hint of cooperation.[91] This did not mean being "pro-West" as the policy later came to be understood. The framers of the resolution had England in mind as the main power involved. In this early period Martin Tranmael and Halvard Lange conceived of a possible "third force" of Socialist Europe between the other major poles.[92] As Udgaard has described quite concretely, during 1947 "bridgebuilding" increasingly was interpreted within the Labor Party in ideological terms, meaning joining with other countries in which socialist parties were strong, to exert influence on the international scene.[93] The socialist view of international politics (like the traditional American view) "masks space relations" (in William T.R. Fox's phrase).[94] Bevin, although he shared socialist ideals, was to emphasize this to Lange (as the British did to the Americans).

It is clear that at this point Norway was probing in a variety of directions. At a Nordic Foreign Ministers' Meeting February 23-24 1948, Lange took up the question of defense cooperation, suggesting that the Nordic countries should discuss cooperation in military production and supplies. The others agreed in principle--the Danes seemed particularly receptive--but this was left for further discussion by the defense ministers.[95] While nothing directly emerged at this point, this was part of the background to the May proposal by Sweden.

The crucial juncture for Norway was March 1948 when Lange sounded out both the British and American ambassadors about their countries' assessment of Norway's situation, and willingness to aid Norway militarily if necesary, when Lange had a long and significant discussion with Bevin, and when a high official in the Norwegian Defense Department traveled to Washington to investigate the possibilities of obtaining military supplies (and perhaps more diffuse assurances).

Against the background of the events of January and February (especially the Soviet note to Finland) and a combination of rumors (later traced to the Communists, especially Danish Communists, and to diplomatic reports that an invitation like that to Finland might be extended to Norway), Lange asked both the British and American ambassadors how their countries would evaluate Norway's situation and whether they would give military aid in the event of the worst happening.[96] Both Ambassadors raised the question in return of how Norway felt about even broader cooperation, for example with the Brussels Pact, just then being established.[97]

A week later, on March 15, Lange had a crucial conversation with British Foreign Minister Bevin, who made clear that while Britain was sympathetic to Norwegian problems, Norway's hope lay in having the United States associated in an arrangement which would then be strong enough to help Norway too. Britain's reevaluation of its strength, indicated the previous year when it handed over responsibility for Greece and Turkey, preceded the Norwegians' appreciation of Britain's declining capabilities. Combined with this was the first inkling of the intimate relationship which was being fostered between the foreign policy-makers in London and Washington. Bevin, in fact, had oriented the Americans in advance about the meaning of his January 22 speech in the House of Commons, but at the time, the Norwegians knew nothing of this.[98] Now Lange was told, in strict secrecy, of the developing plans to incorporate the Brussels Pact into an Atlantic alliance.

The picture that Lange received in this discussion, both of England's declining capabilities, and of the resolute and single-minded strategy of Bevin to involve the United States in the defense of Western Europe, was enormously important. First, it cut short the "third force" line of thinking. Second, it cut short thoughts of essentially bilateral arrangements with Britain. Third, it opened a whole new, Atlantic, perspective. Years later Lange was to recall the main lesson: Bevin had stressed that whatever reservations about the United States Lange and he might have as social democrats, "they are our sheet anchor".[100]

The first fact of life for the Norwegians was that Britain alone did not feel able to supply protection to Norway. The second was that Britain's major energies were now being devoted to eliciting the commitment of the United States to the defense of (unspecified parts of) Western Europe. The third was that if such a commitment could be obtained, the British would encourage the inclusion of Norway in any arrangement.

Also during late April 1948 Deputy Minister in the Norwegian Defense Department, Dag Bryn, went along on a mission to the United States with the head of Norway's Bank, Gunnar Jahn.[101] The official purpose of the visit was to negotiate a loan, but Bryn had talks with military advisers in the Pentagon, as well as in the State Department about the possibilities of obtaining weapons and about more general defense questions. The responses from the Pentagon were very cautious. It was clear that they feared an overextension of American promises of protection in the current situation when they felt they did not have the requisite strength to follow through if necessary. Despite the fact that the State Department view was quite different--more optimistic and more political--the Norwegians were exposed to the American defense decision-making process and to considerations of the practical difficulties of the developing Western strategy. The scope of American efforts was uncertain.

Thus by the time Undén came to Oslo, the Norwegians had had some first hand discussions with both the Americans and the British. British strategy aimed at a minimum to avoid anything which would discourage American involvement in Europe. Bryn's visit made clear why. At this point, then, there were two uncertainties: would the Americans commit themselves to Europe's defense, and if so, that would be the geographical scope of the commitment?

One should note here an asymmetry in the Danish and Norwegian positions in these formative months of the Atlantic pact. Denmark owned Greenland and the Faeroe Islands in the North Atlantic. These were crucial defense areas for the Americans, Canadians, and British. According to Herbert Feis, as early as May and June 1948 Denmark was considered a candidate for membership, although there is no evidence available about whether the Danes knew this at the time.[102] Norway sounded out the possibilities as early as March but although it was unofficially encouraged, it received no definite answer until September, after the summer consultations of the original seven countries[103] (Sweden had been sounded out, but refused).

If Norway wanted to keep the Atlantic option alive, it had to work with Britain, which was the major power eager for Norway's inclusion; it also had to develop its own assessment of the evolving American policy, its likely direction and requirements. Once it had been established that the Scandinavian pact could not be entirely self-sufficient but would need both arms and aid, those advocating the Scandinavian option also had to consider the American attitude toward such a pact.

In order to understand the problem for the Scandinavian countries in assessing the American response, one must know something of the development of American policy of that period, of the dispute which surrounded it, and of characteristics of American politics which affected that policy.

One must recall that this was less than a year after the announcement of the Marshall Plan, and while its organization, guidelines, and financing were all in their initial stages. There were several ways in which the Marshall Plan approach affected American foreign policy in general. The political and economic strategy behind the Plan required intra-European cooperation as the price of American aid; it considered the economic resources of the European continent as a whole, and asked Congress for allocations on a Continent-wide basis. This tended to reinforce the American tendency to think of "Europe as a whole" rather than of individual countries.[104]

The Marshall Plan model was essentially based on George Kennan's conviction that America should support European initiatives; it was to supplement, not substitute for, European political leadership.[105] This model was now generalized to the military field (although in a way which Kennan himself found alien).[106] Bevin's original idea had been to broaden the 1944 Dunkirk treaty (between England and France). The American reaction was to suggest instead the mutual support model of the recently concluded Treaty of Rio: "an attack against one is an attack against all".[107]

Recent interviews with John Hickerson and Theodore Achilles, who headed the European Division of the Department of State at the time, convey the give and take involved in developing the NATO plan. In December 1947 as the London conference (on Germany) broke down, Marshall and Bevin had conferred. At this point, said Hickerson, Bevin was thinking of "two circles", a tight inner one bound by treaty, and an outer one, including the United States and Canada, with fewer commitments.[108] Achilles said that it was Robert Lovett--through whom everyone reported to Secretary of State George Marshall--who insisted that the Europeans show what they could and would do. This led, in Achilles' opinion, to some "Alphonse and Gaston" behavior; the Brussels Pact was part of this, he thought.[109] Thus even before the "Bevin plan" speech, feelers had been extended to the Americans. Marshall, however, had asked for evidence that the Europeans were really determined to defend themselves.[110] In other words, certain psychological tokens of mutuality, solidarity, joint involvement were required.

In addition to the side-effects of the Marshall Plan, several specifically American preoccupations may have influenced the general direction of the American response (preoccupations better understood with hindsight). Both the tendency to think about foreign policy in universalistic terms and the intense concern to avoid repeating Woodrow Wilson's failure to obtain Congressional support, may have reinforced what Theodore Lowi has labeled "oversell", a characteristic of the American system which he attributes to its basic structure, the separation of powers.[111] It was important to the American Administration that any pact have a purpose and a participation which were publicly acceptable and for which public sympathy could be obtained.

On the recipients, as well, the Marshall Plan left traces. Van der Beugel, who was then the Dutch Foreign Minister, noted that Europe, for the first time, was exposed to the problems of American foreign policy-making.[112] European diplomats found themselves considering, if not actually participating in, Congressional-Executive relations. The American Administration solicited Europeans from Marshall Plan (OEEC) countries to speak before Congress; Ole Colbjørnsen, the Norwegian Labour-Party economist and planner, was one, for example.[113] Regardless of their original strategic preferences, European policy makers had to begin to consider what could be "sold" to Congress, and on this question there were differences. Europeans had to make their own judgments about which strategic concepts were likely to prevail within the United States, and what, if anything, they could do to influence the outcome.

Concretely, there was some evidence of dissent from the evolving NATO conception. Walter Lippmann (who was not part of the American Administration of course, but whose voice was listened to)[114] was one who opposed several key concepts in the developing strategy. The alternative he advocated rested on bilateral guarantee pacts between the United States and specified countries in Western Europe, the purpose of which would be to make clear the American commitment to defend them.[115] The prewar error of ambiguity which might provoke aggressive miscalculation would be corrected, but the geopolitical specificity of American interests would be maintained.

In early 1949 Lippmann wrote columns with an extended explication of his (alternative) conception.

> The real defense against aggression is not a policy of military containment. It is a policy of the balance of power. For if the Soviet Union has or had an idea of military aggression, what has restrained her or will continue to restrain her, is not the local capacity for resistance but the certainty that the total power of the United States would be involved.[116]

This balance of power was to be achieved by a non-aligned "buffer belt" consisting of Scandinavia, a neutralized Germany, a neutralized Australia, Italy and possibly Spain. Soon after he made clear that his assumption was that these states be "...determined to defend their independence and assured of support if they are attacked..."[117] This idea of a series of unilateral guarantees ran directly counter to the main assumptions upon which the Brussels Pact-NATO strategy had been built. It envisaged, in fact, a unilateral guarantee by the United States of the entire border with Eastern Europe. Lippmann's ideas on Scandinavia, clearly more compatible with the Swedish view, the independent defense pact alternative, were a part of his total European strategy.

Lippmann, therefore, would have been interested in the type of plan an independent armed Scandinavian defense pact represented.[118] Both he and George Kennan in the State Department no doubt would have been open to a beneficent understanding with such a pact.[119] The questions for Scandinavian leaders were: "what was the likelihood of such ideas prevailing in Washington? "if they did not prevail in general, could exception be made for Scandinavia?";

"would the behavior of the Scandinavians make any difference to the outcome?".

There are two different strategies open in a situation of an evolving policy. It is possible either to latch on to the view most likely to succeed and hope to be carried along "in its wake", or to argue that one ought to be considered an exception to the main lines of policy. The Norwegians tried the first and the Swedes and Danes the second. In an unconstrained situation all three countries most likely would have preferred to have their pact proposal considered "on its merits", that is to say, in isolation from the general strategy which was evolving. Their argument would have been roughly as follows: we are genuinely democratic, reliable, inwardly cohesive countries; this is the real "commitment"--all the rest is superficial; will you help us if we help ourselves and each other? Had the substance and tone of the reply been, "Yes, we will not only supply you arms on favorable conditions and with priority, but we will consider that is taking care of the stability of your corner of the world you are making a contribution to the common weal," then it is most likely that all three countries would have joined in a Scandinavian pact, even without formal guarantees by treaty.[120]

But one of the problems of foreign policy in a country such as the United States, where foreign affairs and diplomacy have never been the exclusive prerogative of the Executive, is that of devising a broad policy line which can be explained to the public. Particularly if mobilization--men or money, not just words--is required, this is a necessity. No matter how wise, a policy of extreme differentiation from situation to situation is difficult to maintain, not only from the point of view of decision-making--as the literature on organizations should tell us--but also from the point of view of winning political support for the policy.[121] American policy had to be comprehensible in its main outlines to Congress and the public at large.

All these factors tended to evoke a reciprocal response from Europeans negotiating with the Americans, because _they_ were single-mindedly trying to involve the Americans in Europe and had to take the American political system into account. The Dutch Ambassador told his Danish colleague--as late as February 1949--that he feared "that Scandinavia's position could come to wreck the chances for getting the United States for the first time to bind herself to defend European countries against attack".[122]

It is in this context, then, that Lange reiterated his formulation that Norway's (or, if the pact materialized, Scandinavia's) defense problems must be viewed as "subproblems" (delproblemer) of the Western defense. To expect a special relationship was unrealistic.

In Sweden, American responses were judged differently. It will be argued below that this may well have had to do with the fact that Sweden's fall-back position differed from that of Norway. In addition, however, the Swedes believed that the position of the American government on supplying arms did not simply reflect the situation of scarcity of the available supply compared to the probable demand, but that it was a strategy; it was being used as pressure to prevent the Scandinavian negotiations from succeeding.[123] As the SFK report revealed, Sweden too would be dependent on outside (American) sources for certain supplies[124] within the Scandinavian pact, and Swedish representatives on the SFK also agreed that if attacked, aid would be needed "in the initial phase".[125] But the Swedes believed that the Americans would supply needed material and aid because it was in their own interest, and regardless of their commitments. Supplies might not, however, be obtainable immediately.[126]

There is also the question of whether the Swedes thought the dissenters would succeed in influencing the evolving American policy. The Swedish Ambassador to Washington, for example, is said to have been friends with Lippmann. Lippmann's views were widely reported in the Scandinavian press. In any event, the Swedish strategic response was to prescribe a fait accompli; the three countries ought first to agree among themselves on an independent defense pact and then approach Washington to support it.

The initial Danish evaluation of the American response was optimistic and close to Sweden's; we may speculate that it may have been affected by the asymmetry mentioned above. Because of its possession, Greenland, Denmark may have been more certain of its Atlantic option.

The Danish Ambassador in Washington, Henrik Kauffmann, argued later that timing would have made a difference. Had the three countries jointly requested aid to an independent pact in the summer of 1948, before the NATO negotiations had proceeded too far, they would have succeeded.[127] He implied that before the general strategy was frozen, special arrangements would have been easier.

Even in the later period, Kauffmann maintained, had the three announced that their pact was a fact, and had they been prepared to broaden it to measures creating economic unity, the project would have won sympathy because of the American interest in regional integration in Europe. Even without such plans, there would have still been a "chance" for a joint démarche to have won acceptance and weapons supplies, "if not right in the first round, then at a little later point in time",[128] although almost certainly without binding assurances about priority and favorable payment conditions. Thus in the later period, Norway's conditions could not be met.

By February 1949--when the impression had been created in the United States that the Scandinavian pact negotiations had failed, although Lange was still discussing its possibility[129]--Kauffmann thought that aid to such a pact would have a chance only on conditions such as those suggested by Canada's Lester Pearson: that Greenland and possibly the Faeroes be included in the Atlantic Pact, and that a connection be established between the Scandinavian and Atlantic pacts--"more than the exchange of information between military attachés and 'occasional visits' of officers". Although Kauffmann still recommended trying to agree on these conditions in order to save the Scandinavian pact, they were clearly unacceptable to Sweden.[130]

Assessments of the Deterrent Effect of the Proposed Pact

The second issue on which each country had to formulate an opinion was the value of the proposed Scandinavian pact as a deterrent. There have been two attempts at characterizing the strategic theory of Norway in this period, neither of which allows one to distinguish appropriately between the strategies of Norway and Sweden. Philip Burgess argued in an analysis of the defense pact case that Norway's concern was to avoid being a destabilizing power vacuum, tempting preemption, while Sweden relied on a kind of balance of interests among the blocs.[131] The idea of "vacuums" by itself begs the question. Sweden as well as Norway. abhorred (power) vacuums, but, as we shall attempt to show Sweden had a different conception of what it took to fill them.

Likewise Nils Morten Udgaard's thesis that Norway after the Second World War returned to a "balance of power" strategy does not help us differentiate the ways in which Norway's and Sweden's strategies differed.[132] In addition to its other ambiguities,[133] the concept of the balance of power does not by itself tell us whether the aim of a country is to create (or help create) a balance, or rather to exploit for its own purposes what is assumed to be a preexisting balance. Although small powers may well ask themselves how an international balance may be created, the actual policy problem for them is rather: given a state of imbalance (or one of balance, or one of change) what shall we do? They do not "optimize" in foreign policy (create balances), but rather take major constraints as given, major questions as already settled, and therefore "suboptimize" (exploit balances).[134] Both Sweden and Norway relied upon a developing "balance" between East and West. The SFK report, with its emphasis upon the need for early aid in the event of attack, supports this. Where the Norwegians and Swedes differed was first in their evaluation of what would most likely call forth this needed aid, and secondly, in their strategies for deterring attack in the first place.

The difference between Sweden's strategy for deterrence and Norway's is captured by Glenn Snyder's distinction between "denial strategies" and "punishment strategies".[135] Sweden relied first upon a large and costly defense system to support its strategy of denying Swedish soil to a potential enemy except at what it hoped would be prohibitive cost. Secondly, it relied on the self interest of the Western powers to induce them to come to its aid once it proved able to withstand the first assault. This served as a defense strategy. The ambiguity of whether it would in fact be aided, was considered sufficient deterrence as well. The spirit is one of cool calculations of profit and loss. Swedish Defense Minister Allan Vougt illustrated this early in 1949 when he argued that the assumption had been that were a Scandinavian pact well equipped, any attack upon it would have required a large operation; this would have been "avkylande", literally, "chilling" to a potential aggressor.[136] (The word Vougt did not use was "avskräckande", literally, frightening off or deterring).

A rather different answer emerges when the Norwegians asked "what would fill the vacuum?". It was intimated in the important speech by Foreign Minister Lange on April 19, 1948, a speech which received wide attention in Scandinavia and which may have stimulated the Swedish pact offer two weeks later. Lange commented:

> But in a state of such sharp opposition as we are witness to, there always lies before us the possibility that a great power can occupy a strategically important area, which is not defended, or which it believes it can occupy without appreciable sacrifice, [and] in the belief that such an occupation will not lead to war.[137]

The idea was that what might be needed was not only the denial of gain to an aggressor but the threat of war, including counterattack. As the Scandinavian negotiations ended early the following year Lange again referred to becoming part of a new balance by cooperating with an area strong enough to represent a real power factor.[138] The next month he told the Labor Party Congress that not only Norway but also Norden was "...too small a unit...for us to be a power factor strong enough to deter all [parties] from attacking..." His impression of the Atlantic Pact which was still being worked out was that "...there is good hope for a form which will give us the security which lies in [the fact] that all the world knows that an attack on any part of Norwegian territory will be equivalent to an attack on the United States of America".[139] This deterrence theory, then, relied more heavily on the threat of punishment than on the denial of reward.

An implicit Danish theory of deterrence is even harder to discern. There were even fewer public statements by Danish officials than by Norwegian or Swedish officials in this period. The official Danish explanation stated that the Danish position in the negotiations had been that "an alliance-free, mutually binding Scandinavian defense union with assurance that the necessary supplies can be obtained from outside..." was the best solution for Scandinavia. That was the Swedish position plus <u>one</u> of the Norwegian stipulations.[140] The Danes never openly posed the questions of a choice between the two conditions.

But the Danes did adopt as central to their position a complementary thesis, familiar at the time, which one might call <u>the non-provocation thesis</u>. If deterrence is a method of persuasion,[141] then another form of it might be to convince the opponent that one is not worth bothering about. This means either making oneself inconspicuous, or being actively reassuring. In fact, most foreign policies combine deterrence and reassurance in some degree, but the Danes emphasized the latter when they argued that "an alliance-free union...could contribute to a relaxation [of tensions] and [to] peace."[142]

We must digress here to observe that in making this argument the Danes had a particularly hard row to hoe. The Soviet Union's position beginning long before and continuing through the period of the pact negotiations, was that there was nothing to choose between Scandinavian adherence to a Nordic and to an Atlantic pact. In attempting to influence them to remain isolated and neutral, the Soviet Union lost the opportunity to influence the real choice being made. Even early in 1947 Soviet papers were making accusations of secret pacts with the West. During the tense month of January 1948 the Soviet military journal and radion repeated accusations made by the Danish Communist newspaper of secret agreements between the United States, Great Britain, and Scandinavia. From their point of view, in this era before neutrals were wooed, it made no difference whether the Americans controlled directly, or through "an ostensibly 'neutral' alliance".[143] It was thus more difficult for the Danes to make persuasive the argument that membership in the Scandinavian pact would antagonize the Soviet Union less than would membership in NATO.

The Danish position is usually described and self-described as one of mediation between those of Norway and Sweden.[144] Internal Danish disagreements, which will be discussed below, contributed greatly to this. But the position was "overdetermined". Structural factors can also account for it.

First. because of its ownership of Greenland, strategically vital to the developing Western alliance, Denmark must have been relatively confident that it would continue to be welcomed as a member of the Alliance. Given the ideological cast of international relations at the time, it would be unlikely that any of the Western powers chiefly concerned (the United States, Canada, Britain) would propose an arrangement to keep Greenland in but Denmark out, unless that were the specific wish of the Danes. On the other hand, the Danes also knew definitely that Sweden would not consider a defense pact with Denmark alone.[145] The significance of this asymmetry of position between Norway and Denmark is that _if_ Denmark preferred the Scandinavian solution, its possibility of attaining it depended on Norway's choice, or, to put it another way, upon bringing Norway and Sweden together, which is what Denmark tried to do. The mediator role had foundation in the bargaining constellation and in Denmark's particular position within it.

There was a second individuating feature in Danish strategy and diplomacy, the evidence of which has sometimes been remarked on but not accounted for. There is a striking contrast between what appears as an active posture of Norwegian diplomacy in the 1948-49 period and a passive posture of Danish diplomacy. Again, in the view of this writer, this can be explained both deterministically by its historical antecedents, and functionally, as serving a purpose (or at least being believed to serve a purpose).

Let us begin with the contrast. The picture has already emerged of Norway's active, alert seeking for information, opinions, assurances, ties. The precedents and channels of Norway's wartime associations especially with Great Britain, but also to some extent with the United States, have been noted by many. Some point as well to the cosmopolitan upbringing of the Foreign Minister and his fluency in French and English as contributing to the ease of communication. Clearly also Norway conducted a policy of continuous, intimate orientation of both sides, Great Britain and also Sweden and Denmark, perhaps in part to avoid suspicion of playing a double game in the dual and delicate negotiations going on. Thus, for example, although it did not consult Sweden or Denmark before sounding out the British and American ambassadors in Oslo on March 8, 1948, it did notify them immediately of what it had done.[146] Likewise, it insisted on orienting Britain (who was very suspicious of Sweden's influence) on the Scandinavian discussions.[147] We see how active Norway was in seeking and receiving, giving and getting, information.

By contrast, in the same situation and time, Denmark seems extremely passive, It initiates little so far as one can tell, either vis-à-vis the West or the other Scandinavian countries. Perhaps the only exception to this picture is the recurring characterization of Danish Prime Minister Hans Hedtoft as particularly eager for the Scandinavian pact, and as taking whatever opportunities he could to mediate between the other two countries. It was Hedtoft who worked for the Uddevalla meeting among the three Prime Ministers in December 1948; he urged Erlander to compromise further to obtain Norway's acceptance; this Erlander did.[148]

On the other hand, although the Danes initiated little, they readily responded to the initiatives of others. When Lange raised the issue of some degree of cooperation on military production and rearmament at the Nordic

Foreign Ministers' meeting in February 1948, the Danes seemed more interested than the Swedes.[149] When Sweden notified the Danes (April 30, 1948) that they were about to propose a Scandinavian pact to Norway, and that, contingent upon Norway's response, would extend the invitation to Denmark, again the Danes were positive. The picture then, is not of indifference, but of unwillingness to assume the initiative. Why?

Long after the period we are discussing, the Danish historian, Troels Fink, who in 1948 had been a consultant in history to the Danish Foreign Office, commented that he had been surprised that Denmark got a guarantee from the United States (meaning within NATO):"it is without any analogy".[150] Johan Holst has pointed out that the analogies people refer to most often are "local" analogies.[151] What then, had been Denmark's experience?

Danish pessimism was based on its vulnerable geographical situation and its historical experience of being unable to find protection, defense, allies. From the days of the defeat by Prussia, to the interwar years, no other powers had been willing to aid Denmark or to promise to do so. In the 1930's Denmark had been forward in attempting to elicit protective cooperation both from England and from the other Scandinavian countries; its efforts had met with failure.[152] The Danes' reading of this experience resulted in their geographically-based attitude of "realpolitik"; just as their experience with respect to outside aid had been uniform, their view was relatively static. Other states would give help based on their interests (not Denmark's); there was little scope for altering the appreciation of their interests so as to include Denmark's; politics (active efforts) would not pay. Mary Dau's account reflects this when she relates: "The West coast of Jutland was turned toward Britain; but Denmark was, as often repeated, a Baltic state, and in saying that one was back in the old question of how important the Baltic was for the Western countries".[153]

A corollary to this was the view that even if Denmark should obtain a treaty, it might well be undependable (since, in the last analysis the other party would decide whether or not to uphold it, based on its own interest). Denmark had signed a treaty of non-aggression with Hitler's Germany in 1939, and that had not prevented Hitler from overrunning Denmark. Treaties were often paper.

What, then, could Denmark reasonably do to obtain not only allies but dependable allies? The answer was an extremely cautious strategy. It was possible, and perhaps probable, that nothing could be done, that no one would assume responsibility for the Danish heartland.[154] Within the Western alliance the defense of Danish territory by the alliance might depend on whether they wished to defend Germany to the Elbe, or to the Rhine. Based on their experience in the Second World War, the Danes distinguished between a defense of freedom" (frihetsforsvar) and a "local defense" (lokalt forsvar); if an alliance would give only the former (implying the possible occupation of Danish territory until some future liberation) it would not be worthwhile; only if the alliance accorded strategic importance to the latter, the defense of Danish territory, would it be worth it. Was there any way to judge in advance whether this were likely?

What looked to outsiders like meaningless passivity, might well be seen as a technique for obtaining politically reliable information. The Danes did not exclude the possibility of alliance, but they did not actively seek it for fear that they actually might be biasing the information they obtained. If others were genuinely interested in an alliance with Denmark, they would take the initiative.

Internal political, and external structural factors made the mediating role functional for the Danes. Their historically conditioned pessimism and their extreme insecurity about the reliability of any guarantees suggested a passive strategy as a technique of weighting the information they received. The style of, as well as the implicit theories behind, Danish policy in this period can be explained with reference to their situation.

Having dealt with the mediation role and the relatively passive posture of Denmark, we shall return to our discussion of the implicit theories of deterrence held in the three countries, and the different evaluation of the Scandinavian and NATO pacts in terms of them. In the opinion of this writer, there was a strategic view which almost succeeded in satisfying the requirements of both the denial school and the punishment school, and almost succeeded in bridging over the differences between them. That view might be called the "critical mass" theory. The Danish Ambassador Henrik Kauffmann stated one version of this:

> If the three Nordic countries had established a defense union, an attack on one of them would have brought about such an extensive

> fire, that it would have released a reaction in the American people, which would have meant an American declaration of war.[155]

The Norwegian and Danish members of the SFK stated a more cautious version in their summary:

> Provided that the three countries are united in a defense union, it is more likely that an attack on Scandinavia will release a reaction from powers outside Scandinavia. To the extent that an aggressor must reckon with an active reaction from the other great powers, it will be the most important preventive factor, in that the aggressor must assume that an attack on Scandinavia will loose countermeasures with the input of the Western powers' coordinated economic and military strength.[156] (emphasis added)

The idea that if the group were big enough (important enough all together), an attack upon it would be answered by more than its own forces, fits parts of the opposing theories neatly. It requires that the three do no more than "deny" their territory to the aggressor, yet invokes a "punishment" threat as the real deterrent. If this theory is invoked the question becomes "will an ambiguous interest by the Western powers be considered a sufficient risk by a potential aggressor, to discourage his attack?". Given the divisions within each country about foreign alignments as we shall see, there was strong incentive to hope or believe that it would.

Assessments of the Domestic Political Situations

We have seen that the three countries differed in their estimates of the likely American response to a Scandinavian plan. Their individual theories of deterrence imputed different significance to that response as well: for the Norwegians, a favorable American response was crucial; the Danes were close to them; the Swedes, given their denial theory, made the American response less pivotal. However, for all three there seemed to be potential attractions in the critical mass theory. Why was it, then, that the three failed to make a joint effort which would have been the only conclusive test of the American response? What would have been lost by trying? For the answer we must turn to the differences among the three in the political risks and constraints of their domestic politics. The argument is that the Norwegian decision-makers calculated that domestic pressures would have jeopardized their fall-back position if they tried the Scandinavian option and it failed. With the fall-back position in doubt, the attempt was too risky, and was turned down.

In all three countries there were traditions both of cross-party cooperation and of Government-Opposition parties' cooperation. The degree of such cooperation varies, of course, with the country and the strength of the Government's base. In Denmark, where minority Governments have been the norm, cross-party cooperation has been most pervasive.[157]

The Swedish situation could be described as "consensus with nuances"; this was revealed in the negotiations. Within the intricate parlance of neutrality politics, from which none of the Swedish political parties ever really deviated, the Liberals and Conservatives were somewhat more openly sympathetic to the West. Some of the leading independent Liberal newspapers openly advocated joining NATO, a real break from what had been practically unanimous agreement on neutrality;[158] however, this did not succeed in altering even Liberal Party policy, much less that of Sweden.

These subtle nuances reappeared in the final stages of the formal negotiations, when the question arose whether Sweden was stipulating as a condition that Norway and Denmark should be able to acquire weapons from the West. The governing Social Democrats and the Agrarians wished to omit this formal condition while the Liberals and Conservatives wished it to be a stipulation in the Swedish offer.[159] There were thus indications that a policy which did not really deviate formally from neutrality, but which at the same time maximized the possibility of Western aid, would be politically attractive. The "critical mass" theory would have obvious appeal.

A moderating consideration for Danish policy makers was the strong tradition of pacifism which went back to the nineteenth century and to the fruitlessness of border disputes with Prussia. One of the most famous Danish political slogans in defense debates had been Hvad skall det nytte?, "To what purpose?" or "What's the use?"[160] One of the "four old parties" of Denmark is the Radical Left Party, formed in 1905 as a pacifist reaction to the military policy of the time. Until after World War Two, the Radicals and Social Democrats had cooperated in electoral pacts and parliamentary support. Now the Socialists were in power, a minority government with only 57 out of 149 seats; their traditional ally, the Radicals, could be expected to object vehemently to a change from the policy of neutrality.[161]

This left its mark on the Danish debate. In contrast to the Norwegians, the Danish spokesmen never publicly mentioned any possibilities other than the Scandinavian one, or isolated neutrality. This may be attributed to concern about the Radicals.[162] On the other hand, the Liberals and Conservatives were for the Atlantic option, and in fact were critical of the Government for seeming to have no position of its own and just "mediating".[163] One can see why the "critical mass" idea, which might win the cooperation of the pro-Western Liberals and Conservatives, and yet retain the Radicals who voted against NATO ultimately, would be most appealing.

In the pivotal country, Norway, the opposition parties were solidly for cooperation with the West as early as the beginning of 1948,[164] but the governing Labor Party showed early and significant divisions. Besides the divisions within the governing party, there was the issue of potential Communist Party strength; their vote-getting power had not been tested in a national election since 1945 when they had won 11.8% of the votes. These divisions affected three aspects of Norwegian decision-making as we shall see. First, some key decision-makers were won over--temporarily--to the "critical mass" theory. Second, the tempo of decision-making and the timing of negotiations were affected. Third, the willingness to take risks was reduced.

A recent historical account, Knut Einar Eriksen's DNA og NATO (The Norwegian Labor Party and NATO. The fight within the governing party over Norwegian NATO-membership, 1948-49), reveals for the first time the dimensions of the division within the Labor Party over aligning Norway with the developing Western alliance. As part of his research, Eriksen surveyed the Labor Party press all over the country. In the period January to mid-February 1949, 10 newspapers followed the foreign policy leadership's line, 22 the opposition line for a Nordic defense pact without ties to the West, and 12 out of the 44 were insufficiently clear on the issue to be categorized.[165] Within the Labor Party's Storting group, Eriksen estimates that until the Party Congress a majority were for the Nordic solution. Even after the Congress vote, and after group leader Oscar Torp's pointed assertion that the Congress was the Party's highest organ (and therefore that the Party parliamentary caucus was obligated to obey it), the vote was 35 to 23 with, even more significantly, 18 absentees.[166] The leader of the opposition group was Olav Oksvik, a veteran in the Party; Oksvik had been a member of the Cabinet in 1947-48. He clearly opposed any Western alignment, even if the economic costs associated with other strategies were to be greater.[167] As early as April 1948 he had offered a resolution within the Labor Party's Storting group, enjoining Nordic defense cooperation on the basis of unconditional neutrality in any great power conflict.[168] He predicted that three-fourths of the Party would share his view of this issue, and, according to Lange's account, just before the Party Congress Oksvik felt confident enough to assure Swedish and Danish Socialists that two-thirds of the Congress would oppose the Government's foreign policy recommendations. Those listening to the debate at that Congress and judging audience reaction, were unsure until the end how the vote would go. Although it went overwhelmingly--and then, in the Labor Party tradition, unanimously--for the Government's policy, it took several days to persuade Oksvik to be bound by the Congress' decision.[169] His absence, and that of 15 others during the Storting vote on NATO membership on March 3, 1949, was a demonstration of disapproval.[170]

The bitterness over the rapidity of the decisions which has surfaced periodically over the following twenty-five years, reflects the persistence of the opposition within the party, as well as the difficulty they had in organizing at the time to counter a policy which was contingent, evolving, and therefore not easily grappled with. (Eriksen argues as well that the opposition, given its numerical strength, was reticent in opposing the Government, partly due to ingrained Labor Party norms which accord substantial authority to the leadership, partly due to Party loyalty).[171]

It also represents the general problem of differential rates of learning between leaders and followers. The leadership had long been receiving information not only about the visible and traumatic events like the coup in Czechoslovakia or the Berlin blockade, but also the continuous tug of war in every international forum, in the postwar conferences, in the United Nations, in the recently reactivated but secret negotiations with the Soviet Union over Svalbard (Spitzbergen). They had been privy to and involved in discussions with their counterparts in other countries. To them the decision seemed the end of a long process. What is clearer to an outsider is the rapidity of the reorientation for people outside those circles. While in October and December 1947 and again in January 1948 there had been elaborate orientations by Foreign Minister Lange in the Storting, these had either been secret or quite cautiously worded. The change of tone in Arbeiderbladet, the Labor Party's Oslo (and main) news organ, between the fall of 1947 and late spring 1948 is equally striking--particularly with respect to the "capitalist" world, America in particular, and the desirability of associating with it. Arbeiderbladet's editor sat on the Party executive. As Erikson showed, many of the provincial Labor newspapers did not change their outlook. The main point is that to the dissidents the decision to join the Atlantic pact seemed a rushed, panicked, decision; to the foreign affairs leadership it seemed the fruit of a year and a half of thought, negotiation and discussion.

The dissenters believed themselves to have the ear of Prime Minister Gerhardsen. It has been said, in fact, that the fight was one "for Einar Gerhardsen's soul".[172] In fact Gerhardsen's role was different at different times. In January 1948 it was he who was clearly for the Bevin plan, (while Lange argued that opinion, especially within the parliamentary Labor Party might not be ripe for a full-fledged campaign).[173] This early decisiveness in itself did not betoken a pro-Western-alliance proclivity. Gerhardsen undoubtedly felt that neutrality was no firm rock, and the Bevin plan was the first palpable indication of possible aid. Moreover it came from a Labor government. Once the Swedish offer arose as an alternative, and once the United States, and not Britain, began to be seen as the major ally, Gerhardsen had second thoughts. Soon after Undén's inconclusive private discussion with Lange in May 1948, it was Gerhardsen who raised the Scandinavian possibility publicly.[174] In December 1948 again, it was the three Prime Ministers who were optimistic. Finally the Karlstad draft agreement, which otherwise seems so inexplicable against the background of the distinctly Western-oriented New Year's Day statements of the Foreign and Defense Ministers, was due to Gerhardsen's strong desire for a Nordic arrangement.

Yet the final decision was to opt for the Western plan. What, then, outweighed Gerhardsen's preferences? There were, so far as one can see, two factors. First was his focus, both because of the electoral situation and because of the trade unions, on the relatively large Communist vote. Udgaard points out that while the Labor Party vote was down slightly from the last prewar election in the mid-1930's, the Communists had jumped from 1.9 to 11.9% in the 1945 elections, even higher in the cities, and to 22.9% in strategically vulnerable Finnmark in the North, where Soviet troops had been the liberators and had withdrawn peacefully.[150] In the 1947 local elections the Communist Party had retained 10.04% nationally, although in the cities its vote had dropped almost 4%. Still, the Communists remained important competitors at grass roots level. They had strength in certain trade unions, such as the merchant marines in Oslo and Bergen, and in Norsk Hydro (the state electricity company). The next national elections were to be held in October 1949, half a year after the decision. Both Gerhardsen and Konrad Nordahl, the head of the Trade Union Federation, were worried about disruption, particularly in the unions.[175] This was to influence Gerhardsen's attitude toward risk and speed as we shall see.

Gerhardsen was anything but a one-man show. His conception of a Cabinet, according to his explanation several years later, was "a collegium".[176] His positions were the result of the intimate give and take of opinions especially among trusted Labor Party comrades. Thus, when Oscar Torp, chairman of the Parliamentary Labor Party, argued in the time between the Karlstad and Copenhagen meetings, that the acceptance of the Swedish-Danish *fait accompli* tactics was too risky, Gerhardsen was willing to listen.

Torp's argument was that if the Swedish-Danish plan were tried, and if, as seemed likely, it failed to win the American support it sought, it might boomerang. He argued that a hostile attitude would be created in Norway toward the Western powers, which would make difficult the fall-back position of an Atlantic alliance.[177] In other words, Torp's thesis was that this was "too risky a game" (*for høgt spel*) as Lange was to say many years later.[178] Torp, in the words of another of those who had worked with him on the trip to Washington, was important in judging "what the traffic would bear". In Lange's later assessment, "Torp was a deciding factor".[179] Thus the combination of recognized divisions within the Labor Party, and the fear that these could be played upon, led the Prime Minister to reconsider the Karlstad draft.[180] Uncertainty about the ability of the Government to swing public opinion behind the second-best option should the first fail, combined with the assessment that it probably would fail--the Americans would not be persuaded--reduced the Government's propensity to take the risk of opting for an independent Scandinavian pact without prior American assurances of support.[181]

What had happened at this point was that the same old divisions had reappeared in the "intermediate" theory. The idea of a "critical mass" could be used as a theory of deterrence, as a theory of defense, or as a theory of bargaining for support to the pact. As a bargaining tool it took the form of the proposal for a fait accompli: the three were to decide on the pact and then ask for outside aid. As a theory of defense, it assumed the "widespread fire notion" that an attack on such a large and important area would call forth aid (with or without promises). As a theory of deterrence it assumed that such a calculation would be made in advance by a potential aggressor. Even if the theory of defense were accepted,[182] it would be possible to consider the bargaining strategy unlikely to succeed or the deterrence strategy too uncertain.[183] For Hauge, the theory of defense was defective since it excluded cooperation among defense staffs; defense must be prepared for.[184] It is likely that Lange had been especially dubious about the bargaining strategy. Hauge, Lange and Torp had had experience dealing with extra-Scandinavian authorities directly. Now Gerhardsen was also persuaded that to bet on this was taking a big chance with domestic public opinion, an argument to which he was particularly sensible

One might conceptualize it this way. If one assumed that some kind of Scandinavian pact was the first choice of all three countries (leaving open the question of whether and what kind of ties with the West it might have), then what becomes relevant is the order of the second and third choices, because that affects the calculation of opportunity costs by each country's leaders. The preference order was: Denmark: Scandinavia West, alone; Norway: Scandinavia, West, alone; Sweden: Scandinavia, alone, West.

What is usually thought of as the "fall back" position might also be conceived of as the "opportunity cost" for each country's policy. Thus Torp's argument was as follows: the risk of the fait accompli tactic is that it endangers our fall-back position (given the political climate in Norway); the "opportunity costs" of the first preference strategy are very high. On this ground alone, such a decision was subjectively more costly for Norway than for Sweden.

But why were the Norwegian and Danish decisions different? What accounts for the subjective differences in their costing? One explanation was suggested by Lange in 1966. There was, he argued, a "difference in sentiment (atmosphere)" in the two countries which affected their evaluations of risk. He attributed this to the role which the Nordic identity had played in the resistance of the Danes to the Nazis. In Norway, he noted, the British connection outweighed this:

> In the resistance against Nazi pressure for uniformity, consciousness of the distinctively Nordic, of community with the other countries in Scandinavia, had been for most Danes an important source of strength, and Nordic cohesion and solidarity were included as a central value in the thoughts they had of developments after the war.[185]

The point of view which has been developed here suggests reinforcing circumstances. The Danes evaluated the Scandinavian alternative as less costly first because they believed this first option had a higher probability of success than did the Norwegians, and second because they had greater certainty of a viable fall-back position should their first preference fail. The Danes, like the Swedes, believed the United States would act in its own interest once it saw that a pact had been established, and would support it with the necessary supplies. Since in their view the probability of success was higher, the degree of risk was lower. However, should mediation fail and therefore their first preference fail, the onus was unlikely to be on Denmark, something which would help domestically if the Government had to recommend its fall-back position. We shall see why.

The domestic political difficulties for the Danish Government came more from the right of the Social Democrats, than from the Left. Birgitte Westerholm points out that the parliamentary situation explains a lot. The governing Social Democrats had only 57 out of the 150 parliamentary seats. The Communists (9 seats) were now morally and politically isolated. The traditional coalition partner of the Socialists, the Radical Left party, socially reformist but also, as we have explained, neutralist and minimalist on defense, also had too few seats (10) to complete a majority. On the one hand this meant that even if the Social Democrats wanted to include the Radicals in their tacit coalition, they could not forget the other, larger non-socialist parties, the Liberals (Agrarians) and Conservatives. On the other hand it was known, Westerholm suggests, that these two, which favored the NATO option or at least pushed for a position close to that of Norway, would nevertheless support the Scandinavian plan if it could be negotiated.[186] In my view this means that the Liberals and Conservatives were banking on

Norway to hold out to insure Western support to such a plan. In any event, Westerholm concluded that this meant that these two could be ignored and the Government could then concentrate on placating the Radicals whom they wished to retain as partners on issues of domestic politics.

For this purpose, the mediator strategy, finally coming down on the Swedish side, was serviceable. Should the Radicals' (newly) preferred Scandinavian option[187] fail, they would have only isolated neutrality to fall back on. While this continued to attract some--as evidenced by both the speeches of Radical spokesmen in the March 1949 parliamentary debate and by the 9 (out of 10, all but the party leader) Radical members of parliament who voted against joining NATO--pure neutrality and a minimum defense policy had been discredited by the recent war; the 'never more a 9th of April' theme could be (and was) mobilized against them.[188] By comparison with the Norwegian situation, the Danish Social Democratic Government had more of a potential challenge to its fallback position on its right, but was able to neutralize it by its choice of role in the Scandinavian negotiations.

Suppose the Scandinavian pact were to fail due to American refusal to supply arms and goods with the necessary speed and on favorable conditions? Would the second preference, alignment with NATO, be jeopardized? On the left, the Government faced a situation which also different from that in Norway. The Communist vote in Denmark in October 1945 had been even higher than that in Norway. 12.5% compared to 11.8%. However, in the national elections of October 1947 that vote had shrunk to 6.8%.[189] (By comparison in Norway where the Constitution permits no parliamentary dissolutions, no national election had been held since 1945. The local elections of 1947 had shown some Communist decline, especially significant in the cities, but as we have indicated before, the overall figure remained high (10.04%) and high especially in north Norway. Both the Communist vote and Communist activity in key labor unions remained a source of anxiety to the leadership). In Denmark, then, fear of a Communist-provoked backlash with appeal within Social Democratic ranks was not salient. Moreover, externally, their ownership of Greenland gave them a valuable negotiating asset with respect to NATO itself.[190] Because their fallback position was not potentially jeopardized, their first preference, the Scandinavian pact, was subjectively less costly.

An interesting case which illustrates the difference in the Norwegian and Danish responsiveness to this aspect of the decision is the difference in the timing of the choice of NATO. When the Norwegian delegation returned from their Washington trip in February 1949, both Lange and Torp felt that diplomatically there was nothing to be gained by hurrying; they advised a broad effort to orient the public on the issue. The problem of public opinion in Norway had been sufficiently salient for them to have mentioned it to Bevin in discussions in England on the return trip. To the surprise of both Lange and Torp, Gerhardsen determined that once the Government was decided that the Atlantic option was both viable and necessary, it had to move rapidly. He decided to bring the issue up for decision at the upcoming Labor Party Congress--rather than, for example, call an extraordinary Congress at a later date--which previously had been arranged for 17-20 February (beginning two days after the delegation reached home).[191]

At the Labor Party Congress the debate on foreign policy "guiding principles" (Retningslinjer) took all of one day, February 19. (NATO was never specified by name). Gerhardsen alluded to the fear that delay might "open possibilities for the Norwegian Communists, in coordination with Soviet authorities, not least via Soviet radio and press, to influence Norwegian opinion with threats and frightening propaganda".[192] A firm decision, he thought, would halt the Soviet pressure, recently evidenced by the two Soviet notes to Norway. The rapidity of Norway's decisions in the Labor Party, in the Storting, and in joining the NATO planning group, are explicable by reference to its decision-makers' uncertainty with respect to domestic reactions in contrast to the Danes' probable estimate of the domestic situation in Denmark. We can, therefore, distinguish the reasons for, and the style of, Norway's choice not only from those of Sweden, but from those of Denmark, by reference to the concept of opportunity cost.

Conclusions

In sum, Sweden believed that the American position on weapons' aid was a tactic, and was willing to gamble that a fait accompli strategy would obtain aid after a while. Its theory of deterrence was one of denial, and extension of a pact to Scandinavia could have the advantage of achieving a critical mass" which would give greater incentive to the Western powers to aid if any part of Scandinavia were attacked. Essentially there was domestic unity on this position although some versions of the "critical mass" theory (nearer to the Norwegian versions, where the Western powers understanding was a premise) appealed especially to some opposition parties' members. Because of this basic unity of public opinion, Swedish decision-makers were willing to gamble on the chance of Western sympathy for an independent Scandinavian pact, because in the event that they lost the gamble, their fall-back position would remain unimpaired; the subjective opportunity costs of their first preference were not high. Sweden's effort throughout the negotiations was to protect the credibility of its traditional policy either for the pact which would be created or for its fall-back position of complete independence.

Denmark, because of its position in the negotiations, took on the role of mediator. In its own policy it supported both the "critical mass" theory of deterrence (near the Swedish view) and the need for assurance of aid (nearer the Norwegian view). Until the last moment, Denmark refused to choose between these two, but finally opted for the independent Swedish strategy. It wavered in its assessment of what was possible to obtain from the United States, but was willing to take more of a risk than Norway because it was surer, for external and internal reasons, of its fall-back position. But after Norway chose NATO, Denmark had to follow.

Norway believed that the American position on aid was essentially informative and not strategic in intent; it had to be seen in the light of the general American strategy which was unlikely to be changed in its essentials, one of which was the concept of mutual commitment. This general strategy was also seen by and large as good because it committed the United States to Europe, and created the conditions not only of a power balance but of a core which could be extended to Scandinavia. Norway's basic deterrence theory was one of punishment, not denial, although on this there was probably internal disagreement. What was crucial in deciding which deterrence theory would be tried was the sense that public opinion could not be swung rapidly with the leadership should the risk of deciding on a neutral pact be taken and fail, and the fall-back position need to be revived.

Divergencies in the assessments of the likely American response, of basic deterrence strategies, and of the domestic constraints of each country, account for both the variation in the strength of the preference for a Scandinavian pact, and for the variation in estimates of the viability of a fall-back position. The different fall-back positions can be taken as the opportunity costs of the first preferences. In turn, they determine the critical policy decisions, and thus the failure of the attempt to create a Scandinavian defense pact.

CHAPTER THREE

DISPARITIES, STRATEGIES, AND OPPORTUNITY COSTS: THE PROPOSED SCANDINAVIAN COMMON MARKET, 1947-1959

In the case of the defense pact negotiations we saw how differences in the judgment of the importance and probabilities attached to crucial dimensions of the defense problem led to opposing policy decisions. In particular, the countries' differing fall-back positions meant that for each the plan had different opportunity costs.

The negotiations for a potential Scandinavian economic market reveal first how differing attributes of the parties, namely their relative strength, affected the way they sought to accomplish their purposes, that is, their strategies in negotiations. These strategies nonetheless were not absolutely static; after all the negotiations continued sporadically for over a decade, from 1947 to 1959. Changing internal and external circumstances altered the opportunity costs associated with the plan, and soon, the appreciation by each country's leaders of those costs. This resulted in changes in each party's negotiating position. The second point this chapter demonstrates, then, is how changing opportunity costs change bargaining positions. Thirdly it shows the rather subtle way in which a commitment becomes an element in the costing of a decision. Both "why the countries wanted what they wanted" and "how they sought to achieve it" are illustrated by a study of the economic discussions. Finally, the economic issue had several characteristics quite different from those of the defense pact issue; a Scandinavian economic market was a low priority in all the countries, yet it had high political "visibility". The peculiar combination contributed, as we shall see, to the negative diplomatic spiral in which few political resources in any of the countries were invested in its attainment.

A Brief Chronology

At the end of summer of 1947, the same summer in which representatives of Western European and North American countries met to establish the organization of the Marshall Plan, the Scandinavian Foreign Ministers announced that they intended to set up a "cooperation committee of experts" to discuss Nordic economic cooperation, including the removal of customs duties. The "cooperation committee of experts" was established in February 1948.

Its mandate was:

> as a contribution to the general economic recovery after the war to take up the questions which are of common interest for the economy of the Nordic countries. The Committee shall especially investigate the possibilities
>
> (1) to introduce a common Nordic tariff as a prerequisite for a Nordic customs union
> (2) to reduce the tariffs and limit the quantitative restrictions among the Nordic countries
> (3) to broaden the division of labor and specialization among the Nordic countries in cooperation with the individual industrial branches and industrial and trade union organizations,
> (4) in connection with which the possibilities of furthering new production to supplement the countries' economies,
> (5) and to further the cooperation on trade policy vis-à-vis the outside, which already obtains.[1]
> (numbering added)

There was no word from the Committee until, in a preliminary report in early 1950, it concluded:

> that a customs union would benefit Scandinavia as a whole,
> that there would be transitional difficulties for industries in all three countries,
> that to ameliorate these, the reduction of trade restrictions would have to be successive over ten years.

The Norwegian members of the committee stressed that a customs union would present such serious problems for Norway that only "if special measures to balance the development within the customs union area were first taken" would the union be a net gain for it. The committee's conclusions was that the problems were of such magnitude that at present there was no basis for agreement.[2]

By all rights, the matter should have been buried. Upon Norwegian initiative, however, the Committee was given a new mandate in November

1950: to investigate those industrial areas for which an elimination of restrictions among the countries would be a common interest. Thus what the committee was now to discuss was a partial free trade area, that is, the elimination of intra-Nordic customs barriers in certain areas without touching the issues of a common external tariff, or of free trade in the rest of the areas.[3]

Again, nothing was heard from the committee until the flurry of activity generated by the establishment of the Nordic Council in 1953. At that time the several previously established Nordic committees were asked to make reports to the Council's first session. The Committee on Nordic Economic Cooperation met twice early in 1952 to discuss the forthcoming report, but could not agree and left it to each country's delegation to write its own statement. The Nordic Council was presented with a plethora of diverse documentation both from the Committee itself and from its national components.[4] The same disputes which had been evident in the initial 1950 report surfaced again in the national interpretations of the Committee's mandate, its results, and method of work. The Nordic Council could only unanimously urge the Committee to complete its report, and note that "closer economic cooperation"--the formula which bridges the gap in viewpoints, and commits no one to anything--would strengthen the economies of the Nordic countries.[5]

In March 1954, the Committee submitted its final report to the Governments. Again, it had split conclusions. The Swedes and Danes wrote their report together and ended on an optimistic note, while the Norwegians wrote a separate and pessimistic sounding report. <u>For the first time</u>, the Swedes and Danes acknowledged the need for something other than purely transitional measures in order to avoid disruptions in the Norwegian economy; the need for "capital transfers" was made explicit, which contrasted with the 1950 report. The report concluded that the Governments should take up negotiations in the twenty-one industrial sectors which had been investigated by the Committee, beginning with those eight areas in which there had been little or no opposition.[6] The Norwegian Committee members commented that:

> ...an arrangement purely on the basis of tariffs would have to be of relatively limited extent for the present, if the advantages and dis-

advantages were to be distributed approximately equally among the countries.[7]

The Norwegians argued that if there were to be any further investigation, it would have to be on a different basis: political discussions would have to include the possibility of credits and loans; the interrelations of the parts of the agreement would have to be acknowledged. The report indicated that the two views had come closer than before, but not close enough for joint conclusions.

Yet just a few months later there did seem to be a cautious reorientation by the Norwegian Government. In June of 1954 a Government report to the Storting had a new tone, compared with that of Norwegian representatives in the reports of January 1950 or March 1954. The Government paper gave a variety of arguments for further economic cooperation of different kinds in Scandinavia, but the most interesting point was the general one: that it did not terminate the discussion, as one might have predicted from the March document, but rather kept it alive.[8]

The new momentum was evident at the second session of the Nordic Council in Oslo that August. Norwegian Prime Minister Einar Gerhardsen contended that "it is now time" to prepare a Nordic common market and implement it in the near future. A recommendation was passed by the Council supported by all the Swedes and Danes, and by the Norwegian Labor Party members but by none of the Norwegian opposition parties' members.[9] It urged the Nordic Governments: to establish conditions which would permit a common Scandinavian market in as large an area as possible; to investigate a common external tariff, reduction of internal Scandinavian tariffs and other restrictions "at a rate considered compatible with each country's special circumstances"; to take up concrete tasks in the areas of research, power, etc.; to establish responsible organs charged with the above tasks.[10]

The upshot of the year's activities was the October 1954 Cabinet level conference at Harpsund, Sweden, headed by the three Prime Ministers. It resulted in an upgrading of the Scandinavian negotiations. The Ministers of Trade were to direct the investigations, assisted by civil servants, and in contact with economic organizations[11] representing major economic interests.

The significant change, then, was that politically responsible ministers were now involved, because it is clear that the mandate was no stronger than that of 1948. The new committee, the Nordic Economic Cooperation Committee (NECC), was to "survey" Nordic trade to see where tariffs might be eliminated with "overwhelming advantages for all three countries". They were also to "investigate whether there are areas of production" which would be advantageous to exploit cooperatively.

The NECC took up first the 33% of intra-Scandinavian trade which was "relatively free", then other areas stipulated in the mandate ("chemical and pharmaceutical, iron and steel, electrometallurgical and electrotechnical, metal and metal half-processed industries"). On its own initiative (i.e. with the consent of the "Cooperation Ministers", the Ministers of Trade), it added the area of machinery which accounted for another 10%, bringing the total over the GATT requirement for permissible discriminatory arrangements. Nevertheless, the new negotiations do not seem to have been conducted in any essentially different way (such as to facilitate concessions across the sectors or between the customs union and the other issues). It looks as if little political evaluation and direction were given until the final stages in 1958.[12]

In January 1955 the third session of the Nordic Council received a report on the Harpsund arrangements but did not debate it. At mid-year a statistical study of inter-Nordic trade was published, and in January-February 1956, at the following Nordic Council meetings--the first in which Finland participated--a report from the NECC was debated. In the summer of 1956, Finland joined the NECC negotiations.

The farthest point which the negotiations reached was described in the NECC's July 1957 report and in the supplement to it, published in the fall of 1958. Its main outlines were as follows:[13]

1. A common external tariff. Abolition of tariffs among the (now four) Nordic countries, covering 80% of intra-Nordic trade, and effective immediately.

2. Transitional arrangements (mostly five, sometimes ten, years): in Finland and Norway for the machinery and electrical engineering industries; in Denmark for the removal of some quantitative restrictions; in Finland and Norway for the removal of export restrictions on timber and scrap iron.

3. Exceptions should be made only after consultations with the others although the national state remained the final judge.

4. The remaining 20% of intra-Nordic trade was: agriculture (8.6%), fish (2.5%), industrial goods (8.3%). It was recommended that fish be included; agricultural decisions would have to be dependent on European decisions.

5. The aim of the market would be to change the structure of industry to make it competitive on world markets; thus there would be no subsidies of weak industries.

6. Conditions of competition could not and should not be coordinated but in the control of "harmful monopolies" Norway wanted much stronger legislation than did Sweden and Finland.

7. The report included lengthy but vague discussions of cooperation in production, research and education, balance of payments problems, commercial policy.

8. There was also an agreement for a cooperation organization for the iron and steel industry.

9. A Nordic Investment Bank was suggested along the following lines: its purpose was "to strengthen the Nordic economy" (Nordens ekonomi) by investing "in projects of Nordic interest", where two or more countries would be affected or where the long run effects would be beneficial to the region as a whole. "In special cases" funds could be used for "alleviating transitional difficulties arising from the common market" such as helping firms which had to make new investments to remain competitive, or providing new employment for those displaced, but not helping to maintain uncompetitive firms.

   The bank would grant loans or guarantee loans either to countries or firms. "Operations should be governed by banking principles" and the allocation of loans should be without regard to allocation among the countries, or to whether the recipient is a public or private firm. The initial capital was to be 300 million dollars subscribed by Sweden, Norway, Finland, and Denmark in a ratio of 2:1:1:1, which approximates the ratio of their national incomes. In addition there was an arrangement by which Sweden was to count the payments which the others owed it for postwar loans as part of their share. The bank itself was to obtain loans on the international market, and, in fact, the major part of the funds were expected to be so obtained.[14]

On the prodding of the standing Economic Committee of the Nordic Council, the NECC produced a supplementary report, not covering the whole 20% of remaining intra-Nordic trade as requested, but covering up to 91.6%. Even that report was, however, still inconclusive. The full Nordic Council again urged the Governments to negotiate on the basis of, but not to be bound by, the reports (i.e. the widest possible mandate). At late as May 1959 real negotiations continued, with the NECC agreeing on further protective measures: some tariff increases, longer internal tariff transitions, and special measures for textiles. However, at the top level Nordic meeting in July, the work of the NECC was declared done; no action was taken. In effect, this was a decision against the Scandinavian option, and for the European Free Trade Area.[15]

Disparities and Strategies

Nordic Economic Cooperation, 1947: A Joint Diplomatic Ploy

The prospect of Scandinavian economic cooperation arose in a special context. It was first raised by the Norwegians in July 1947, when the Scandinavian countries met to coordinate their positions for the forthcoming meetings of the Marshall Plan countries. The communiqué reveals that they suggested that such cooperation include "the coordination of the countries' investments".[16] At the end of the summer it was evident that the countries did not have a unified position on the degrees of participation in the Marshall Plan arrangements. However, they took note of the American interest in a European customs union, and upon a Danish suggestion agreed to set up a "cooperation committee of experts" to discuss Nordic economic cooperation including the removal of duties among their countries.[17] "This decision was later announced to the Marshall Plan conference in Paris by the Danish delegation".[18]

Thus two things had happened: first, the American insistence on a unified plan for a reduction of the barriers among Marshall plan countries had stimulated (at least pro forma) discussions on a European customs union. In reaction to this, the Scandinavian countries had announced their own regional negotiations to avoid being pressured to involve themselves more seriously in the larger group. Secondly, in this ploy, the content of the original proposal was changed from a proposal for joint investments (possibly with capital transfers) to greater attention to a customs union.[19] This coincided not only with American preferences which made it diplomatically useful, but also with Swedish and Danish preferences as is clear from all subsequent negotiations. The Norwegians thus became involved in discussions on much broader grounds than those they originally had proposed, as the mandate to the joint committee, worked out in February 1948, makes clear.

The diplomatic use of the Scandinavian "investigations", first pointed out in a dissertation by Per Olaf Jonsson,[20] is illustrated by the reports of the fall of 1949 when Paul Hoffman gave his famous "integration" speech to the OEEC Foreign and Finance Ministers in Paris. He argued then that it had been on the basis of "this promise" (of integration) that Congress had passed the Marshall Plan, that such integration required fiscal and monetary coordination and looked toward the "creation" of a single European market. But, he added, "there are other arrangements which I am convinced , will also turn out to be steps toward the same objective, "namely groups of two, three or more cooperating countries. Hoffman stressed the "urgency" of such measures because of the short time remaining to the Marshall Plan itself, and because it would give "new impetus" to American support through 1952.[21]

Years later Norwegian Foreign Minister Lange recalled that the unanimous reaction of the three Norwegian delegates (himself, Finance Minister Erik Brofoss, and Chief Delegate to the OEEC, Arne Skaug) had been that the Americans were trying to force integration on terms which were unacceptable to the Norwegian Government as social democrats.[22] They saw this as an effort to curtail economic planning. Interestingly enough, however, American press reports understood from Lange only that he "generally approved" Hoffman's proposals, although with "some qualifications".[23] His visit to Harriman and Hoffman was reported by The New York Times under the headline, "Scandinavia Plans to Speed Forming of Customs Union".[24] A few days later even Paul Hoffman was saying, "We would like to see a grouping of the Scandinavian countries which are complementary economies" (sic!) which does not sound as if he had been discouraged.[25] The point is simply that there were strong diplomatic incentives for a show of progress toward economic unity. This would also account for the prolongation of the investigation after the January 1950 report which found no basis for agreement.[26]

Bargaining Strategies: Expansive versus Distributive

While the reason that the negotiations were started made them *pro forma*, the differences in national position were genuine, based on genuine assessments by national leaders of the needs of their respective countries. Two different negotiating positions emerged, the Swedish-Danish, and the Norwegian. These remained relatively unchanged until the middle of the 1950's. Sweden and Denmark were interested in a common market (a common Scandinavian tariff against outside countries, and the elimination of tariff barriers between the participant countries), or at least a free trade area (the elimination of the internal tariff barriers, but the retention of separate tariffs vis-à-vis the outside world).

In contrast, Norway was interested in two quite different possibilities. Norway's major underdeveloped resource was water power, transformable into electricity *if* sufficient investment capital could be obtained. Therefore Norway probed the possibility of joint investment projects. Insofar as Norway was interested in an expanded market, it conceived of such a market as broadening the division of labor and specialization among the Nordic countries. (This might contrast, for example, with an economist's conception of division of labor among regions or industries, a view which does not pay attention to national boundaries).

What is suggested here, is, first, that the Swedish-Danish position and the Norway position represented two distinct and recognizable bargaining strategies, the forms of which can be described by concepts from game theory. Second, our hypothesis is that the two strategies are understandable as a strategy of the strong and a strategy of the weak respectively. We shall pause briefly to explain the concepts.

Game theory distinguishes two polar types of games. The first is a "fixed sum" game where the area of negotiation is fixed and the sole rational strategy for any player is a "distributive" strategy, that is, one which concentrates on settling the shares of the respective players, the division of the pie. Since any increase for one means a decrease for others, concern for ones net gain coincides with concern for ones relative gain. The second type of game is a "variable sum game" in which there are possible solutions which could"benefit both parties, or at least...the gains of one party...need not represent equal sacrifice by the other".[27] In such games there are different rational strategies possible. A distributive strategy is, of course, one. But an "expansive" strategy, that is, one which concentrates on increasing the joint gain, the size of the whole pie, is also possible. These expansive and distributive strategies are of course the polar extremes. Most real life strategies combine elements of both. Characterisations are, therefore, of the predominant orientation.

Walton and McKersie, who have used these game and strategy types in analyzing labor negotiations, have explained some of the dilemmas involved in choosing an appropriate strategy in a non-fixed or variable-sum game.[28] If the player follows the distributive, purely competitive strategy, he runs the risk of losing opportunities for maximum gain (i.e. for increasing the whole pie, and through that, the absolute size of his share). If he follows instead a purely expansive strategy, he runs the risk of being taken advantage of if the other party plays a distributive game.

One would think that a sequential strategy, first expansive, creating the highest possible joint gain, then distributive, hard competitive bargaining over its division, would be optimal. However, it is difficult psychologically; it is not easy to shift gears in that fashion, for example to be first open, then closed, with information. Moreover, and very significantly, some high joint-gain solutions inherently provide one party with what the other may consider "disproportionate" gains. Although in game theory this dilemma is solvable with "side-payments", that is extra inducements outside the original area of bargaining, in practice this is often unlikely.

> The disadvantaged party may not have the distributive bargaining power or skill necessary to compel the payment when the time becomes appropriate. It is also possible that the advantaged party will not accept the need for this action, arguing that the shares should be allocated according to "where the chips fall".[29]

If, in ambiguous or clearly variable-sum games, there is no best strategy, who is likely to select which strategy? What are the characteristics of parties who bargain _as if_ the games were primarily a fixed sum, that is, bargain distributively, and those who bargain _as if_ the game were primarily variable sum, that is, bargain expansively? To my knowledge, game theory does not specify.

Since the expansive strategy leaves open the question of distribution, the question of who will choose that strategy may be rephrased as: "under what circumstances will a party be willing to leave open the question of distribution?" The contention here is that a party will be likely to do so when it has confidence that, should the necessity (in its view) arise, it will be able to influence the distribution of joint gain at a later stage. The obverse of this is that a party less confident of its ability to influence the outcome later on, will be less likely to opt for an expansive strategy. Instead it will be particularly concerned from the beginning with the distribution of gains. What we are suggesting is that the party which feels itself to be advantaged in the negotiations will tend to follow a primarily expansive strategy, while the party which feels itself to be disadvantaged will tend to follow a primarily distributive strategy.[30]

With some exaggeration, the Swedish position may be characterized as a "let the chips fall where they may" solution, and the Norwegian position as one that distributive arrangements ought to be worked out in advance to prevent an improperly skewed distribution of benefits and losses.

An example of this is the 1950 joint Report of the inter-Scandinavian committee. It made only one concession to the distributive worries of the Norwegians: the customs union which would benefit all of Scandinavia, should have transitional rates of tariff reductions. The Norwegians on the committee added that "special measures to balance the development within the customs union..." were needed.[31] According to a senior Danish civil servant on that committee, the "special measures" had been discussed in 1949 at a meeting "on the highest political plane". The proposals were for loans from Sweden and Denmark to Norway, and the problem, as he later explained to a meeting of Scandinavian economists, was "how can one create a balance among the participants if one agrees that a customs union would give economic advantages...".[32]

The argument here is that Sweden's strategy was basically an expansive one and Norway's a distributive one. (Denmark's line was usually indistinguishable from Sweden's). Sweden's aim was to expand market opportunities for its thriving industries, and its main argument was the comparative advantage thesis of classical economics: all parties would gain by the increased division of labor in a larger market. Norway, on the other hand, conceived of a prearranged division of labor, with the common external tariff giving a form of guaranteed marketing possibilities.

Our hypothesis has been that there is a connection between a sense of being advantaged, a sense of efficacy, and the tendency to choose an expansive strategy, and likewise a connection between a sense of being disadvantaged, and the tendency to follow a distributive strategy. Furthermore unless there is evidence to the contrary, it is assumed that there is a rough correspondence between circumstances of strength or weakness, and self-evaluation, although the latter is frequently far from perfect, or may lag behind changes in the objective situation. The sense of capability or incapability is neither random nor capricious; it can be explained in terms of previous experience subjectively assimilated. (This is not to imply that it is appropriate to the current situation, to current tasks, current opportunities or current negotiations).

Initial Disparities

From what has been said one would suspect that there were general disparities in capabilities among the Scandinavian countries, and of course to anyone familiar with these countries they were obvious.

Before the Second World War, Denmark had been the wealthiest of the Scandinavian countries; while it had been occupied during the war, it did not suffer great destruction. Its development had been based on being a commercial center, an *entrepôt*, and on its export of agricultural commodities. Not until the mid-1960's did its industrial exports exceed agricultural exports. Sweden replaced Denmark as the economic leader after World War II. Its natural resources, such as the enormous iron mines of the north, were the basis for an iron and steel industry and later such products as its famed ball bearings and machine tools. Thus it had the possibility of a more differentiated economy than those of Norway and Finland, with whom it had in common a wealth of timber from vast forests. By the 1950's Sweden was the most highly industrialized of the four. In intra-Scandinavian trade it had a balance of payments surplus with each of the others. Moreover it had emerged from the war with sufficient capital not only for its own needs, but also enough to be a lender nation.[33]

Norway was the poorest of the three countries. Only three percent of its land was arable, and its industrial resources were sparse, with the exception of its numerous waterfalls which could be developed to generate electric power. Industrialization had come late to Norway. In addition, during the war it had lost half its huge merchant marine which had been its main source of foreign exchange. The far north had been laid waste by the retreating Nazi occupiers; reconstruction was the order of the day.[34]

Economic disparities are not the only ones worth mentioning. Sweden was a former Great Power with a long diplomatic tradition; Norway was a relatively new state with only a short history of independent diplomacy since 1905. There was also the contrast between the state whose neutrality policy had succeeded in keeping it out of a world war, and one whose policy, also one of neutrality, had not. Here again, Denmark takes a middle place, being a country long independent and formerly much larger, but nevertheless dragged into the recent war against both its will and its neutral policy.[35]

Evidence that the parties' views of themselves corresponded to these objective disparities in their situation, is fragmentary, and as is natural in a bargaining situation, partially obscure, It does, nevertheless, suggest the patterns we have described. For example, as will be shown below, the Norwegian Federation of Industries tended to view the Scandinavian market as a limited pie, and Norway's share unlikely to increase either absolutely or relatively. Or, take an opinion of a former Norwegian Government member: Halvard Lange explained many years later that the investment fund requested by Norway would have been "a token that Sweden would help the weak brother".[36]

Reinforcing Factors: The Governments' Domestic "Terms of Trade"

Thus far it has been argued that there is a certain logic in the situation of being stronger or weaker which predisposes toward adopting an expansive or distributive orientation respectively. This is a tendency, one dynamic among others, which in some situations may be reinforced and in others outweighed. In the Scandinavian case there were several reinforcing historical and political factors.

Differences in bargaining strategy were reinforced by differences in

1) the basic economic strategies pursued domestically, 2) the degree of cross-party consensus on these economic lines, 3) the political histories of the governing Social Democratic parties, and 4) the parliamentary base of the respective governments.

First, the basic economic strategies pursued in the three countries after the war, differed. In Norway investment was massive, financed by extremely heavy taxation (holding consumption low), and a deliberate import surplus. Investment opportunities were channeled directly from above; the "home industries", those producing exclusively for the home market (usually consumer goods), were denied investment funds, while export industries were encouraged. Gross domestic investment as a percentage of gross domestic product was 35-38% between 1950 and 1958. Gross fixed capital formation as a percentage of gross national produce was 30-38% between 1953 and 1956.[37]

How were the Norwegians able to carry out such a program? The keynote in Norway was <u>gjenreisning</u>, reconstruction. The experience of solidarity among all the democratic parties during the war had diminished the sharp socialist-nonsocialist political antagonisms of the prewar years.[38] The Government-in-exile in London had worked out a program of direct controls for the period immediately after the war and, in consultation with the Employers' Federation and Trade Union Federation, a program of wage and price stabilization as well. The coalition government of liberation had an economic "joint program" agreed to by all.[39] Even after the victory of the Labor Party several months later, there was substantial agreement about economic priorities. With the goal of reconstruction common to all, the high investment-austerity strategy was basically non-controversial, although the allocation of investments might be in dispute.

The most important "planner" of the Norwegian economy was Erik Brofoss, who was Minister of Finance from 1945 to 1947, then Minister of Trade until 1954 when he was appointed to head the central bank.[40] Brofoss was described by James Reston as a "Crippsian" in outlook on life, but another journalist (who called him a "firebrand who seems to create constant controversy") perceptively remarked that he "could not help feeling that (Brofoss) is not treating the capitalists as badly as they say, and that they are not opposing him as much as he seems to believe".[41] A comparison of the tone of the economic debate in Norway with the much sharpter debates in Sweden or Denmark, would seem to bear him out.[42]

In Sweden, and particularly in Denmark, the dominant economic philosophy was much more liberal. In contrast to Norwegian direct controls, which continued until 1952 to 1954, Sweden and Denmark used indirect economic measures. In the mid-1950's a Danish Social Democratic Finance Minister argued that fiscal and monetary policy must be used solely for countercyclical policy; tax and inheritance laws should be the only means of affecting consumer choices. To the same audience the Norwegian Liberal, Gunnar Jahn, who had previously headed the Bank of Norway, argued to the contrary that a "planned economy" implying "control over consumer behavior" was necessary to achieve social goals, such as the combination of a desired distribution of income and price stability.[43]

Why should there have been such differences, especially among the Socialist parties of the three countries? If one looks first at Denmark, one notes that in contrast to Norway, the wartime Resistance movement had no real postwar plans for anything except purging the Government and changing the foreign policy leadership. Even though the Resistance movement had representation in the first coalition cabinet, they conceived of their task as apolitical. There was no agreed economic policy.[44] In addition, in both Sweden and Denmark, the non-socialist parties were more ad adamant opponents of economic controls than was the case in Norway.

A more profound answer lies in the historical development of social democracy in the three countries. In both Sweden and Denmark, labor movements had arisen before the achievement of democratic suffrage and responsible government. The fight for the franchise encouraged the cooperation of socialists and liberals and drew socialists into calculations of electoral, as well as organizational, strength early on. Ideological rigor --and inbreeding--declined. By contrast, the Norwegian party had developed after the fight both for suffrage and for parliamentary control, and therefore had few incentives to ally with others. The Norwegian party is conventionally considered to have been the most "radical", as it was the only Western European party to join the Comintern (briefly).[45] The important point, however, is that its isolation left its ideas relatively intact for a longer period, and the practice of cross-party cooperation was muted until 1940. The consequence was a difference in the economic philosophies of the Norwegian, when compared with the Swedish and especially Danish, socialist parties.

Although having a more radical economic philosophy than its Swedish and Danish counterparts, the Norwegian Labor Party, when in power, was a majority government which the other two never were. This was partly an artifact of the electoral system in Norway which rewarded the largest party very highly; even changes in 1952, lessening this bias, did not eliminate it, or the Government's majority in parliament.[46] By contrast, the Swedish Socialists, also in power throughout the period, never had a majority in parliament, although they had nearly the same electoral base. Instead, they had a minority government from 1945 to 1952, thereafter until 1957 a coalition with the Agrarians, and then again a minority government. The Danish Social Democrats also had minority and coalition governments, and were sometimes entirely out of power. From 1945 to 1947 they were out of office; from 1947 to 1950 they formed a minority government; from 1950 to 1953 an Agrarian-Conservative coalition held office; from 1953 to 1957 there was again a Social Democratic and Radical majority, followed from 1957 to 1960 by a majority coalition of three parties including the Socialists.

Finally, John Sanness suggests the possibility of a strictly situational explanation for Norway's planned approach and Sweden's and Denmark's more liberal ones. They may well have been dictated by the differences in economic constraints and possibilities in the three countries. Norway had both the need for extensive reconstruction due to wartime damage--a need which facilitated political consensus on economic policy--and the possibility of a planned program due to its ability by its exports to earn the hard currency needed to obtain investment goods. Sweden also had hard currency exports but its need was not pressing and political differences on economic policy were great. Denmark had relative need--it had not been destroyed during the war, but its economy had stagnated--but it could not earn hard currency with its exports; a high investment austerity program was not a necessity for Sweden, then, while for Denmark it was an excluded option.

All these differences, the more radical history of the Labor Party in Norway, its firmer parliamentary basis, the degree of cross-party consensus on the reconstruction and general economic program, the economic situation itself, reinforced the Norwegians' view of the propriety of a planned approach and suspicion of market forces. These attitudes underlay the distributive approach to the Scandinavian negotiations, an approach which insisted on calculating and apportioning prospective joint gains. Conversely, the superior economic position which made the expansive approach to the negotiations a natural for the Swedes and Danes, was reinforced by their own more liberal economic policies at home, by the early "liberalization" of their Social Democratic Parties, the earlier traditions of cooperation across parties, and the greater strength of the opposition parties in their current political systems, measured both in parliamentary strength and in fierceness of tone on economic issues.[48] We can see, therefore, not only the logic of the negotiating positions but some of their historical and political underpinnings as well.

Changes in Costing. 1. Norway, 1954*

Incentives to Change

If the basic goals and strategies, and the historical and political factors which supported them, were accurately described, when and why should there ever be movement from the initial diplomatic positions? One example of movement was that of Norway's partial change of position in 1954. Just four months after the second Nordic committee had reported, with split conclusions and very pessimistic words from its Norwegian members, the Norwegian Government itself reopened the issue in a report to the Storting, and a few months later the governing Labor Party's representatives voted together with the Swedes and Danes in passing an encouraging recommendation by the Nordic Council. Why was there a change, and why was the change only partial?[49]

---

* For a table of events, see pp. 105 - 107

TABLE 1. TABLE OF EVENTS IN THE SCANDINAVIAN AND EUROPEAN NEGOTIATIONS 1954 - 1959

European Events	Date	Scandinavian Negotiations
	1954	
	March	Report of the expert committee appointed in 1948, to the Governments. Sweden and Denmark write joint conclusions; Norwegian delegates write separate conclusions.
	June 18	Norwegian Ministry of Trade report to the Storting. Tone more positive.
	August	Nordic Council 2nd session, in Oslo. Swedish and Danish delegates plus Norwegian Labor Party delegates vote for recommendation to the Governments to negotiate a Nordic market. Norwegian non-socialists abstain.
	October 3-31	Harpsund meeting, Sweden. Government delegates headed by Prime Ministers agree on new mandate to a Nordic investigating committee to be appointed under the direction of the "Cooperation Ministers" (Ministers of Trade) from each country. (Committee hereafter, NECC.)
	1955	
	January	Nordic Council 3rd session. Report on Harpsund. No debate.
Messina. European relance.	June	
	July	Nordisk samhandel (Inter-Nordic trade), a statistical study, published.

European Events	Date	Scandinavian Negotiations
	1956	
	January - February	Nordic Council 4th session. Report on the wo rk of the NECC (dated December 12, 1955.) Debate. First session in which Finland participates.
	August - fall	Finland joints the work of the NECC.
	1957	
Maudling Commission begins European Free Trade Area discussions within OEEC. (Sixteen nations).	February	Nordic Council 5th session. Debate on Nordic market, against the background of the European free trade area plans.
25 March 1957 Rome Treaty signed.	March 25	
	July 8	Report from NECC on 80% of Inter-Nordic trade: Nordic Economic Cooperation.
	November	Nordic Council's standing Economic Committee recommends drawing up plans for the remaining 20%.
	1958	
	January	Nordic Council 6th session. No debate.
	fall	Plan for all but agriculture in inter-Nordic trade, or for 91.4%.
Maudling negotiations break down	November	Nordic Council's 7th session recommends that the Scandinavians negotiate on a Governmental level.

European Events	Date	Scandinavian Negotiations
	1959	
	January 24-25	Governmental level meeting.
EFTA discussions, Oslo. (The Outer Seven).	February 21	
	May	NECC meeting. Further concessions on textiles, transition measures, external tariffs.
	July 10-11	Nordic Council praesidium and the Economic Committee of the Nordic Council meet at Kungälv.
	July 11-12	Nordic Governmental level meeting under Prime Ministers. NECC work declared finished.
Formal negotiations for EFTA, the European Free Trade Association.	July 20-21	

There were two possible sources of change which this writer could identify. They concerned the evaluation of the domestic and the external environment respectively. The first is that by 1954, when Norway's industries had been rebuilt, its appraisal of its competitive abilities within a Scandinavian grouping changed.[50] (Why this should not have affected the "experts" on the Nordic committee a few months before, is unclear). This was the period in which direct controls were being lifted from the Norwegian economy, making cooperation with others easier. Brofoss himself maintains that he had told those who raised the idea soon after the war, "come again in five years".[51] He was no protectionist per se although he had felt Norway too weak just after the war to participate. He saw the value of larger markets and greater stimulus to industry. It has also been argued that participation in the Marshall Plan had been a learning experience; exaggerated fears of interference with domestic prerogatives, and of the effects of the liberal trade strategy on the economically weaker, had been allayed.[52]

But more than this permissive condition was needed if Norway were to regard the customs union not just as a quid pro quo but as desirable in itself. Brofoss himself has given one explanation of the change. He related that in the fall of 1951 he had met and worked with Jean Monnet on a NATO committee for the financing of infrastructure. He was both "fascinated" with and "sceptical" of Monnet's ideas, but had returned to Norway with the conviction that a "constellation" was developing in Europe.[53] He advised the Government: "Now the point is to prepare Scandinavia for a new situation".[54]

Brofoss' motive, then, in suggesting a new Scandinavian opening was to enable Scandinavia to "stand together vis-à-vis the Continent", not for their potential economic complementarity, then, but for their potential cohesion and potential leverage.

Was this a consideration of "high politics" coming unexpectedly from the Minister of Trade rather than from the Foreign Minister? Only partly. Brofoss remembered that during the interwar years the big powers had played off the small for their own trade advantage.[55] Now there was a chance to avoid this happening again.

In addition, some specific economic considerations seemed to dominate his thinking. The Marshall Plan funds were tapering off, and Brofoss feared that the liberalizing effect of the OEEC might fade as well. If convertibility of currencies to dollars were achieved, as was then being bruited, the big powers, particularly Germany, might seek to discourage imports which had to be paid for in dollars, or to demand dollars in payment for their exports. If so, Norway, which traditionally paid for its imports from Germany with sterling, would be hurt.[56] Brofoss wrote memos with these views to the Prime Minister, took up the matter with the Cabinet, and, in the spring of 1954 "lectured" the Nordic labor parties' cooperation committee on the implications for Scandinavia, and the need to cooperate. This resulted in a Norwegian Cabinet decision authorizing the June 1954 Government report which suggested the partial change of policy. (The report itself, written by Dagfinn Juel of the Ministry of Trade, was toned down because of internal disagreements).

Brofoss was, at the time, rather alone in many of these evaluations. What persuaded the Government to go along far enough to allow him to try out his ideas? In 1952-53 the old NATO--anti-NATO split within the Labor Party surfaced in dissension about the (post-Lisbon) defense plans. Brofoss noted that it was "in that context" that he raised the Nordic consideration.[57] The inference might be that the plan had some attraction to the Cabinet in showing that a Nordic policy could be combined with the Atlantic policy, an attempt to cater to the anti-NATO wing of the Party.

Brofoss was quite close to Einar Gerhardsen, who had been Prime Minister from the end of the war until November 1951 and was to be again in January 1955. Not a Cabinet member (but leader of the Labor Party Storting Group) in 1954, he was nevertheless a central figure in all top Labor Party discussions. Gerhardsen is said to have relied heavily on Jens Christian Hauge and Erik Brofoss in his years as head of Government, and when retired mentioned Brofoss as among the five or six with whom he had had "especially good cooperation". It is likely that Brofoss was able to persuade Gerhardsen.[58]

Impediments to Change

The incentives to change have been located in the Government's evaluation of both domestic and external consequences of the Nordic option (and its competitors). The impediments to change will be sought in the same sources. The possible domestic losses involved in the Nordic option included, in the view of Government members, disrupting the consensus which obtained on industrial policy, a possible drop in the current level of investment, and possible electoral losses. To understand how external costs were judged, one must answer the following questions: how did others in the Government "read" Brofoss' analysis of the changing international environment?, how did they see that environment themselves?, what sort of problem did the Scandinavian economic option pose for Norway's foreign policy generally? What follows will show what kinds of costs, domestic and external, may have been calculated in the decision. It will argue that the joint effect of these considerations resulted in a low politicization of the issue. This, in turn, led to a negative diplomatic spiral which was unconducive to a Scandinavian agreement.

Domestic Costing

To understand considerations which must have been of concern to the Norwegian government, one must know the positions of the major economic interest groups in Norway, and be aware of the tight integration of these functional groups into the political parties. Two of the groups, agriculture and labor, had formal positions worked out at the Nordic level by their organisations. The Nordic Farmers' Central Council had concluded that a Nordic customs union was unobjectionable so long as agricultural products were excluded. Both in Sweden and in Norway agriculture had a "special position" since the Government was committed to deliberate equalization of agricultural and industrial incomes through systems of subsidies. Agriculture therefore was excluded from the beginning.[59]

Likewise, the trade unions attempted to formulate a joint Nordic position. In 1951 a report of the Nordic trade union federations sounded rather sympathetic to the Norwegian view; it reversed the NECC emphasis by giving "industrial cooperation" priority over "trade policy cooperation". Industrial cooperation was specified as long term investment through a Nordic Investment Bank--the first public mention of such an arrangement--

to which funds were to be subscribed by the countries in the same ratio as their populations. The Bank was to aid agriculture as well as industry. Most significantly, the report explicitly linked investment credits to the reduction of intra-Nordic tariffs.[60]

However, the report never seems to have had the status of an official position in any of the national trade union confederations. It was rather considered a "contribution to the discussion" by the unions, given relatively little play in the respective trade union journals, and almost no follow-up.[61] In fact, there were reservations in those Norwegian unions which were attached to the "home industries"; they tended to share the views of their industries.[62] In general, the labor federations' views were not far from those of their governments: in Sweden, more liberal in economic outlook, in Norway, more planning-oriented.

Industry, in Scandinavia, spoke on the national plane, exclusively through Federations of Industry and Export Associations. They sent commentaries (uttalelser) on the Nordic investigations to the Government, and in addition were involved in subcommittees of the NECC, dealing with the various sectors of the economy. At the end of 1949, for example, the Norwegian Federation of Industry presented a statement to the Government--a statement it did not make public until just before the 1954 Harpsund meetings --the fundamental argument of which never changed. Several of the arguments were conventional: that Norway would lose her freedom of action in trade negotiations with those outside powers upon whom she was primarily dependent (i.e. England); that a joint tariff would increase the cost of important Norwegian goods, making them uncompetitive; that trade diversion would invite reprisals; that given the fact that there were currently fewer barriers to Norwegian goods in the other Scandinavian countries than the reverse, Norway had the fewest markets to gain.[64]

Two features, peculiar to Norway, were asserted to make Norwegian industry uncompetitive with its Swedish and Danish counterparts. There was the home industries' capital starvation, a policy which the Federation did not dispute, but whose consequences for competition it underlined. Secondly, the more stringent tax, depreciation, and other regulations in Norway, would have to be "equalized" with those of the other two countries.

Could that be done, asked the Federation, except in an economic union, or even an unionstat, a political union?[65] The Federation thus attacked the Government's regulations (an old bone of contention on the domestic scene) and, at the same time raised a double spectre: Norwegian industry competing under unfavorable circumstances or Norway once more in a "union" with Sweden, words which had negative historical resonance.

Just as every man is expected to have his group in Scandinavia, every group is expected to have its party. The political parties in Norway reflected the preoccupations of the interest groups, and, in the case of the Liberals and Agrarians, added some new anxieties. After 1954, the Labor Party officially was favorable to investigating "Nordic economic cooperation". Opposition within the Labor Party must be discerned in terms of relative enthusiasm, and the relative importance given the issue. The Opposition parties, however, were very vocal; the Government faced a solid front. At no time did the Government succeed in obtaining nonsocialist support even for its cautious endorsement of a common market under certain conditions, and as one among several forms of economic cooperation.

Two major threads bound the opposition political discussion together. The Conservatives echoed the arguments on the unequal competitive position of Norwegian industry. Since they were also maintaining that a customs union would therefore require substantial policy coordination, and since there was a move in the mid-1950's towards fewer and less direct controls within Norway, one would have thought that agreement by industry or the Opposition to a common market with Sweden might have been used to buy Norwegian Government agreement to lower taxes for industry. Conservative Storting member Harald Torp discerned one such hint and commented, "I dare say such a revamping could be worth a mass".[66] On the whole, though, this did not seem to be offered by the Government, and the Conservative opposition centered on the potential threat to industry.

The Liberals, the Venstre Party, might have been expected to concentrate on limiting foreign ownership and foreign capital. Historically the party had mobilized around the fight for parliamentary government which became connected with opposition to the Union with Sweden. In the Liberal heyday, just after independence in 1905, "concession laws" with strict limitations on foreign ownership of natural resources had been passed.[67] Bent Røiseland, Liberal leader, did stress the need for careful control of foreign capital during a debate on a Norwegian-Swedish electricity agreement in May 1954.[68] Traces of old emotions may have been left after all. Leading Liberals like Gunnar Jahn (head of Norway's Bank) and Jacob Wörm-Müller, had grown up in the era of the Union fight and were generally negative.[69]

However, the heart of the matter was really a different issue, the balance of large and small industry, and of urban and rural life. Røiseland, and the representatives of the Agrarian Party as well, seemed more sympathetic to foreign capital if it were to be used for "a broader economic base in the small towns".[70] Although Lars Evensen, Labor's representative, argued that water power was the only advantage that the rural areas had, and that if it were not exploited now, the rural exodus would increase,[71] the argument failed to have effect. Jon Leirfall of Bondepartiet, The Agrarian Party, pointed out that precisely the most dispersed industries, for example, textiles, furniture, leather goods, were the industries considered by the Nordic committee most ripe for rationalization within a common market.[72] The spectre was raised of the Nordic plan interfering with Norway's distriktspolitikk, regional planning. Since regional cleavages are among the most salient in Norway,[73] this was politically sensitive. In June 1956, there was a motion at Venstre's convention to make the Nordic market an issue in the next elections, raising the possibility of a confrontation along these lines.

There were three types of possible losses to the Norwegian Government in this political situation, The first is a function of the potential relationship with the other Scandinavian countries within a common market; this surfaced most often as the issue of coordinating economic policy. To put the issue bluntly: whose economic policy would be favored in a future common market, and whose disfavored?

A fundamental fact which must be remembered here is the significantly higher rate of investment by Norway than by Sweden or Denmark. If the elements of economic policy (wage rates, interest rates, taxes) were coordinated, or if Norway's investment level were reduced to that of Sweden, for example, the rate of its development program would be greatly reduced.

Knut Getz-Wold, one of the top Norwegian civil servants involved in the Nordic negotiations, concluded, in an analysis early in 1955, that therefore the economic policy of a proposed Nordic group would have to concentrate new investments in Norway. This, in turn, would mean a palpable reduction in Sweden's and Denmark's own investments.[74] A year later he repeated: "It will therefore be necessary that the other Nordic countries join in bearing a part of the reduction in our high savings rate which may be a consequence of a common market and a coordination of economic policy."[75]

A second potential loss, involving Government relations with domestic interests, emerged from the viewpoint of the Ministry of Industry. There was fear of pushing the Nordic plan against a united opposition because the problem was, in their view, not just economic but "psychological". If the plan were put through against industry opposition, it would "take the enthusiasm (gløden) out" of industry. (The head of the Ministry, Lars Evensen, came from the trade union movement which had never been fully persuaded that rationalization would not harm them.)[76] For the Government, then, there were thought to be serious costs in breaking the relative consensus on industrial strategy. This tends to confirm the general points made by writers like Samuel Beer and Stein Rokkan on the power and informal sanctions of organized functional groups in democratic politics with managed economies.[77] It may also account for what one of the Nordic Market's Norwegian proponents considered to be a protectionist attitude within the Norwegian Government itself: he remarked sarcastically "the only thing they were willing to put on the "free list" was communion wafers!"[78]

The third possible loss was, of course, electoral. The opposition taken together represented 53% of the voters; as noted earlier, although Labor had a parliamentary majority, it did not have an electoral majority. It is difficult to estimate the direct fear of electoral losses, but at the very least it had some effect on the Government's sense of legitimacy. Interviewed years later, former Prime Minister Einar Gerhardsen argued, "With such great opposition it would have been neither right nor defensible to drive (the decision) through". He was asked how this differed from those times when the Labor Party had succeeded in putting through domestic reforms against the wishes of the Opposition? Gerhardsen replied that if it is "a question of principle" then it is "in the party program" and then the Government is "bound" to act on it. Since the Opposition had always complained about being "uncertain" (for example, as to the possibility of nationalizations), the Labor Party's position had been that, against a unified opposition, it would force through only those things which had been promised in its program "in order to remove one factor contributing to [such] uncertainty".[79]

One might consider this an attempt to explain away the Government's indecision, or, as one of its former members put it, its "lack of political courage". But such a judgment would not illuminate just what the Government feared--or counted as probable losses--at the time, as we have tried to do, nor would it explain why such "courage" was lacking. It would also give too little weight to normative influences. Clearly Gerhardsen was juxtaposing two norms: that of mandate (via election on a Party program or platform) and that of consultation (with social forces outside the Party). While not technically a minority Government, the Labor Government was actually based on less than a majority of votes. In such a case, <u>and</u> in the absence of a clear mandate from within the Party, the norm of consultations was felt to be even stronger than usual.

In such a situation the minimum which seems to have been needed was something either to buy off the opposition, or go to over their heads to the electorate. One of the Swedish negotiators expressed this when he said that he had felt the Norwegian Government needed "something to point to".[80] Thus even when, in the spring of 1954, the Norwegian Government position had changed so that they now too regarded a common market as desirable, they needed something which would be a visible gain, something to tempt at least part of the opposition, or attractive enough to use in an election fight.

External Costing

If one turns to impediments to change in the Government's position arising from its evaluation of the world outside Norway, one may begin by asking how Brofoss' perceptions and prescriptions were likely to have been met by his colleagues. There were several themes in Brofoss' argumentation which may well have been met with scepticism.

First, others may have "heard" Brofoss' politico-economic evaluation of the directions in Europe against the background of other foreign policy evaluations he had made in the past. Brofoss had written the August 1947 white paper which advised against close involvement in the Marshall Plan for fear of limitations on Norway's economic planning, and for fear of an American economic recession. He advised belt tightening rather than American loans, and in fact it was these fears which were the reason for the very small amount requested by Norway the first year of the Marshall Plan (an amount which he later called "indefensible".[81]) As late as February 1948 (that is, after the Czech coup and the Soviet note to Finland) Brofoss stood out among the prominent Norwegian socialists for his reserve toward the Western powers.[82] Moreover, two other themes were prominent in his thinking: small powers at the mercy of big powers (a theme which had, of course, been dominent in Norway before the war)[83] and also distinct anti-German sentiment.[84] These, taken together, might help account for the incomplete acceptance within the Norwegian government itself of his proposal of a Nordic strategy.

There is little evidence that the Norwegian leadership took seriously the rise of an enduring Continental grouping until the nineteen sixties.[85] The external environment was changing but ambiguous, and lent itself to divergent interpretations. The Nordic market could obtain a hearing, but it did not stimulate the determined political leadership evidenced in the Nordic Pact versus NATO choice, where the time horizon had been shorter, and the alternatives relatively clearer. Brofoss himself cited the Foreign Minister as a supporter of the Scandinavian market and said that it had been Evensen who had been the chief skeptic (for the domestic reasons suggested above). But the main preoccupation and main danger to the Labor Government then was the defense appropriations issue. It took a long time to get even a partial decision on a Scandinavian market because "other games" were being played, and this game was very secondary.

Did the divergent foreign policies of the three countries, alliance and nonalignment, preclude a common market among them? There is no evidence that such a market would have been considered contrary to either policy. Nor were there fears that other important states might interpret it that way.

If, however, one asks whether the disparate policies made agreement less likely, more nuances emerge. One such is that only half a dozen years before, Norwegian foreign policy had undergone a major reorientation. As has been shown, its outcome had been by no means a foregone conclusion. In Scandinavian politics the "Nordic" alternative has functioned as a "privileged means"[86]; that is, in any situation in which there is dissatisfaction with current policy, a "Nordic" solution is certain to be suggested. It is quite possible that any plan which seemed to revive a Nordic option (in which Sweden would be a neutral pole), might be viewed as a burden to the general policy of alignment on which Norway had so recently embarked.

To make the point in a different way, one might argue (a bit perversely) that had Norway's alignment policy been undisputed at home, been supported by a very solid consensus including within the governing party, this very fact might have facilitated a Nordic economic agreement in this period. That is to say, had there been no fears that an alternate policy pole might be encouraged, the potential foreign policy losses would have been minimal. Moreover, time and energy would not have had to be diverted to guarding domestic flanks with respect to the main foreign policy posture, as for example in the periodic fights over defense expenditures.

We can draw three conclusions from this: <u>it was not the fact of different foreign policy main lines per se which caused the failure of agreement</u>. The ways in which these main lines affected the economic market problem were more subtle. First, <u>the Foreign Office had no special reason of its own to add its weight to the proposal</u>, particularly in a situation in which the economic ministries, Industry and Trade, were divided. (Brofoss had identified Lange as having been positive toward the Nordic market, but clearly it was not one of Lange's main causes.)[87] Second, probably the <u>main</u> impact of the NATO line on the Scandinavian market issue <u>was the priority for such directly connected sub-issues as defense appropriations and the defense strategy</u>. This made it critical to conciliate the opposition (to NATO) wherever possible. (Brofoss claims, for example, that concessions on agricultural subsidies were traded for support on defense. It is perhaps not coincidental that Oksvik, the leading spokesman for those who disagreed with the NATO line, came from an agricultural area.)[88] Such concerns absorbed political attention and energies and diverted them from any Scandinavian plan. Had there not been a major dissenting, if publicly nonvocal, wing of the Labor Party there might well have been a greater chance for a Scandinavian economic agreement, the differences in major foreign policy lines notwithstanding! Third, therefore: it was not the fact of, but the degree of support for, alignment which made cooperation with a non-aligned state more difficult. Finally, the aggregate effect of these weak positive incentives, and weak-to-strong negative incentives was "low politicization", that is, little political direction, little involvement by parties, press and public opinion. (Such behavior may also of course result from total lack of interest, but that was not the case here.) Robert Lieber has shown in his study of the politics of British entry into the ECC that the normal process of deciding politico-economic issues is one of "functional" (interest group) representation. Although there is always some degree of "insulation" from straight interest-group bargaining, he argued, the degree of "politicization" to counterbalance such sectional bargaining varies widely at different times.[89] Low or incomplete politicization does not mean the absence of a political decision, but rather, permissive politics, an implicit decision not to mobilize or expend political resources on the issue.

The 1954 change by the Norwegian Government can be understood as "low politicization" of the issue. It has been suggested that Oscar Torp, who was Prime Minister for three years (end of 1951 to end of 1954), was a weaker Government leader than Gerhardsen who both preceded and followed him. (Apparently Gerhardsen had been outstanding both in his ability to manage the left wing of the Party--the dissenters on foreign and defense policy, of whom some of the important ones also disputed the changing economic policies of the mid-1950's--and in his ability to counterbalance the propensity of the Cabinet members each to develop his exclusive bailiwick.) It is possible that this particular situation also contributed to the partial decision or low politicization of the Scandinavian proposal in 1954.[90] Be that as it may, changes in the Cabinet did not substantially alter the fate of the Scandinavian plan.

The issue was weakly politicized in all three countries (as will emerge below), and the negotiating process, even when finally on the Ministerial level, reflected this. The Ministers who officially headed the NECC, met periodically, but, according to one of the Swedish civil servants, there was no "political evaluation" until 1958; the Ministers contented themselves with receiving the reports of the NECC civil servants.[91] Years later in Scandinavia, there was criticism of what was called "the method" of "investigating first and taking a political decision after".[92] Without some prior political definition, there was no aggregating principle, no definition of the national interest in the light of which sectoral interests were to be considered. When this happens--and trade policy is perhaps most conducive to this pattern--"nibbling" by interest groups is inevitable.[93]

Changes in Costing. 2. Norway and EFTA, 1956 - 1959

In the period mid-1954 to mid-1956 the external situation was more favorable to the possibility of a Scandinavian group than it had been before or was to be thereafter. The alternatives were few and, with the developing European group, the costs of remaining unorganized were rising. Nevertheless the ambiguity and uncertainty of external changes weakened these incentives, and failed to counteract domestic opposition which remained constant.

In the following years the opportunity costs of a Nordic plan rose. Denmark's farmers began to turn their attention to the Continental market, which did not exclude agriculture as did the Nordic plans; the Danish Government said publicly that it could not wait upon Nordic plans indefinitely.[94] By January 1957 the Maudling Committee was discussing a sixteen nation grouping, and a European option was clearly part of Scandinavian considerations.

To say that Europe was an option is by no means to say that it was clear cut. There was uncertainty as to whether the sixteen nations which negotiated within the Organization for European Economic Cooperation would be able to agree; ultimately they did not. Moreover, while options imply choices which are mutually exclusive, in this case there was a question whether a Nordic and a European plan might be combined.

Once a European formation was a likelihood, neither those who had supported nor those who had opposed the Nordic plan previously considered such a plan apart from a connection with Europe. Those who had opposed it naturally saw the European market as an additional and persuasive alternative. Those who had been in favor of the Scandinavian group now suggested a Nordic common market within a European Free Trade Area. This would have meant: a reduction of tariffs among the Nordic countries at a more rapid rate than between them and the other European countries; common tariffs from which to begin the transition to a free trade area in Europe; common tariffs against non-European nations.

The proponents of the Nordic-within-a-European plan had two arguments. In their view the Nordic market would help formerly protected industries to adjust to the free trade area; it would be an adjustment in two steps. Opponents refuted this, saying that two transitions instead of one would only be an incentive to erroneous planning and investment; as Bent Røiseland, the Venstre leader, put it, the two plans were not "concentric circles".[95]

Their second argument was more serious; the cohesion and thus bargaining power of the Nordic group would be increased. This had always been one of the main reasons for the Scandinavian proposal; the possibilities were simply more concrete in the context of the proposed European market. Even after the breakdown of the sixteen nation negotiations, and during the new seven nation talks which eventually resulted in the European Free Trade Area (EFTA), some continued to hold the view that (despite Britain's displeasure), Scandinavia had sufficient leverage to insist upon a Nordic group inside EFTA.[96] Their opponents pointed to the absence of any agreed Nordic plan, and also to the fact that since EFTA had been conceived of as a negotiating instrument vis-à-vis the European Economic Community (EEC), an internal Nordic group would only disrupt EFTA's purpose.[97] At this stage, then, although the Scandinavians did continue to negotiate, and did in fact negotiate further concessions, the Nordic option was most likely a fall back position.[98]

One possible serious incentive for a Nordic plan has gone unmentioned until now--Finland. Finland had joined the Nordic negotiations in mid-1956. It was not clear whether the Soviet Union's changed view, which permitted Finland to join both the Nordic Council and the market negotiations, would also extend to its participation in a European Free Trade Association. It has been suggested that if Finland had not been able to make arrangements with EFTA (or even if it had asserted that it would not be able to do so), then the others would have put great effort into a Scandinavian customs union within the EFTA bloc.[99] But this conjecture was never put to the test. At the final Nordic meeting in July 1959, Finnish Foreign Minister Karjaleinen said that Finland could consider any group which did not have political conditions; that was understood to include EFTA.[100] EFTA, which included the British market, and which now seemed able to encompass also Finland, appeared to have more advantages, and fewer disadvantages, than did the Scandinavian alternative.[101]

A Diplomatic Spiral

By diverting attention and expectations, EFTA exacerbated the interaction pattern which had developed before: a negative diplomatic spiral of expectations. The elements of this spiral were uncertainty, low priority, and simultaneously, visibility. So long as the Nordic market proposal was defined as an issue of trade policy, it remained low priority for all three countries because the Nordic market at that time was only about 15% of the trade of each. The incentives for any fundamental changes in domestic economic policy in order to make gains in this area were correspondingly small.

Paradoxically, although accorded low priority, the Nordic market negotiations were highly visible, because economic issues in general are highly visible in Scandinavia. The ideological impetus of the large Social Democratic parties has been, to a large extent, economic betterment. Politics has been relatively consensual; other cleavages are few. All the countries are extremely dependent upon foreign trade, the balance of payments providing an obvious bellwether for national prosperity.[102] The national press gives much attention to, and explanation of, economic issues. Rudimentary aggregate economics is taught in the schools, providing an economically literate public. Each sector of the economy is organized nationally, and the norm of consultation of the relevant interests is a powerful one. Given this setting, economic issues may have a better chance of being solved within a consensual framework, but may be relatively more controversial in the sense that other things are less so.

Particularly from Norway's standpoint, the effects of the proposed plan were uncertain. When there is major uncertainty of the distribution of future gains, problems of location tend to outweigh the prospect of joint gain, particularly, as we have seen, for the weaker party. However, sometimes side-payments (bargaining exchanges outside the particular area being negotiated), can either substitute for, or be a symbol of, trust. The significance of such payments may be: "We are all in this together and are sharing the risks involved". Norway wanted some assurances that the problems which might arise would not be its alone.

On the Swedish side there was one distinct disincentive and other factors which may be considered as lack of potential incentives. Swedish industry had favored a customs union but never joint investment or capital transfers.[103] The Norwegians were discouraged very early. In June 1954 just before the Norwegian Government's unexpectedly open report, Swedish Prime Minister Erlander noted that Brofoss had the erroneous view that Sweden had no compelling reasons for large domestic investments and, having no balance of payments problems, would be a natural exporter of capital. "This is surely over-estimating our economic strength and putting our capital requirements too low", he said, adding that Sweden was on the "threshhold" of a period of increased investments both private and public.[104] Although Swedish Minister of Trade Gunnar Lange did say at one point in 1956 that there were "significant questions" which could not be solved without public assistance,[105] Swedish industry clearly disagreed. Future capital needs of the Swedish economy were discussed at a Stockholm Chamber of Commerce meeting in February 1956 where Marcus Wallenberg, Sweden's most important banker, noted, for example, the enormous capital input required for automation.[106] None of this pointed to favoring capital investment in Norway.

Moreover, the Swedish Government's own liberal viewpoint fostered the attitude that since joint gains were expected, including gains for Norway, Sweden should not have to "pay" to boot. Sweden would attempt to convince the Norwegians that their arguments were erroneous. "Well-founded technical argumentation by which the economic advantages of the project could be demonstrated", as one analyst has described it, characterised Swedish diplomacy from the start.[107] Likewise, Bertil Ohlin, who had been the head of the Swedish Liberal Party, and long interested in Nordic efforts, maintained in an interview many years later, that the negotiations were not "crude horse-trading".[108]

To the extent that the emphasis on trust and risk-sharing is correct, it is clear that a purely expansive strategy and style which eschewed "horse-trading" would be ineffectual. Why had Sweden chosen such a style? Amitai Etzioni has suggested that elites within a group may be willing to expend "utilitarian assets" in exchange for "some symbolic (identive) gratification"; Sweden, he noted, because of the others' resentment of its history as the dominant power vis-à-vis Norway and Finland, foresaw little possibility of leading a Nordic group.[109]

One can go further along this line with the concept of opportunity costs. Sometimes countries - or their leaderships - see themselves as having, (or aspire to), a distinct role in the world: bridge-builder, leader of the free world, peacekeeper, policeman of the world, homeland of the revolution, and so on. One role which (particularly since the days of Dag Hammarskjøld) has been available to Sweden, among imaginable possibilities, is that of mediator between East and West. Since Nordic ideology emphasizes egalitarian cooperation, and in effect denies the possibility of leadership, and since the dominant foreign policy lines of the others might inhibit such a mediating role for Norden anyway, then a specifically Nordic role may never have seemed worth an expenditure of resources; there were alternative role possibilities.

Finally one must add that the hesitation of the Norwegian Government to invest politically in the issue can hardly have encouraged the Swedes to be more forthcoming.[110]

Denmark had the reputation of being the most "pro-Nordic" of the countries.[111] As the defense pact discussions showed, this seems to have influenced its position. What possibilities did it see for a Nordic market, and how did it think they could be achieved? The Danes shared with the Swedes the view that the common market itself should be the focus of discussion. Financial questions were "not serious" according to one of the top Danish civil servants who had sat on the NECC and its subcommittee on financial questions. Of course, Denmark would be "quite neutral" if Sweden wanted to provide investment funds; Denmark's role, however, was neither to pay money nor to receive money from others.[112]

The Danish position had its foundation in the perceived minor importance of the Nordic market for Danish goods. Agricultural products, Denmark's main exports, were in those years excluded from the proposed common market arrangements. The structure of protection for Danish industry at this time was also different from that of the others: first, frequently no or low tariffs on raw materials were combined with tariffs on processed goods, giving a high net protection to industry. More important, although Danish industrial tariffs were low on the whole, the number of quotas was high.[113] To broaden the negotiations beyond just tariffs, then, was to affect Danish industry and industrial strategy more seriously.

The Danish position was no doubt reinforced when Denmark's interest turned to Continental Europe. By 1957-58 this certainly was so; it has been suggested that the shift of Jens Otto Krag from Minister of Nordic Cooperation to Minister of Foreign Economy in the new Danish coalition government of 1957 indicated this change of interest.[114] Half a year earlier Krag had begun to say publicly that Denmark could not wait indefinitely.[115] Denmark's sensitivity to new opportunities arose from the fact that while its trade with Scandinavia had remained at 14% of its total trade between 1952 and 1956, trade with England had declined from 33% to 28%, and that with the Continent had risen from 29% to 33%.[116]

Some concessions were made by Sweden, but late; the context had already changed. First, there were improvements in the offer concerning the Nordic Investment Bank. Sweden offered in 1957 or 1958 to contribute almost all the capital for the Bank by counting as the contribution of the others their payments on postwar loans. Secondly, in 1959 longer and unilateral transition arrangements were offered. Particularly Norway and Finland would have transition arrangements of up to twelve years for certain disadvantaged industries; in some cases they would open their own markets only gradually while having immediate access to the Swedish and

Danish markets. These concessions were characterized by a later Norwegian economic survey as "quite significant", and by Getz-Wold, as "in the end large, one-sided, and favorable".[117] There was some indication that the Norwegian textile industry might be persuaded, although officially the Norwegian Federation of Industries presented a solid front.[118] But attention was already dispersed between Scandinavia and Europe; the concessions came too late.

Thus Denmark and Sweden shared the view that a common market was or should be the focus of discussion. Denmark was "neutral" on the question of side-payments to Norway, most of which would not come from Denmark. Because of the structure of its economy, Denmark was especially alert to the variety of European options. It did not contribute directly to the diplomatic spiral in Scandinavia, but may have hastened it. Because the Swedes had a low estimate of the will or ability of the Norwegians to push through a Scandinavian plan, there was little incentive for them to grant further concessions; Denmark would offer little, and was open to other plans; the Norwegians expected few significant concessions, and therefore, were hesitant to develop a domestic political campaign on behalf of the Nordic Plan. This negative diplomatic spiral helped defeat the plan.

Changes in Costing. 3. Sweden and "Nordek" 1968 - 1970. A Comparison

The most conclusive evidence of the effect of additional incentives deriving from other foreign policy interests and goals is from a later period. Sweden's position in the negotiations of the 1950's is illuminated by contrast with its behavior in the late 1960's in the "Nordek" negotiations. Our intention is not to make a comprehensive study of the Nordek case or its various phases, but rather to use it to shed light on Sweden's behavior in the earlier negotiations.[119]

After the failure of the Scandinavian negotiations of the 1950's and of the Maudling negotiations for a sixteen nation European market, the three Scandinavian countries joined EFTA, the "Outer Seven". Finland, too, developed an arrangement called FINEFTA which is the same in all but name.

The economic results of the EFTA arrangement for the Scandinavians have been highly rewarding, and in ways which were not anticipated. For example, the Norwegian opposition of the 1950's had emphasized that a strictly Scandinavian market would shut them out of the English market toward which they were much more significantly oriented.[120] When asked why they were willing to open the Norwegian market to the seven, but not to the other Scandinavian three alone, the answer was because of anticipated gains in the volume of sales outside Scandinavia, primarily in Britain.

Even before the breakdown of the large scale negotiations, the Scandinavians made inquiries in the summer of 1958 about the possibility of forming a British-Scandinavian free trade area, should the sixteen nation negotiations fail. The British refused to discuss it at that time. When there was no hope for the large group, they made clear that they wanted Switzerland and others to be included. Although the Scandinavians continued their internal negotiations, and even made further concessions and tentative plans, in February 1959 following a routine UNISCAN meeting, the British, Scandinavian, and Swiss representatives slipped away for secret discussions of a smaller free trade area.[121] The reason for the Scandinavian participation in these less desirable fall back negotiations was the value placed in all the countries on the British market.

Ironically enough, rewards came from a different direction. Because of the slow rate of growth in Britain, the British market did not prove to be the major gain. (In fact, as early as 1961, Brofoss compared British and Continental growth and urged a reorientation towards the Continent.) Instead Sweden proved to be an expanding market for the newer industrial sectors of Denmark, Finland, and Norway, even though it continued to maintain a positive trade balance with each of them. The Scandinavian economies proved to be considerably more "complementary" than previous over-simplified analyses had suggested.[122] "The text book writers were righter than they thought", as one of the Norwegian civil servant negotiators put it.

In 1968 there was an ambiguous Danish initiative for renewed negotiations on Nordic cooperation. This Nordic market plan - intended to include Finland - came to be called "Nordek". My focus here is only on the Swedish position, and my thesis is that the fact of an enduring EEC grouping with a common external tariff was the incentive for Swedish eagerness for a Nordic grouping. The index of this is the improvement of their offer in the face of a reduction of their anticipated economic gains, by comparison with the 1950's. Evidence on the reasons for the improved offer is provided both by the circumstances under which it was made, and by Swedish statements.

In the Nordek negotiations Sweden offered to contribute more than ever, including contributions to joint funds for transitional measures for industry and for structural reform in agriculture. As of 1969 Sweden had offered to pay 25% of a joint bank of 50 million dollars plus 46% of three funds for agriculture, fishing and industry, or about 290 million dollars. This 340 million dollars compares with the 1958 offer of 300 million dollars (when Sweden offered to increase her contributions to the investment fund by forgiving old loans). On the other hand, whereas in the 1950's it would have obtained a joint tariff wall around the Scandinavian countries, now there would be only joint tariffs against non-EFTA countries. Whereas in the 1950's there would have been a gain from the removal of tariffs within Scandinavia, by 1968 all intra-Scandinavian industrial tariffs had been eliminated in accordance with EFTA rules. Thus the offer was increased and the anticipated economic gains were decreased. Clearly mere economic calculations do not account for this position.

The changes become explicable if one observes the context and notes the articulated concerns of the Swedes. The context of the renewed discussion was the experience of the veto of British (and with it Scandinavian) adhesion to the European Economic Community in 1961 and again in 1967. While Norway and Denmark had applied both times for entry, Sweden's Social Democratic Government had decided that entry would be incompatible with its nonalignment policy. In 1961 Sweden applied for "association", to the vehement dismay of the opposition parties , one of which campaigned (unsuccessfully) on a platform of "Yes to Europe". In the second attempt in 1967, Sweden submitted an "open" application which stipulated that its adherence would have to be compatible with its foreign policy, but which left the question of status open for negotiation. Again the Liberal and Conservative Parties opposed this as inept diplomacy and urged instead an application for membership, with reservations to be negotiated. Early in 1968 when the EEC Commission reported on prospective members, it discussed Norway, Denmark, Ireland, and the United Kingdom but did not mention Sweden; the position of the Commission was that the applicant itself must decide what status it was applying for.

From industry and government sources there are statements which confirm the interpretation that Sweden's offer to Scandinavia in the 1960's was correlated with its hope that a Nordic group would mitigate the burden of a neutral foreign policy which, it felt, limited its ability to make political commitments to the EEC. Svenska Dagbladet and Dagens Nyheter, the largest Conservative and Liberal papers respectively, urged the Swedish Government to be generous in the financial aid parts of the Scandinavian package, advice very different from that they gave in the 1950's.[123] Svenska Dagbladet also editorialized that after the "unfortunate form" of Sweden's 1967 application to the EEC, a Nordic organization could undeniably "mean much for keeping Sweden in the same category as Norway and Denmark".[124] When Prime Minister Tage Erlander was asked how far Sweden was prepared to go in meeting Danish and Norwegian demands for agricultural and industrial assistance, he said, "How interested one is depends upon the weight one attaches to a common Nordic stance in the European context". The draft treaty of July 1969, which stipulated the achievement of a complete customs union within five years as a condition of the Swedish contribution, was the "needed evidence" (manifestation som behøvs) of the unity of the North.[125] Dagens Nyheter went so far as to suggest that perhaps the Swedish government need not even insist upon that condition; even a modified customs union would serve the same purpose.[126] These comments support the interpretation that the Swedish interest in a Nordic customs union in the late 1960's was that it might decrease the risk of isolation from a possibly enlarged EEC, and increase Swedish leverage in the future EEC negotiations by consolidating ties which would make it almost impossible to be left out. (Of course, precisely the factor which made Sweden more eager, created problems for Norway and Denmark.)[127]

Conclusions

In the 1950's the question of a Scandinavian market was a low priority issue but highly visible and characterized by the uncertainty of the calculations. Its low priority derived from the small percentage of the trade of each country directed at the Scandinavian market, and from the other opportunities for trade expansion through the general European liberalization efforts. Its high visibility was due to the relative importance of economic issues in Scandinavia, as well as to the integration of national interest groups into the political parties and in advisory relationships to the governments. For Norway, economically the weakest, these characteristics, combined with its uncertainty about the effects of a future market, led to a need for tangible and visible gain to persuade either key interest groups or the electorate.

General foreign policy considerations contributed to the Norwegian position mostly by their absence; that is, they provided no additional inducements to support a Scandinavian pact. The market was certainly not precluded, but neither was its value enhanced by non-economic considerations. The result was low politicization of the market question. Nor, during the 1950's, were there additional inducements stemming from major foreign policy considerations for the Danes or Swedes. For Sweden, the possibility of an international mediator posture, and the egalitarian relationships among the Nordic states, may have lowered the relative attractiveness of a specifically Nordic role. Moreover, there was no evidence that the Norwegian Government would invest its prestige in a Nordic plan. The consequences were the need for side-payments for one party, Norway, and the lack of incentives to make them by the others, particularly Sweden. By comparison, in the 1960's when Sweden was specifically interested in maintaining a "low profile" with respect to its non-alignment policy in order to facilitate its negotiations with the ECC, this provided the additional inducement to offer side-payments even for what was an economically less rewarding package.

Several conclusions may be drawn. First, rarely is purely economic calculation sufficient for incentives on all sides to "converge" on an agreement. With hindsight and the experience of EFTA, it is clear that a Scandinavian agreement at least from the mid-1950's would have been profitable for all. However, uncertainty about its effects prevented it. A related conclusion is that incentives from other policy areas may supply the needed "grease" for an agreement, particularly if those incentives are a bit diffuse and therefore not easily calculable for a quid pro quo. Here Sweden's position in the Nordek negotiations, in comparison with the negotiations of the 1950's, provides a ready example.

More generally, what explains changes in bargaining positions is changes in costing. The three examples here, the Norwegian partial change in 1954, diversion in the EFTA period, and the Swedish offer in Nordek, illustrate the point that changing appreciations of relevant internal or external factors bearing on alternative options change the opportunity costs of the plan under discussion and thus lead to changes in bargaining positions.

Finally, low politicization of issues may keep relations among countries relatively unheated, but may also be conducive to negative diplomatic spirals such as the one here, in which the perceived low priority, Norway's unwillingness to expend political resources for the Scandinavian market, became a disincentive to Sweden to expend its political resources and create the needed additional inducements.

CHAPTER FOUR

REDUCING COSTS: "THE NORDIC PARLIAMENTARY COMMITTEE FOR FREER COMMUNICATION, ETC."

Are policies and problems which seem to have a relatively high technical component--or at least have a low partisan-political component--equally amenable to analysis from the costing perspective? Or are they better understood by those theories which emphasize the technical links among problem areas in a modern society? There is one case, where we can make a rough comparison (although not a definitive test) between types of explanation. The relatively successful efforts to reduce hindrances to communication within the Nordic area seemed to this writer to be an interesting approximation in practice of the neo-functionalist model, discussed in Chapter One. It appeared to be a case of "sneaking up on sovereignty",[1] of reformers nibbling at technical areas in order to reach if not absolutely central areas, at least those more controversial than could be tackled fruitfully at the time. Nils Andrén had caught this feeling and described the relationship between the passport union proposed by these reformers, and the labor market which followed it, as one of "spillover".[2] Finally, the Scandinavians had considered themselves to be good "functionalists" in the long European debate between federalists (those who wanted a federation of Europe) and functionalists (those who wanted to start with cooperation on immediate, practical, and less controversial matters) within the Council of Europe; had they perhaps practised this "functionalism" at home in Scandinavia?

The case of "The Nordic Parliamentary Committee for Freer Communication, etc." is only an approximation of the neofunctionalist model, although sufficient, in the opinion of this writer, for our purpose, which is to compare two starting points for analysis of cooperative measures. The approximation is not perfect because the neofunctionalist model specifies the establishment of an organization to which is granted definable powers within a specific area. The area should be of some centrality so that technical-economic links will connect it to other areas of the economy and therefore to other decision areas. The major hypothesis is that "spillover" will tend to occur; spillover is described as a process in which the "groups" affected--interest groups presumably, also states--realize that in order to accomplish the original tasks allocated to the agency, the scope of its authority will have to be expanded.

In the Nordic case, the agency which was established was a committee of members of the parliaments of the countries. It had only two powers: to investigate (a broad) problem area and report to the Governments; to call on experts in the bureaucracies of the individual countries for testimony and assistance. Decisions were still reserved to the states. Nor was the area of investigation central to the economies or politics of the countries, although it touched both in interesting ways. Nevertheless, the Governments did follow through on most of the recommendations made by the Committee; it was relatively successful in its efforts, and was eventually institutionalised as part of the Nordic Council system.

Did a version of spillover occur. Did that account for the progression of reforms achieved? Or does a calculation of costs and benefits, attributed by assumption to the states-as-actors, better account for the outcomes? The substance of this chapter is that the costing perspective tells us more about the establishment and successes, and also about the difficulties encountered by this interparliamentary Committee, than does the neofunctionalist hypothesis. "Spillover", however telling as a metaphor, is inaccurate either as a description or as an explanation of the successive developments after the Committee's establishment. Instead, what seems to have happened is first that the Committee was quite successful in reducing the costs of various measures (in comparison with the status quo) to the Governments involved, and second, that outside factors contributed, coincidentally at times, to reducing these costs as well, thus making the Governments more willing to entertain suggestions they previously had rejected.

A Nordic Entrepreneur: Rolf Edberg

In 1951 those eager for closer relations among the Scandinavian countries had been disappointed twice, by the decision on the defense pact proposal, and by the negative report of the previous year on the possibilities of a common market. Nor had negotiations for a joint electricity project succeeded. In general, as Christian Lange has shown, contacts among the countries were at low ebb.[3]

One person thought that what was needed was "an act of good Nordic will",[4] some sign that not all Nordic projects were doomed to failure. He was Rolf Edberg, a Swedish Social Democratic newspaper editor and member of parliament from Värmland, one of the provinces bordering Norway. Even before the end of the second world war Edberg had written a pamphlet called "Tomorrow, Norden".[5] As will emerge, he had a sense for the symbolic; he thought of his initiative, a proposal for an inter-Nordic parliamentary committee to look into the possibilities for eliminating restrictions on communications in Scandinavia, as "a quiet beginning to something which in substance can be characterized as a Nordic citizenship".[6] Within the labor movements, the idea of the free movement of labor had long had a place of honor. Edberg, however, did not make his argument on either ideological or partisan grounds, but rather harkened back to the state of the civilized world before World War I, when neither passports nor visas had been required in the European countries west of Russia.[7] The present state of the world was such, he observed, that when Ernest Bevin had been asked to name his most distant foreign policy goal, he replied, "Just to be able to go down to Victoria Station and take a ticket to where the hell I like without a passport".[8]

The way Edberg went about introducing his proposal is significant. He obtained the co-sponsorship for his proposal of an inter-Nordic committee from the leaders of all Swedish parties in the Riksdag. His social democratic colleagues, Hans Hedtoft in Denmark, and Trygve Bratteli in Norway, agreed to introduce similar measures in their respective parliaments.[9] But in the three countries cross-party, not just partisan, support was garnered. The first move was thus political in that it sought and obtained the backing of the leadership of the parties in each country. If a Committee of twenty

MP's -- five from each of the four countries (including later Finland) -- seems unwieldy, it permitted the representation of all major political parties in these multi-party countries. At the same time the move was non-political in that it raised the question above party politics, as well as above the politics of national interest. This initiative was taken by legislators, then; its political meaning was the reestablishment of political ties among the Scandinavian countries.

The Committee also provided a form of political tie with Finland. Until 1956 Finland was not a participant in the Nordic Council (although it did participate in some inter-Nordic expert groups); parliamentary contacts maintained through the Committee were considered especially valuable. The Committee was discrete in the way it publicized its work in order not to politicize the matter and thus jeopardize Finland's participation. Swedish Prime Minister Erlander and Foreign Minister Undén were said to have suggested, for instance, that the term "passport union" be avoided; the Committee spoke of "easing inter-Nordic communication" instead.[10] Within Finland itself there was little publicity, either in parliament or in the press since the matter was considered too sensitive.[11]

The Parliamentary Communications Committee: Strategies and Goals

Characteristic for the Committee was the speed with which it was established, and with which it presented its recommendations. The parliaments requested such a committee in the spring of 1951, and it was established in July. Within half a year, by January 1952, the first recommendations were presented to the governments.[12]

Discussion of various amelioration measures, such as a possible "Nordic travel card" to replace the formal passport, was rejected at the first committee session. Such measures had been proposed with little success in the past. The Committee decided to work for a full passport union (i. e. the elimination of the need for passports for travel among the countries of the union). "I considered that as a political decision", Edberg later said,[13] although actually the Committee members did have to confirm their "decision" with the national authorities; by the second full meeting, agreement was confirmed.[14]

A crucial decision was in effect to shift the burden of proof to those who would attempt to uphold the existing network of border regulations. The Committee, of course, worked with technical experts, but it did not begin by having them explain and justify all the rules as they stood. Rather it decided to ask, "Suppose that there were no border restrictions at all, what controls would one then find it necessary to institute in the current situation?".[15] It thus established a concrete goal for its own work, and a method, both of internal operations and of public presentation, which would be favorable to action rather than to inaction.

The mandate of the Committee was limited to investigations, but was broad and vague on the scope of the investigations. The Committee was "to investigate the possibilities of facilitating communication (samfärdseln) among the Nordic countries, and in various ways to further freer association (umgänge) among the peoples of these countries". As Edberg conceived of the purpose, "The work of the committee was limited to the frontier formalities - in the widest sense of the word".[16] Thus the committee had a concrete goal, the passport union, as well as long term diffuse goal which the achievement of such a union would not exhaust. The former was constantly cited, even when for the tactical purpose of getting changes started, it was divided into smaller sub-goals, phases or steps; the latter was useful for expanding the scope of the Committee's concerns.

Finally, the Committee deliberately decided to utilize, rather than refrain from, publicity of its work. It issued press releases after its meetings, and held press conferences on its reports. Its intent to create a favorable climate of public opinion is clear, although this also may have been simply the spontaneous reaction of Edberg as a journalist.

The Work of the Parliamentary Communications Committee, 1952-1956

Within four years, 1952-1956, the Parliamentary Communications Committee produced twelve reports dealing with passports, customs allow-

TABLE 2. REPORTS OF THE NORDIC PARLIAMENTARY COMMITTEE FOR FREER COMMUNICATION, ETC. A TABULAR SUMMARY.

Report No.	Source	Date	Topic(s)	Aims	Reasoning Criteria	Detailed Recommandations	Degree of Achievement
1	SOU 1952:4	Jan 1952	PASSPORTS part (1) Scandinavians in inter-Nordic travel.	Goal - full passport union including: 1) no check at internal borders; 2) no passport needed within Nordic countries, and no time limit on stay; 3) check on non-Nordic only at outer borders.	Concrete suggestions limited to what could be achieved by administrative action in order to be in effect before summer tourism.	1) No check on Nordic citizens at the internal borders; 2) No obligation for Nordic citizens staying up to 3 months in another Nordic country, to have passports. 3) No obligation to register for Nordic citizens staying without paying, at private homes in another Nordic country.	1) & 2) implemented June 1952. 3) unimplemented.
		Apr 1952	CUSTOMS	1) To liberalize existing quantitative restrictions on goods traveler brought back with him. 2) To free ordinary traveler from customs inspection.	Same - as above. Rules should be such as would satisfy the reasonable wishes of travelers and therefore make obedience more likely; should make inspection as a rule unnecessary; should be easy to be informed about.	1) A common and specific upper limit of about $50 be set on the value of goods brought in for private use (rather than separate restrictions on individual items). 2) The only special exceptions to be on liquor and tobacco; Committee had suggestions on common limits for these. 3) Elimination of duplication of controls on both sides of the borders. 4) Actual inspections of those who did not declare dutiable goods be reduced to random samples.	1) Sweden implemented by summer 1952. 1) & 4) implemented by 1956. 2) Some but not full implementation; widely different starting points. Problem of sale of duty-free goods on ferries between Sweden and Denmark and Sweden and Finland. 3) by 1963 - customs stations at the internal borders had been reduced from 75 to 22, thus reducing duplication of controls.

TABLE 2 (Cont'd)

Report No.	Source	Date	Topic(s)	Aims	Reasoning Criteria	Detailed Recommendations	Degree of Achievement
3		Apr 1952	CURRENCY	1) That other forms of currency controls be used rather than checks at the borders. 2) Liberalization of permissible amounts.	Given the disparity of economic policies and situations, currency restrictions could not be lifted entirely. Each national group made suggestions regarding possible change in its country's policies.		1) The governments reduced currency checks to random samples by 1953. 2) Some liberalization of permitted amounts. (OEEC also recommending liberalization at this time.) 3) Until late 1960 Norwegian citizens still needed a passport to buy foreign currency for travel abroad; in reality, therefore, they still needed a passport even for intra-Scandinavian travel.
4	SOU 1953:4	Jan 1953	PASSPORTS part (2)	See Aims for Report No. 1 above.	Reservations concerning the elimination of the work permit could be dealt with in a separate convention like that between Denmark and Sweden for a free labor market (1946).	1) Elimination of the residence permit (uppehållstilstand) and 2) of the work permit (arbetstilstand) for Scandinavians in other Scandinavian countries. 3) The elimination of these would eliminate the need for a passport for those staying longer than 3 months, which was also recommended.	1) Free labor market for unlicensed and non-professional labor signed March 1954. (See below)

TABLE 2 (Cont'd)

Report No.	Source	Date	Topic(s)	Aims	Reasoning Criteria	Detailed Recommendations	Degree of Achievement
5	SOU 1953:5	Jan 1953	MOTOR VEHICLES	Elimination of restrictions on vehicles among the Nordic countries.		1) Elimination of the temporary (1 year) importation papers for vehicles. 2) Checks to be only random samples. 3) Elimination of road taxes for the same (1 year) length of time. 4) Norden to be a common "carnet"-area. 5) A driver's licence from one Nordic country ought to be exchangeable for one from another Nordic country without further tests.	1) While Denmark eliminated the need for importation papers for different categories of vehicles in 1953, 1955, and 1958, and Sweden in 1954, Norway and Finland, which were attempting to discourage the importation of cars, and feared that this might be used illegally, did not. 2) In 1958, Norway instituted random checks and Finland also reduced restrictions. (Note: coincided with Council of Europe urging; nine nations reduced restrictions in 1958 and others declared their intention to do so.) In Sweden random checks had already been the practice. 3) In Sweden temporary elimination of road taxes had also already been the practice. 4) No progress until 1958 when Council of Europe abolished the carnet system altogether. 5) 1956 - Mutual validation of each others' drivers' licenses agreed.

TABLE 2 (Cont'd)

Report No.	Source	Date	Topic(s)	Aims	Reasoning Criteria	Detailed Recommendations	Degree of Achievement
6	SOU 1954:7	Jan 1954	PASSPORTS (part 3)	See Aims for report No.1, above.		1) No checks on passports for non-Nordic citizens at the internal borders. 2) Rules for visas and the exclusion of undesirables be co-ordinated by the four countries. 3) Length of stay without the uppehållstilstand be uniformly three months. (Norway's rule was two months.)	1) Agreement signed July 1957 and put into effect May 1958 that passport checks for non-Nordic citizens would be made at the external borders except for random checks at internal borders. 2) This presupposed similar visa policies. It included regulations for deportation and the treatment of foreign ship and plane crews (Iceland signed this agreement in 1966.)
7	SOU 1954:20	May 1954	POSTAL RATES	Unification of rates. Inclusion of rates to other Scandinavian countries as domestic rates.		1) For letters of less than 500 grams, domestic rates to apply on letters to other Nordic countries. 2) For letters 500-1000 grams, inter-Nordic rates be reduced to lower than the prevailing rates for international mail.	1) Achieved with the exception that Denmark permitted letters of up to only 20 grams in inter-Nordic mail to go for the same price as domestic mail of up to 50 grams. 2) Rejected by the "Nordic postal conference", one of the regular meetings of the representatives of the postal administrations, whose own investigations had led to the conclusion that this suggestion would both complicate rates and be uneconomic, especially since ordinary letters were frequently sent by air within Scandinavia. (See Committee's Final Report, below; they disagreed and repeated the recommendation.)

TABLE 2 (Cont'd)

Report No.	Source	Date	Topic(s)	Aims	Reasoning Criteria	Detailed Recommendations	Degree of Achievement
8	SOU 1954:20	May 1954	TELEGRAM RATES	Same as Report No. 7, above.		1) Domestic rates for telegrams in Norway, Denmark and Sweden to apply to telegrams to all of them. 2) Unified rates between Finland and all three, and between Iceland and all three, to be negotiated.	1) & 2) accepted and negotiated by July 1955.
9	SOU 1955:3-4	Dec 1954	POSTAL RATES	Miscellaneous matters all concerned with unified Nordic rules and the application of domestic rates to Nordic communications.		1) Domestic rates on printed matter, business letters and sample products, under 1000 grams should apply to inter-Nordic traffic as well. 2) Rates for different weights be the same for inter-Nordic as for domestic mail. 3) Domestic book rates ought to be used for inter-Nordic mail. Ultimately Nordic rules defining the contents of such packages ought to be worked out to replace the international rules now in use.	1) & 2) not implemented as of the Final Report in 1956. Unified January 1957. 3) partially implemented: domestic rates would apply to inter-Nordic book packages as of January 1957. However, the Nordic postal conference rejected the idea of Nordic rules to define the contents as unduly hampering administrative changes in each country.
10	SOU 1955:3-4	Dec 1954	TELEGRAM RATES	The purpose was to improve the possibilities for good news coverage of other Nordic countries by reducing Nordic telex and teleprinter rates to subscribers.		Rate reductions suggested for subscribers.	Implemented by 1956.

TABLE 2 (Cont'd)

Report No.	Source	Date	Topic(s)	Aims	Reasoning Criteria	Detailed Recommendations	Degree of Achievement
11	SOU 1955:33	Sept 1955	TRAFFIC RULES	Unification of rules.	Particular concern, Sweden's left handed traffic rules. Statistical accident record presented. Dissent over whether a problem primarily of one country should be taken up by a Nordic group.	Report with statistical evidence for the "practical value" of a change to right handed traffic. No formal recommendations.	Report just prior to a consultative referendum in Sweden (October 1955) at which right handed traffic was resoundingly defeated. Party leaders agreed in 1963 to put measure through and it was implemented September 1967. Difficult to ascribe to Nordic Council or to Committee.
12	SOU 1956:45	Sept 1956	FINAL REPORT	1) Repeat suggestions made in previous reports and still unaccepted. 2) Call for further liberalizations in some cases where the principle had been accepted. 3) New proposals. 4) Call for the establishment of a smaller, permanent Nordic investigating committee to carry on Committee's work.		a) Renewed recommendations: Report No.1, recommendation 3 (no residence permit for those staying in private homes)	
						Report No.2, recommendation 2 (re duty free liquor & tobacco)	Common liquor & tobacco rules instituted as of March.
						Report No.5, recommendations 1, 2, 3 (no temporary importation papers, and no taxes on cars temporarily in the country, Nordic "carnet" area.)	
						Report No.6, recommendation 1 (no passport checks on non-Nordic citizens at internal borders)	
						Report No.7, recommendation 2 (different and unified Nordic rates on 500-1000 gram letters.)	Again rejected by the postal authorities.

TABLE 2 (Cont'd)

Report No.	Source	Date	Topic(s)	Aims	Reasoning Criteria	Detailed Recommendations	Degree of Achievement
12 (cont'd)	SOU 1956:45	Sept 1956	FINAL REPORT			b) Liberalizations:	
						1) Larger amounts of foreign exchange for travel purposes to be permitted.	
						2) Increased amounts to be permitted duty free.	
						3) Extension of the principle of a free labor market to other types of jobs.	This has been negotiated job-type by job-type, for example for doctors, for dentists, for nurses.
						c) New Proposals:	
						1) No requirement to list residence, for Nordic citizens living in another Nordic country, regardless of whether living in private or public accommodations.	
						2) Nordic citizens should be able to cross borders at any point, not just at specified border-crossing points. (Or, as an interim measure, elimination of the identification cards which had been issued to those in border areas.)	Never acknowledged in principle or effected. The number of crossing points was increased, however.
						3) An "auto-pass" or something similar to be issued to non-Nordic drivers at the outer borders of Norden.	
						4) That Norway and Sweden establish common customs houses or use common personnel at their check points.	Customs stations reduced (Jan. 1960) between Norway and Sweden, and (Jan. 1963) between Finland and Sweden. Total down from 75 to 22.
						5) Better warning for drivers crossing borders with change from left to right handed traffic (or vice versa).	
						6) Elimination of the necessity for Norwegians to present passports to obtain foreign currency at banks.	As of December 1960, Norwegians no longer needed to show a passport to buy foreign exchange.
						7) A host of specific suggestions for customs liberalizations regarding pets, cycles, carriages, etc., which accompany a person.	

ances, foreign exchange allowances, postal and telegraph rates, and traffic rules--all relevant to inter-Nordic communication and travel possibilities. A fuller treatment of the Committee's aims, recommendations, and achievements is to be found in Table 2 on the following pages. Here, however, their work will be treated selectively, focussing first on the passport issue where their achievements were early and visible. The study illustrates areas of difficulty, obstacles which had to be overcome, ways of overcoming them, <u>or</u> limits to the Committee's effectiveness. Since from today's perspective the establishment of a passport union may seem unremarkable, it is worth underlining what sort of things could be at stake. Where the recommendations of the Committee collided with major domestic economic policies, for example, where they attempted to differentiate Nordic from the rest of international society, where they directed their recommendations to only one of the Nordic states, there they ran into problems.

The passport union was one of the main goals of the Committee. From hindsight this appears not to have been so controversial, but that was neither clear nor certain at the time; in fact, previous attempts pointed the other way.

The first controls had been instituted in World War I. During the inter-war years, there had been vain attempts to have them lifted. The depression, which necessitated food and housing controls, made control of immigration important to the authorities. Racial theories which gave a premium to homogeneity, and the fear of "Bolshevism" brought by refugees from Finland, increased the objections of various bureaucratic authorities. In Sweden, the provincial authorities at first were asked each year whether the wartime restrictions were still necessary, but soon the Justice department just assumed that they were, and stopped asking. The Social Welfare Board (<u>socialstyrelsen</u>) warned against lifting passport restrictions, although it did agree to a special Nordic identification system. Police authorities were always cautious.[17]

At the end of the 1920's, the Nordic authorities finally agreed on a "Nordic travel card", valid for up to six months, but the countries still retained the residence permit for visits of longer than three months. Later on, at Öresund (the crossing between Copenhagen, Denmark and Malmø,

Sweden), Nordic travelers did not have to show identification but simply entered through separate doors; this system was not adopted for the other Nordic cross points, however. During the Second World War there was a full panoply of controls, and although the requirement of visas was removed for citizens of Denmark, Iceland, Norway, and Sweden in 1945, and for Finland in 1949-50, the passport requirement remained.[18] Passports, once instituted, seemed destined to be retained.

Even though the passport question was divided into three parts, all the proposals were submitted within two years (1952-1954) and implemented within four more (by 1958).[19] Against the background sketched, this must be acknowledged a considerable achievement. Where recommendations crossed central economic policies of the countries, progress was slower. Currency liberalization efforts confronted foreign exchange controls, particularly those of Norway. Likewise the elimination of motor vehicle importation papers came up against the fears of both Norway and Finland which as part of their general economic policies were attempting at that time to discourage the importation of cars. In both these cases, acceptance and implementation were slow. There was some currency liberalization relatively soon, although how much was due to the Committee's recommendations, and how much to autonomous economic improvement, or to the simultaneous urging of OEEC, is difficult to judge. Only at the end of 1960 did Norway lift the requirement to present a passport at the bank in order to receive currency for travel purposes. Similarly, Norway and Finland reduced vehicle restrictions in 1958 coinciding with Council of Europe negotiations on this question.[20]

Attempts to differentiate Norden from the rest of the world met with mixed success. As we shall see, the distinction between Nordic and non-Nordic citizens was used to reassure national authorities, and eased reform in some areas, like passports. When the Committee tackled postage rates, it aimed to have Nordic mail treated as domestic mail. This was partially successful (see Table 2). However, when they requested a special Nordic rate (for letters of 500-1000 grams which would not be carried at domestic rates) different from the prevailing international rates, the suggestion was rejected. The "Nordic postal conference", representatives of the national postal administrations who meet regularly, argued that this would only complicate the rates and be uneconomic. The Committee disagreed and repeated this recommendation in its Final Report, arguing that the current rates were "prohibitive" and detrimental to inter-Nordic communications.[21]

The significance of the rejection should not be exaggerated, except that economic considerations were clearly decisive for the administration. This in itself is significant because within most countries mail to distant or infrequently traveled areas is subsidized; political and symbolic factors are influential. On the other hand, most personal letters would be in the under 500 gram category, so that the unification with respect to those is probably the important point.

Recommendations to one country only led to difficulties. In 1955 a Swedish Social Democrat introduced into the Nordic Council, a recommendation to the Governments to cooperate in unifying traffic rules. This sounds innocuous enough, but at the time, Sweden was debating whether to change to right-hand traffic. The Foreign Ministers decided to send the matter to the Communications Committee. The Committee quickly wrote a report comparing national traffic regulations, cataloguing disparities, enummerating accident statistics, and emphasizing the "practical value" of a change by Sweden to the right-hand pattern. Although the Report omitted any formal recommendation, one of the Swedish members wrote a reservation questioning whether it was appropriate for the Committee to make so strong a recommendation for the solution of a current special problem in one of these countries. "That question is of course in the first instance exclusively a Swedish matter".[22] The reaction is perhaps explicable since the report was released a month before a consultative referendum in Sweden on the matter. (The proposal to switch to right-hand traffic was defeated in the referendum by more than five to one.)[23] In their Final Report the Committee again stressed the serious effects of the Swedish system but confined its proposal to a better warning system for drivers going through Sweden.[24]

Although another attempt was made through the Nordic Council in 1961, it is difficult to attribute the final decision to change, made by the Swedish party leaders in 1963, to either Nordic Council or Communications Committee influence.[25] This time the party leaders did not ask the voters. The context suggests that a desire to indicate that Sweden felt itself part of Europe may well have been operative in the decision making.

The results of the Committee's work were significant. They obtained a system of spot checks on passports, identification, and personal customs. They simplified motor vehicle rules, and to a significant extent unified postal, telegraph, and telephone rates. On matters which tended to conflict with major domestic policies, which raised costs, or which were directed to one state only, the legitimacy of the Committee's recommendations were, however, in doubt. Within a few years of the establishment of the Nordic Council, the Communications Committee was absorbed into the Council system of standing committees, and therefore was able to maintain some continuity of membership and staff.[26] The Committee had started a process which would continue after it, and which included keeping unresolved issues on the agenda.

Committee Methods: "Mechanical" or "Purposive" Spillover?

In its aspirations and in some of its methods, the Committee seemed "designed for" what Ernst Haas has called "spillover", the continuous expansion of the tasks allotted to an organization.[27] As we have seen, Edberg interpreted the vague mandate of the Committee as a mandate to investigate "the elimination of frontier formalities - in the broadest sense of the term", and this interpretation informed the Committee's work. Logically, this view could encompass the elimination of any sort of hindrances, direct or indirect, to exchanges of peoples, goods, information, or the adaptation of people to the foreign environment; pushed to its farthest limits, it could border on economic policy (tariffs, customs, the labor market and regulation of business franchises), social and national policy (the status and rights of immigrants and aliens, citizenship requirements), facilitation of the exchange of information, and facilitation of communication between public officials. Operative limits would be set by the skill and persistence of the Committee, the political possibilities, and the domains of other Nordic organs or committees.

Having chosen a goal which left it sufficient room for maneuver, what was the strategy of the Committee? Edberg expressed it this way: "Now we chose to take hold of one detail at a time, fully conscious that the first step must with greater or lesser force, drag the next one with it".[28] A practical spillover theory? What did it mean in practice?

First, it meant that the passport question was divided into several discrete steps, presented and argued a year apart. Stage one eliminated passports for Nordic citizens traveling among the Nordic countries; stage two proposed the elimination of residence permits and work permits for citizens of Nordic countries; stage three proposed that also for non-Nordic citizens passports be checked solely at the "outer borders". Once Nordic citizens did not need to show passports in crossing between their countries, it was difficult to maintain the requirement that they request permission to stay "within three months", no record of their entry date having been established.[29] Stage one thus implied that part of stage two.

The first step also had another implication: travelers had been classified into Nordic residents and non-Nordic residents for passport purposes. Entry points had two marked doors, one for each category; Nordic residents went through one door without a passport check, while others were subject to regular passport inspection. This meant, in effect, that the person categorized himself, or that there was more chance for someone intent on slipping through to do so. Edberg maintained that this "personal passport union" was "never thought of as other than a transition measure",[30] the intent was always the "territorial passport union" which the Committee then proposed - i.e. that the checking of non-Nordic citizens be confined to the outer borders of the area, as well.

Finally, Edberg has stated that the first step also implied that part of the second stage which called for a common Nordic labor market, i.e. the elimination of the labor permit requirement for Nordic citizens. It was a "logical consequence" of the freedom from passports.[31] This case shall be examined separately.

Thus there was a distinct connection, a kind of "mechanical spillover", between step one and step two, and between step one and step three. Were the other proposals of the Committee related in the same way? Two further changes in passport requirements seemed to follow. Checking foreigners only at the "outer borders" of the areas assumed sufficient administrative cooperation among the countries to insure uniform standards for defining undesirables, for deportation and readmittance, etc. Likewise, since criminals could now move more easily among the countries, cooperation among police authorities had to increase.[32]

In fact, practice overtook theory. The police in border areas--whether prior to or in response to the new easing of restrictions is not entirely clear--had developed informal cooperation of their own, in delivering people wanted by the neighboring police authority, directly rather than through the diplomatic-legal procedure of extradition.[33] "In contrast to the traditional conception of the relations among sovereign states, is the new, developing [conception] of the mutual relations of the Nordic states", said the Nordic Council's Legal Committee. "According to the latter Norden is considered as a unified territory in certain respects".[34] The characterization seems apt.

Can one say that initial steps were taken in the belief that they would be sufficient, and that thereafter there was a realization that the task would have to be expanded - the classic "spillover" model? That did not happen here. In the very first report, there were objections from some of the Committee members who foresaw that the consequences of eliminating passport checks for Nordic citizens would weaken the control over non-Nordic travelers within Scandinavia; one of them advised against the first step (elimination of passports for Nordic citizens), and two others advised that the step be experimental, and that it should not be extended to others.[35] Moreover, as we have seen, Edberg has indicated that the original steps were never seen as more than transitional measures. Nor did the Committee fail to say so in its reports.

Was there some kind of "mechanical" connection between the questions the Committee handled, such that solving one problem would automatically lead to undertaking one or some of the others? There is little evidence for this. First, several questions were tackled nearly simultaneously (passport step 1, and customs and foreign exchange restrictions, or passport step 2 and vehicles). Thus one cannot say that by eliminating restrictions in one area, restrictions in other areas became relatively more visible or more confining to the public at large or to the relevant groups within it.

Secondly, except for the three stages of the paspport question, there seems to be only one item, the requirement in Norway that to obtain foreign exchange one had to show a passport, that was "connected" (in this case in the sense that the elimination of the need for a passport would be hollow so long as one could not obtain money for one's trip without it). Yet precisely this item took nearly nine years to put through.[36] Functionalist logic, the logic of "spillover", may have been on the side of the Committee, but the Norwegian Government feared loss of control over the export of capital. Thus it was not at all "automatic" that the logically connected step would be implemented.

One must conclude that <u>the relationship between the measures was simply one of purpose</u>; they were all taken up with a view to contributing to the goal of "freer communication" as the Committee's title suggested. Their interconnections were not technically determined. What connections there were were deliberately created. Haas himself has suggested that Albert Hirschman's notion of a "hiding hand" (the deliberate, purposive tactics of technocrats) may be as applicable or more applicable to functionalist politics than the "hidden hand" theory of the unintended consequences of initial steps.[37]

The extent to which these "reform mongers" were selfconsciously expansionist in their aims should not be exaggerated. Although, for example, outside interest groups sometimes cooperated with or testified to the Parliamentary Committee, there is no evidence that the Committee sought to build support for its work by fostering such connections, which might have transcended national borders. When asked whether the Committee had thought specifically of involving outside organizations, of soliciting ideas for prospective tasks from them, neither Edberg nor the Parliamentary Committee's long time secretary, Axel Gormsan of Denmark, would accept that as a proper characterization. Had there been any thought, for example, of bringing in leisure or tourist or travel organizations in connection with the passport question? Gormsan answered that the question was treated as one of expertise; the relevant experts were considered the police and passport authorities![38] Sten Aminoff, who had been the Swedish secretary of the

Committee, added that in those years, people did not travel so much as they did in later years, implying that the rate of communication was insufficient for pressure group formation.[39]

Nor did outside organizations officially petition the Committee to take up matters of concern, although it is possible that they may have contacted individual members. The main point, however, is that there was no deliberate effort to gain reinforcement from outside groups or to become the focus of demands within the field. There was little effort to stimulate what Haas terms "a realignment of group expectations" which might then introduce new incentives for enhancing the powers of the Committee.[40]

On the other hand, the Committee did deliberately enlist the press. That Edberg himself was a journalist was no doubt relevant here. From the first the Committee publicized its meetings, and issued communiqués. Edberg asserts that this choice of working in the open was "in order to appeal for the general public's interest and support".[41] That this was self-conscious policy was clear; that it contributed substantially to the successes of the Committee is less so. The news items saved in the Nordic Council file on the activities of the Committee, although not a complete collection, are quite few and small. Whether public pressure was ever actually a factor in officials' calculations is highly doubtful.

Encountering the Opposition

Perhaps there was no real need for a strategy if potential opposition was in fact negligible. Were the questions so uncontroversial that the results were a foregone conclusion once technical calculations had been made? There are several indications that this is a distortion of hindsight. That the view at the time was different is indicated in letters in the Nordic Council archives. Written in late 1952 or early 1953 just before the Committee was to submit its reports on residence and work permits, and before the first session of the Nordic Council, the letters show the uncertainties of the time. In one, Edberg wrote that it was "extremely uncertain" whether a recommendation on communications ought to be proposed to the new Council, for fear that it would fail. The other letter, from Frantz Wendt, the Danish

Secretary to the Nordic Council, suggested that the Parliamentary Committee's forthcoming report should not end with suggestions although concrete steps should be mentioned which individual members could take up. This would avoid "loss of face" should the measures not be implemented. In fact, judgments must have differed because the Nordic Council, at its first session, did pass a recommendation with no opposition and no abstentions.[42]

Types of Opposition

What kind of opposition was there, and how did the Committee attempt to overcome it or circumvent it? There was opposition of three types: opposition to the relaxation of passport requirements from those who had particular responsibilities for security, opposition to various other measures when unification meant lowering an already prevailing domestic standard, opposition to measures which were thought to infringe on economic policy.

When the Nordic passport union was established there were fears that the relaxation of controls would permit the entry of criminals, spies, and other unwanted foreigners. There are only scattered indications of this; evidence on the opposition is indirect. No formal statements of opinion (uttalelser) were printed either in the Council's records or in the Parliamentary Committee's reports; they were mentioned only briefly in the latter. The most convincing general evidence is that it took more than four years to agree to implement stage three, the checking of non-Nordic citizens only at the outer borders of the region. The police were afraid of encouraging criminals; there was talk of a Nordic criminal market".[43] Military authorities were afraid of spies, and sometimes police authorities took this up too; provincial authorities in some of the border areas had reservations about both these categories.[44] The Swedish Aliens Commission raised questions about the possibility of deported criminals returning, of foreigners pretending to be Scandinavians--the problem with the transition system, as we have seen--of NATO or Soviet spies whom the other countries would not hinder, of the possibility that the employment situation would change.[45] It is difficult to tell whether there was actually more opposition from within Sweden than from within the others, or whether it was simply more visible.[46] In Norway, for example, when stage two, the common Nordic labor market, came to a vote in the Storting, twelve members opposed it.[47]

The second type of problem which occurred involved "unification down", that is, lowering a standard already prevailing in one of the countries for the sake of unification. It seems to have been possible only if comparisons were difficult to make. One may compare the success in setting a common duty-free limit for travelers, with the incomplete success in unifying the postal rates for letters.

While a common duty-free limit was agreed upon, the Swedish representatives commented that they would have been willing to have had a higher level set, but had chosen a unified rate rather than make a Swedish reservation.[48] It is possible that they were able to do so because prior to this, no explicit monetary level had obtained in Sweden; comparisons of the effect of unification on the domestic rates could not easily be made. The Committee therefore was not in the position of seeming to lower a previously obtaining domestic standard in the name of Scandinavian unity.

By comparison, when the Committee wanted domestic and Nordic postal rates to be identical, the Danes did not decrease the permissible weight of domestic letters which could be sent for the specified price in order to conform to the Committee's recommendations.[49] This may have reflected a larger disparity in domestic and Nordic mail costs for Denmark with its significantly smaller geographic area than for the others. More likely, the main reason was the difficulty in lowering an already obtaining and visible standard.

When the suggestions of the Committee had, or were thought to have, implications for a major economic policy of a country, there were difficulties. The Committee realized this. In Report nr. 2, suggesting a common limit for duty-free items brought with the traveler, they noted that there might have to be exceptions for rationed goods, such as coffee.[50] In its Final Report, the Committee asked for an increase in the common limit "as soon as the foreign exchange situation in certain of the countries permits".[51]

The two striking cases of this kind were the attempt to create a Nordic labor market which will be discussed separately below, and the Committee's proposal that checking foreign exchange at the borders be eliminated, permissible foreign exchange limits be liberalized, and the requirement of a passport to obtain foreign exchange be abolished.[52] This was directed at Norway, which had stricter controls on her whole economy than did either Sweden or Denmark, and which had embarked upon a recovery program resting on a planned but strictly husbanded balance of payments deficit. Norway settled for random checks at the border, and raised somewhat the permissible amounts of foreign exchange obtainable (for all countries in the European Payments Union plus Finland). However, the Ministry of Trade, which had been created to plan and coordinate the recovery program, advised against steps which would essentially undermine the foreign exchange controls which were a part of that program. The Ministry pointed out that of the foreign exchange allotted Norwegian tourists during the previous two years, about 85% had been spent in Sweden and Denmark; given Norway's large payments deficit, liberalization of restrictions was not advisable. The Ministry also feared that further liberalization could lead to circumvention of the rules governing the transfer of capital from the country.[53] It was willing to accept the requirement of a "foreign exchange card" instead of a passport, for purposes of buying foreign exchange, but apparently this was rejected elsewhere in the government, because in its report to the Nordic Council the next year, the Norwegian Government explained that although they had weighed the idea of such a card, they had concluded that a passport was the most effective control, and not difficult to obtain. They were willing to permit an expired passport to be used in obtaining foreign currency of the other Nordic countries.[54] Where Governments believed that measures suggested by the Committee would infringe on important policies, they balked.

Meeting the Opposition: The Committee's Arguments

The means chosen to meet opposition reflect both the style of Scandinavian politics, and the conditions of existence of the Committee itself. Typically, persuasion was "facts". It sometimes looked as if the Committee attempted to outweigh the arguments of those who opposed a measure by the sheer volume of evidence! The reports on the passport question, for instance, are full of statistical date on not only the size, composition and location of the travel streams, but also on the precise numbers and characteristics of those rejected at borders or deported. In examining this question, the Swedish members of the Committee asked to see the reasons for which people had been denied entrance in the past.[55] Statistics from as far back as the post World War I era (when restrictions were first instituted) were obtained. What the Committee found out was that a very tiny proportion of those who had undergone the usual procedures were ever refused entrance. For example, in 1950, of 3.7 million Scandinavians in inter-Nordic travel, only 0.5% had been refused entry. Moreover, some of the reasons which had been sufficient for refusal of entry in the past were so no longer; thus even the historical figures overstated the number of undesirables.[56] The Committee concluded that checking passports, despite "a certain deterrent effect" (en viss preventiv effekt), in general had "slight effect".[57] Likewise statistical evidence was used to show that the overwhelming part of customs revenues were from liquor and tobacco; the Committee could thus suggest dealing with these separately.

A second technique was to distinguish Nordic and non-Nordic citizens. The Committee asked first for the elimination of controls on Nordic citizens. This step was easier to obtain, and afterwards would be used to show that fears had been exaggerated.[58] In other words, it gave Governments time to learn from experience.

The Nordic--non-Nordic distinction was used also in one of the original recommendations that Nordic citizens should no longer be under obligation to report their residence while visiting in another Nordic country. Since this had not been implemented by the Final Report, the Committee renewed its arguments in an interesting way: it now argued that under conditions of a full passport union, the effectiveness of the remaining controls was at stake: "...the authorities can concentrate their attention on non-Nordic citizens within the Nordic area, and escape the enormous burden of work which the checking of Nordic residence reports implies".[59] Both these examples are an interesting indicator of the degree of greater trust of other Nordic than of non-Nordic peoples.

In addition to experimenting with a partial step first, the Committee's case was enhanced by two additional methods, what might be termed the "insurance" features, and the "cost-effectiveness" argument. The first is illustrated by the fact that both with respect to customs and foreign exchange checks at the internal borders, and with respect to passport checks for non-Nordic citizens at the internal borders, the state authorities still retained the right to conduct checks, although the states had agreed to reduce the number of these to only a random sample.[60] The authority of the states was not reduced.

The "cost-effectiveness" type of argument, reflects the "economic" style of political argument in Scandinavia. Not only are economic issues predominant, and therefore more visible, but politics in consensual societies is largely the politics of distribution.[61] Moreover, both consensual politics and a "planning" approach, long fostered by the social democrats, but now generally accepted by all, have required and taught any advocate of a proposal to put a price tag on his suggestion for change or on his defense of the status quo.

In this context it was natural that the Committee defined its problem as an "economic" one - in the broad sense of the term. It asked in its first report "...does a reasonable relationship really obtain between the nuisance value of this checking system to Nordic travelers, and its purpose?"[62] Secondly, as a result of the statistical evidence it had gathered, Edberg noted in his popular brochure, the tiny percent actually hindered "illustrated the disproportion between the apparatus which is maintained and the essential purpose one has in view".[63]

When one examines these two arguments, one notes that the first "disproportion" is between incommensurables. The second really rests on an additional argument: if the large apparatus could indeed stop spies and dangerous criminals, no matter how few, then perhaps it might be worth the trouble and expenditure after all. But in the Committee's view, major criminals and seasoned spies found no difficulty in passing such official controls. This argument, then, was not one of proportion, but rather of whether the instrument suited the purpose.

In another respect, however, one might speak of a "disproportion". When controls had been instituted originally, the Nordic countries had had disparate welfare provisions which applied only to their own citizens; one purpose of passport regulations had been to prevent the entry of others for whom the state might have to assume care. In recent years, however, agreements among the Nordic countries applied such benefits to Nordic citizens working within their borders; thus the same apparatus now really had a reduced purpose, only to deter undesirables.[64]

What the Committee did, then, with their "insurance" techniques and their "cost-effectiveness" arguments, was to attempt to reduce the perceived benefits (in terms of efficient use of bureaucratic resources) of the status quo, and the perceived losses (in terms of bureaucratic opposition and the expenditure of political 'capital' to overcome it) of the proposed reforms, thus reducing the (opportunity) cost of the reform alternative in comparison with the status quo. To a considerable extent, they succeeded.

The Case of the Scandinavian Labor Market: Climate Affects Costing

One of the most widely publicized measures in the Scandinavian system of cooperation is the Scandinavian common labor market. As Einar Løchen pointed out, the EEC, considered a more advanced form of regional organization, did not have such a market until 1970, whereas the Scandinavian labor market was established in 1954.[65] How and why was the market established? Does its history support the idea that it was the result of spillover from the passport union? Would ideas of costs and benefits be of use in understanding this case?

Historical Efforts

The free labor market de facto was simply the result of a Swedish decision. During the war, Sweden had tens of thousands of refugees, mainly from the other Nordic countries.[66] In October 1943 Sweden abolished the requirements for the Nordic citizens to obtain labor permits for work in Sweden.[67] During the war, the Swedish decision was the only relevant one. Afterwards, Sweden, undamaged, and wealthiest of the three, was clearly the one which would attract labor. But there was a symbolic aspect also.

Both for those interested in furthering Nordic ties and for those in the labor movement, the freedom of a worker to go where he wished to seek employment, was a long sought goal. Compared to the long negotiated and half-hearted steps of the prewar years, this seemed a chance for a breakthrough. In 1944 a motion for a Scandinavian Labor Market was made in the Swedish Riksdag, and in the fall of that year it was included in the Swedish Social Democrats' postwar program.[68] It was taken up at the first meeting of representatives of the Nordic labor movements in July 1945. The Danish Social Democratic Party Congress soon after issued a manifesto whose points echoed those of the Nordic meeting, including specifically the Nordic labor market.[69]

Hans Hedtoft, who was then Danish Minister of Social Affairs, invited his Nordic counterparts and their chief advisers to meet in Copenhagen a few weeks later; at that meeting a draft convention for a labor market was worked out. The Norwegian Minister, Oftedal, noted that Norway had not been notified in advance of the plan for a convention, that she needed all her labor force, and could not, as the situation was then right after the war, raise wages to compete "if it should be generally known" that jobs were freely available in Sweden. He suggested instead that those countries which have unemployment notify the others and work through the labor authorities. Sweden and Denmark urged that the convention could be written to take care of Norwegian interests. In fact, a committee including Oftedal, did work out a draft as well as some "prerequisites" for the convention, which specified that a joint labor market committee was to be established among the countries, that no country would recruit labor from the others, and that the convention must obtain the consent of the Storting.[70] Even so, in March 1946 , the Minister had to notify his Nordic colleagues that Norway did not feel that it could ratify the agreement at present, although it hoped to be able to do so in the not too distant future.[71] The Swedes and Danes went ahead and signed a convention on November 18, 1946 ; the effect of this was to eliminate the need for Swedes seeking work in Denmark to obtain a labor permit. For Denmark, it thus reciprocated Sweden's measure of 1943. Thus ended the first stage in the efforts for a Nordic agreement.[72]

In fact, for all practical purposes there was a free labor market.

There were no legal hindrances for Norwegians or Danes seeking jobs in Sweden. (There were no economic incentives for a flow of Swedish labor to Denmark or Norway). The sole hindrance for Norwegians was, presumably, a state of less than perfect information, and the lack of official approval. The major disincentive to an agreement from the Norwegian Government's viewpoint was its fear of losing skilled labor to better paying Swedish jobs, and thus slowing Norway's own recovery program. The labor market was very tight in these years in both countries. These fears continued up to the 1954 agreement.[73] Secondly, Denmark (and Finland) had much higher unemployment rates than did Norway or Sweden, and in Norway, there was nervousness in some quarters as well that there might be an influx of Danish labor which Norway would not have the capital resources to employ.[74] (These two are not necessarily contradictory: an influx of unskilled labor does not replace the loss of skilled labor.)

Given the fact that these worries by the authorities most directly concerned continued, even in the context of Norway's rapid recovery, the question is: what finally persuaded the Norwegian government to overrule its most hesitant parts?

The Spillover Thesis

Rolf Edberg's thesis is one of spillover. "The abolition of the passport requirement was the key". Once the decision for a passport union was taken, the rest followed as a matter of course. The first step, to eliminate passports for those visiting other Nordic countries for up to three months, was limited, Edberg maintained, in order that it could be effected quickly by administrative decree instead of waiting for legal changes. But once the authorities had no date of entry recorded, it was impossible to maintain the requirement that a residence permit and a work permit be obtained within three months of entry. Since the work permit system was handled by the same authorities, the labor market was thus "like a ripe fruit" once the decision for a passport union was acknowledged.[75]

The published sources, and the Norwegian law establishing the labor market, refer to the recommendation of January 1953 by the Parliamentary Communications Committee in their discussions of the background for the treaty.[76] This evidence would seem to support Edberg's analysis.

Relative Cheapening: An Alternative Explanation

An alternative thesis is more convincing, however. As early as October 1951, the Norwegian members of the joint committee for economic cooperation (discussed in the previous chapter) had suggested that the Norwegian government review its position on the joint labor market since the measure would have "significant psychological effect". The matter was mentioned in the Cabinet, although postponed to obtain the reactions of some of the Ministries.[77] The Communications Committee's report was not the only prodding, although clearly the first suggestion had not been sufficient incentive to make the Government press its most reluctant Ministries.

More to the point is the Foreign Ministry's evaluation early in 1953. It noted immediate postwar efforts, the urgings of the Norwegian members of the Nordic Economic Cooperation Committee, the Nordic Parliamentary Communications Committee, the Nordic Council, and domestically, the acquiescence of the Ministry of Social Affairs and of labor organizations, as well as the objections of the Ministry of Municipal and Labor Affairs. The Foreign Ministry's conclusion was:

> Norway is the country which has taken the least positive position in the question of Nordic cooperation in areas concerning economic life, and it is first and foremost with regard to Nordic cooperation and relations with Denmark and Sweden that the Foreign Ministry recommends that Norway adhere to the convention.[78]

This throws a different light on the matter. There is no argument here that it is difficult and/or expensive to maintain the labor permit system without the passport system. It is true that the reasons given by <u>both</u> committees--that the labor permit system was really part of a system used to keep out anti-social and criminal elements, and that therefore it seemed of little use among the Nordic countries, that the measure was expected to have little economic impact, that the measure would have a good "psychological effect"--were cited. However, the Foreign Ministry's own recommendation, was "first and foremost" in order to show its good will toward the other two Scandinavian countries, since Norway had taken hard positions in other negotiations.

This writer concludes that the operative incentives had less to do with spillover, than with what one writer has sarcastically labelled the "phoenix effect"[79]--out of the dead ashes of one cooperative project, arises another. Climate affects costing. In some political climates or after some sequences of events, what might be called a "relative cheapening process" takes place. What apparently tipped the scales against the hesitations of some of the economic ministries, was the desire for a sign of good will after Norway's veto of the two other recent proposals. Thus, what had seemed too costly in 1946 now seemed relatively cheap.[80]

There are usually several components to the policy of a country, subordinate as well as main themes. At any particular time a subordinate theme may be seen as needing reinforcement. This is particularly so if it can be done without conflicting with the main theme. It is also likely to be so if other recent decisions have reinforced the main theme at the expense of the subordinate one. In this case part of the Norwegian foreign policy was a Nordic attachment, although from the late forties on it had been subordinated to the theme of Atlantic association. Precisely for that reason, some way of reaffirming the Nordic theme would be sought, especially some way which would not do damage to the alignment theme, the dominant element of the posture.

The concept of "relative cheapening" is analogous to that of "marginal utility"; as one value is satisfied to a greater extent, others lower in priority become relatively more important; the trade-off among preferences--how much a marginal increment in one value is worth in terms of a marginal decrement in another--changes. In the case of the Labor Market, the Nordic and Atlantic values or policies were not in competition. But having made the Atlantic policy a priority in recent important decisions, the Government was willing to pay more to satisfy the "neglected" Nordic value.

Postscript: The Provisions and Effects of the Nordic Labor Market

To describe briefly the agreement that was concluded, Norway, Denmark, Finland and Sweden (not Iceland) agreed not to demand a work permit of each others' citizens. The assumption, stipulated in the agreement, was that each country should attempt to maintain full employment.[81] The countries promised to exchange employment statistics, information on planned measures and employment opportunities. A committee was established to follow labor market developments, establish guidelines for cooperation among the public labor exchanges, and discuss other related matters of interest.

The common labor market was limited in several important respects. A Protokoll to the Convention stipulated that the agreement excluded the right to establish a business without permission, and jobs for which one needed authorization (professional licences). Special jobs created to maintain full employment would not be open to the citizens of the other countries; nor would jobs in security and defense. Most significantly the Protokoll specified that the Committee was to see what measures could be taken to hinder private labor recruiting across borders.[82]

The treaty did not have much effect on the actual flow of labor.[83] Sweden continued to be the country which attracted significant numbers from the others, but the great increases had taken place in the late 1940s and early 1950s, i.e. before the Treaty. The only exception were Finns working in Sweden whose numbers jumped in 1951 and continued to be much greater than those of Danes or Norwegians.[84] Although the treaty envisioned that the flow would be through the public labor exchanges, which would give individuals information on their "realistic chances",[85] the majority of migrant workers did not use these exchanges; despite previous fears, this was not in fact a problem. Complaints have arisen on several occasions regarding private recruiting by business firms, and the Committee had agreed to ask the firms to stop, and attained the cooperation of the Swedish Employers' Association in doing so.[86] Nevertheless some still goes on.

Is this an integrated labor market? Where recruiting--a form of equalizing access to information, if considered in the economic sense--is frowned upon, it clearly is not. Nor is there a common manpower policy, since each country still continues to institute its own measures to encourage mobilization of labor (vocational training, measures to bring women into the labor force) or mobility of labor (retraining, housing and moving subsidies). Nevertheless, as has been pointed out, the free labor market has been a factor in balancing the labor market of the area.[87] The Nordic Labor

Market Committee has discussed a wide range of issues of general economic policy bearing on the questions of labor utilization, mobilization and mobility; it probably serves as one channel for the spread of innovation in dealing with these problems.

Liberalization has continued, moving into areas, like the professions, which had been excluded by the Convention. Progress has been made in several categories long stymied (often presumably for reasons of nonequivalent training, often more likely for reasons of competitive scarcity). A common market (meaning that a person licensed or trained in one country will qualify for a position in any of the others) has been established for, among others, physicians (1966), dentists (1967), and nurses (1968).

Conclusions

The vision behind the establishment and activity of the Scandinavian parliamentary committee's work was a view of international society and its organization implicit in the following conception of the significance of borders:

> For what is a border, really? Nothing more than a division often the result of historical accident - where one state's administrative authority ends and another's begins. Many times people on both sides of the gate feel greater identity (samhørighet) with each other than with countrymen further within the administrative unit to which they pay taxes, in which they perform military service, and in which they have the right to vote. A border, therefore, ordinarily ought to constitute a well oiled hinge between two administrative units not a hindrance to communications between them, where people's identity is thoroughly checked and their baggage minutely investigated. It ought to constitute an easy and normally nearly invisible transition between two countries...[88] (emphasis added)

This view leads one not to aim at changing the structure of authorities, but rather to soften their often unnecessarily rough edges. It either conceives of or chooses to present the nation-state as an "administrative unit" which permits viewing proposed changes as primarily technical in nature and potentially non-divisive. These kinds of changes men of good will (such as an inter-parliamentary body with interested representatives of all the major political forces) can agree upon.

The Committee's strategy was to reduce the costs to the Governments of the reform in comparison with the status quo. Reducing costs means concern with the subjective cost estimates of the decision makers. Thus teaching and learning are relevant. Here, the parliamentary composition of the Committee was helpful. Members of parliament bring with them a public platform from which to interpret the success of one measure or to draw conclusions about the implications for others. The Committee could also "teach" by the way in which it framed the problem. It made two contributions to the presentation of the problem. First it reversed the burden of proof by investigating what was now needed rather than what ought to be retained from former systems. Secondly it "taught" also by its "economic" definition of the argument, asking "...does a reasonable relationship really obtain between the nuisance value of this checking system to Nordic travelers, and its purpose?" The "disproportions" they observed were, as we have noted, really comparisons of incommensurables, but political learning frequently has such elements.

The Committee was also able to obtain and endorse "insurance features" which served the same purpose of making the measures cheap for the Governments, while facilitating the aim of the Committee, better communication. Such insurance elements, as was evident also in the case of economic cooperation, may be necessary conditions for taking steps which are thought--often very exaggeratedly--to involve risk. In the communications area, in all cases where controls were "lifted", they were in fact merely reduced to spot checks, thus not actually reducing the authority of the Governments, or preventing their use in unusual cases; on the other hand, they did reduce the time consuming burden for the public.

The friendship of countries has been called (by Richard Neustadt) "the friendship of machines" to emphasize the enormous domestic complexities and mechanical difficulties of cooperation, even given basic good will.[89] It was the Committee's combination of being able to reverse the burden of proof, and simultaneously, by the inclusion of insurance features, to reassure the functional and regional bureaucracies that their ultimate authority was not being eroded, which was particularly useful in such a case where obstruction came from bureaucratic rather than partisan sources.

In the sense that the work of the Committee was concerned "only" with such bureaucratic resistances, it was not politically partisan. However, that is not to say that the secret of its successes was "technical" either. A comparison with similar efforts of the Council of Europe makes this point strikingly.[90] The Scandinavian Committee's techniques were dependent upon prior political good will (although not approval in detail); the Governments had implicitly agreed to consider forthcoming Committee proposals according to political (if not instead of, at least as well as, bureaucratic) criteria. It was understood before the establishment of the Committee that proposals would not remain the sole province of agency or department heads to be decided on a least common denominator basis. (Legally, of course, this still could have happened, but the political assumptions were otherwise.) Success was not guaranteed; the Governments were perhaps not yet decided, but they were declaring themselves open to being convinced. It would be up to the Committee to help the Governments override the objections of their own agencies (which are never likely to see any exercise of authority as unnecessary or any reduction of prerogatives as desirable) wherever it could be made safe and defensible in their eyes to do so. The Committee's tactics of shifting the burden of proof and giving attention to statistical data fitted this task perfectly. The comparison with Council of Europe efforts also indicates that the implicit greater trust of other Nordic (compared to most non-Nordic) peoples, helped Committee efforts.

The cost-reduction view of the work of the Committee best accounts for the slowing down of the Committee's progress in areas touching on major economic problems and policies, such as the liberalization of foreign exchange for travel purposes. Where Governments considered potential costs high, progress was slower. Such facts could not be accounted for by functionalist logic.

From both the establishment of the Parliamentary Committee itself, and from the agreement on a formal Scandinavian Labor Market, a second major conclusion emerges. Climate affects costing; a measure deemed by Governments too costly at one point, at another may seem relatively cheap.

Finally, apropos Scandinavia, (and not our theories) the Scandinavian Parliamentary Committee for Freer Communication, Etc., given its aims achieved considerable success in making intra-Scandinavian borders well-oiled hinges in the communications among their countries.

CHAPTER FIVE

THE COSTING PERSPECTIVE

The general, but also tautological, answer to the question of why so few and weak joint institutions were formed among the Scandinavian countries in the postwar period, was that there was no convergence of policies. The costing perspective, illustrated here, helps us understand why this convergence did not take place. Attributing a kind of cost-benefit analysis to states-as-actors, more precisely to those acting on behalf of states in so far as they have assumed official, state roles, is, it is true, a metaphor. Yet we hope to have shown that it is a fruitful one in explaining state policy. What we are saying is that it is as if there were state actors, and as if 'they' went through a process of costing. What this aids us in doing is connecting the intellectual process of decision-making to social processes and social attributes impinging upon it. It focusses on the questions which must have been asked, the dilemmas which must have been confronted, and examines the factors affecting the answers given.

Such a perspective helped us highlight several questions which had to have been considered by all governments in the decision situation of 1948-49 in which they had the choice of creating an independent Scandinavian defense pact or joining a Western alliance: what would be the likely American response? What kind and degree of deterrent effect would either pact be likely to have? What would be the domestic political reaction to a government proposal of a Scandinavian pact, an Atlantic pact, or if necessary, one after the other? In each case alternative courses of action were being compared with respect to their likely benefits, losses, and the degree of likelihood attached to each.

Three different theories of deterrence affected the estimates of what would constitute adequate deterrence and what combination of deterrence versus reassurance would be optimal: the denial theory of Sweden, the punishment theory of Norway, and the non-provocation theory of Denmark. Still another theory, that of a "critical mass", held most strongly by Denmark, but appealing to all of them in some degree, almost created a basis for consensus. It failed ultimately to do so. In the assessment which each country's leaders had to do, the fall-back position of each can be compared analytically to the opportunity cost of the preferred decision (the independent defense pact on the assumption of a "critical mass"). When the Norwegian leaders seriously discussed the fallback position, they feared that the first position was unlikely to be realized, and the fallback was risky in that they might not be able to swing public opinion to it quickly enough. In Denmark, for reasons we have shown, the fallback position was less risky, and in Sweden, it was entirely different. This is a good illustration of the contingent relationships combining external and internal factors, being assessed in such a decision: the probable response of domestic opinion to probable external (American) actions. This one criterion, then, allows us to discriminate the three final positions in the negotiations over a defense pact, and the reasons for them.

As a byproduct of this examination which focusses on the situation of each country, we discovered that Denmark's mediator role was a function of its position in the bargaining constellation: Sweden's invitation to Denmark had been contingent; Denmark was totally dependent upon Norway's acceptance of a Scandinavian pact for its own opportunity to participate. On the other hand, it was relatively certain, because of its ownership of Greenland, of acceptance by the Atlantic pact. The position was 'overdetermined' by the desirability of not giving the Danish Radical Left party any leverage in opposing an Atlantic Pact if the Scandinavian option failed. A further consequence of Denmark's situation (historical experiences as well as geographical location) was not only pessimism about defense but a style of behavior which looked like passivity, but which was intended to evoke unbiased information from the environment (Western or Scandinavian) about the probabilities of having its home territory defended. By contrast Norway's active style can be attributed to its interpretation of its wartime experience that while nothing is guaranteed, politics can pay.

When we turn to the example of the Scandinavian economic market negotiations, our first observation deals if not with style directly, then with something related to it, with strategies. We characterized the strategy of

Norway as distributive and of Sweden as expansive, linking them to patterns observed in the literature of game theory, the predominantly zero-sum versus the predominantly variable-sum orientation to a game. We argued that this related to the general disparity in overall strength between the two, and was reinforced by several specific historical and current differences in the "terms of trade" of the governments of the two countries.

Strategies as well as the more diffuse notion of style of action both deal with "how", the instrumental, how one gets what one wants. Strategy is peculiar to one situation; style indicates something more pervasive. It is learned strategy, strategy consolidated into a habitual pattern. In the language of psychology, not only commitments but also learned "coping techniques" make up character. Such techniques may or may not be appropriate to the task at hand. They are the residues of the past, elements of continuity. In the economic market case, the major strategies--both the objectives and the styles of negotiating--demonstrated this.

In order to understand how the positions of the parties changed over the lengthy period of the negotiations, one must introduce costing, particularly the concept of opportunity costs. That helps us first to understand the partial change in the Norwegian position in 1954, and Norway's and Denmark's loss of interest in the context of the EFTA alternative in the late 1950s. It also explains the more generous Swedish position in the Nordek negotiations of the 1960s, in the new situation of a consolidating and attractive EEC. As the costs, measured by comparison with the net benefits of other opportunities, changed, so did the positions of the parties.

To make the point even more general, other games affected the economic market negotiations game. At the very beginning, the Marshall Plan context is important in understanding the significance of the early, unsuccessful but never-quite-terminated negotiations among the Scandinavian countries. Later, the NATO game was one which required constant attention from Norwegian leaders. As we have indicated, it was the sense of fragility of the Labor Party support for the defense policy that pushed it continually to the top of the leaders' agenda, and forced them to expend political capital on that, to the detriment of other issues. A related point here is that a major commitment affects other issues in rather complex ways.

Here, not the fact of the Atlantic commitment so much as the sense of its fragility, made it take precedence, particularly in the mid-1950s, when otherwise the time seemed propitious for agreement on the common economic market.

The interaction pattern we discerned among the negotiating countries was one we termed a negative diplomatic spiral. The combination of the low priority accorded to the Scandinavian market (due to the low proportion of intra-Scandinavian trade at the time and, in the Norwegian case, the subordination to defense politics) as well as the high visibility of such an issue vulnerable to organized interest group influence, resulted in low politicization. This meant the unwillingness of goernments to expend political capital tal on the issue, and a downward spiral of expectations by each government of what the other governments would invest in the issue. This was happening in a situation where, we have shown, genuine uncertainty about the results of trade liberalization made the need for reassurance to the weaker party, Norway, imperative. The Norwegian government needed something to point to in a possible election fight; for a long time, the Swedish government had no particular incentives to give it such payoffs. Thus the negotiations were at a stalemate.

One of the conclusions from the case of the economic market is that the tendency of the subjectively weaker party to adhere to a distributive orientation in bargaining will necessitate side-payments from the stronger if a bargain is to be made. The implications of this runs counter to suggestions made both by Amitai Etzioni and by Karl Deutsch.[1] Etzioni argued from the experience of the EEC that although there were "cushioning" provisions such as the EEC's Social Fund and Investment Bank, these were small in amount and limited in time; there were no redistributive measures before integrative ties had developed.

The argument here is a double one: significant side-payments will tend to be needed to make the initial bargain. (One of the Norwegian Labor Party delegates asked rhetorically if Belgium would have joined the EEC without aid to its inefficient coal mines.[2]) Secondly, the line between cushioning and redistribution is one of degree; however, it is possible that the size of the side-payment is not the sole important characteristic. Such provisions *may* supply "something to point to" for the weaker Government, *or* their real significance (to the other Government itself, not just to its public) may be the willingness to share risk, that "we are all in this together".

Because side-payments will be necessary often, the subjectively stronger must have incentives more than sufficient for a strictly calculated *quid pro quo*. In the case of Nordek, the incentives were a long term relationship with the vital European constellation. In another Scandinavian case, that of the formation of the Scandinavian Airlines System, the need of all the Governments to cooperate if they were to reach the minimum viable size for an international airline, led Sweden, the strongest economically, technologically, and financially, to make concessions such as national quotas on pilots, to win an agreement.[3] Reassurance must not be underestimated.

In the case of the successful efforts of the Scandinavian Communications Committee, costing by governments proved a better explanation than did an alternative theory offered, one of "spillover". Descriptively, spillover was weak in that there was little evidence of technical links among the steps suggested by the Committee and implemented by governments. Nor was there evidence that the Committee itself cultivated groups who would or did learn to focus their efforts on the Committee. The costing perspective in this case assumed no momentum from one step to another. It suggests instead that the connections among the steps were ones of purpose; they contributed and were seen to contribute to the same end, facilitating communication among the Scandinavian peoples. As we have shown, the virtue of the costing approach here is that it is able to explain slow-downs as well as successes. In those cases where a proposal was thought to interfere with a major government policy, for example, government controls on currency, progress slowed. The establishment of a common Scandinavian labor market was shown to result not from spillover from the common passport union, but from a calculation that agreement to such a market was now a relatively cheap step. Norway, now searching for a symbol of good will after its refusal in both defense and economic negotiations, agreed to the labor market, which had largely existed *de facto* anyway. Climate, often a product of the particular sequence of events, affects costing. Or, to say it another way, once more other games affected the outcome.

The technique of reducing costs to governments of the variety of liberalizing measures proposed by the Communications Committee was facilitated by two features of the Scandinavian situation. First, the sense of Nordic identity was sufficient to permit a Nordic--non-Nordic distinction in the introduction of some of the proposals; this seemed to have some reassurance effect. Secondly, the Committee really had the political blessing of the governments in the sense that by putting the issue above partisan politics, and in the context of efforts for Nordic good will, the governments were implicitly promising to review the proposals of the Committee using political criteria as well as bureaucratic criteria. The Committee could then see its job as one of helping Governments to overcome the inertia and obstacles of their own bureaucracies. Their cost-reduction techniques of shifting the burden of proof, introducing insurance techniques and so on, were appropriate to and successful in this contaxt. Such a success is not to be underestimated in a world where the friendship of countries becomes more and more the friendship of highly complex "machines".

Whenever there are seriously competitive alternatives open to one or more of the parties, an explanation of decision outcomes must make an "analysis of advantage" for each party. Focussing solely on the attributes of the parties will be misleading. In the defense pact case, such an explanation might exaggerate the certainty of the outcome, an ahistorical view; in the case of the economic market it might underrate the phases of the negotiations and, again, be misled by the final outcome. This is so because choice depends only partly on the attributes of the chooser, and partly on the the situation of choice. An explanation must connect the attributes of the party, as well as his options, with his choice of strategy.

NOTES

Chapter One

The Scandinavian Option

1. For an introduction to Finnish foreign policy see: Finnish Foreign Policy, published by The Finnish Political Science Association, (Helsinki: 1963); Max Jacobson, Finnish Neutrality: A Study of Finnish Foreign Policy Since the Second World War (London: Hugh Evelyn, 1968); Krister Wahlbäck, "Finnish Foreign Policy: Some Comparative Perspectives," Cooperation and Conflict (hereafter C & C) 1969, No. 4, pp. 282-298 (review and discussion of Jacobson); Urho Kekkonen, Neutrality, The Finnish Position (London: Heinemann, 1970), (selected speeches by President Kekkonen, 1943-1969); John H. Hodgson, "Postwar Finnish Foreign Policy: Institutions and Personalities, "Western Political Quarterly, (March, 1962), pp. 80-92; Katarina Brodin, Christian Lange, and Kjell Goldman, "The Policy of Neutrality: Official Doctrines of Finland's Security Policy," ibid., pp. 75-92.

2. Vegard Sletten, Five Northern Countries Pull Together (published by The Nordic Council and under the auspices of the Ministries of Foreign Affairs of the five countries); Joseph A. Lauwerys (ed.), Development of Democratic Thought and Institutions in Denmark, Norway, and Sweden (New York and Copenhagen: 1958). Note also the definition of "culture" given by Hans Sølvhøj, then Danish Minister for Cultural Affairs: "We [Scandinavians] also regard culture as being the way of life for the individual citizen, the daily habits in the home and at work, relationships with fellow-men, the way in which the citizen participates in the government of his country... A consistent democracy means a community in which the individual feels the ties of responsibility for his fellow-citizens." "Nordic Cultural Cooperation," Nordic Cooperation, Conference Organized by the Nordic Council for International Organizations in Europe, Hässelby 2-4 June 1965 (Stockholm: 1965), pp. 99-102.

3. On minorities and immigrant groups in Sweden, see: David Schwartz (ed.), Svenska minoriteter, en handbok som kartlägger invandringspolitiken och befolkningsminoriteternas ställning inom svenska samhället (Stockholm: Aldus/Bonniers, 1966).

4. Einar Haugen in Nordisk Tidskrift, 1953, pp. 240-241.

5. Einar Haugen et al. (eds.), "Historical Background of Norwegian", Norwegian-English Dictionary, Second American Printing with Addendum and Corrections (Oslo: Universitetsforlaget, and Madison, Wisconsin: The University of Wisconsin Press, 1967), pp. 20-34; Einar Haugen, Language Conflict and Language Planning: the Case

of Modern Norwegian (Cambridge, Mass: Harvard University Press, 1966); Stein Rokkan, "Geography, Religion, and Social Class: Crosscutting Cleavages in Norwegian Politics," Party Systems and Voter Alignments, Cross National Perspectives, Stein Rokkan and Seymour M. Lipset (eds.) (London: Collier-Macmillian Limited, New York: The Free Press, 1967), pp. 415-425.

For a fascinating discussion of the use of the language issue in the social mobilization of nineteenth century Finland, see: Roberta Selleck, "The Language Issue in Finnish Political Discussion: 1809-1863", unpublished Ph.D. dissertation, Radcliffe College, Harvard University, 1961. Dr. Selleck uses the case of Finland as a test of Karl Deutsch's social mobilization theory.

6. See the recurrent suggestions in the Nordic Council documents for standardization of Scandinavian names for birds, flowers, etc.

7. For recent changes in party strengths and for the proliferation of tiny parties, see the "Review" section of the annual, Scandinavian Political Studies (Oslo: Universitetsforlaget, New York: Columbia University Press) published since 1966. For the number of seats and percentage of the vote held by each party (in all five Nordic countries) see back cover of Nordisk Kontakt, published biweekly by The Nordic Council.

8. For the British comparison see Samuel H. Beer, British Politics in the Collectivist Age (New York: Alfred Knopf, 1965) (2nd edition with new Epilogue, Vintage, 1969). On the freezing of party formations with PR, see: Stein Rokkan, "Electoral Systems, "International Encyclopedia of the Social Sciences, XII (1968) (hereafter, IESS). "That great carnivore" is the way Francis Hope characterizes the British Conservative Party (in contrast to its Scandinavian counterparts) in "To Young Scandinavians, EEC is Old Stuff," The New Statesman, November 17, 1967. On the stability of Scandinavian parties, see, for example: Bo Särlvik, "Political Stability and Change in the Swedish Electorate," Scandinavian Political Studies, A Yearbook Published by the Political Science Associations in Denmark, Finland, Norway, and Sweden, I (1966), pp. 188-224 (hereafter SPS); Jan Stehouwer, "Long Term Ecological Analysis of Electoral Statistics in Denmark," SPS II (1967), pp. 94-116. On the alacrity with which the old Norwegian parties monopolized the political process immediately upon liberation after World War II, see Thomas Chr. Wyller, Frigjøringspolitikk, Regeringsskiftet sommeren 1945 (Oslo: Universitetsforlaget, 1963).

9. Gunnar Heckscher, "Interest Groups in Sweden: Their Political Role," Interest Groups on Four Continents, edited by H.W. Ehrmann for the International Political Science Association (Pittsburgh: 1958), p. 156. Also: Richard I. Tomasson, Sweden: Prototype of Modern Society, (New York: Random House 1970) Chapter VIII, "Organizations" pp. 242-270; M. Donald Hancock, Sweden. The Politics of Post-industrial Change, (Hinsdale, Illinois: The Dryden Press, 1972), Chapter 6 "The New Pluralism. Groups and System Transformation" pp. 146-169; Nils Elvander, Intresseorganisationerna i dagens Sverige, (Lund, Sweden: C.W.K. Gleerup Bokforlag, 2nd revised edition, 1972).

On the role of interest groups in the organization, morale, and resistance of wartime Norway, see Thomas Chr. Wyller, Nyordning og motstand. En framstilling og en analyse av organisasionenes politiske funksjon under den tyske okkupasjonene, 25.9.40 - 25.9.42 (English summary) (Oslo: Universitetsforlaget, 1958).

For a study of the impact of interest groups on an issue in Norwegian foreign policy see Edgeir Benum, Maktsentra og opposisjon. Spaniasaken i Norge 1946 og 1947. (Oslo: Universitetsforlaget, 1969). Steven Kelman, in a superb reportage, notes that in Sweden even the clergy of the state church are organized. "Letter from Stockholm," The New Yorker, December 26, 1970, p. 39.

10. Ulf Torgersen, "Borgerkrigen som ble vekk," Tidskrift for samfunnsforskning, 1967, Nos. 2-3, pp. 253-254. (This is a review of Harry Eckstein, Division and Cohesion in Democracy: A Study of Norway (Princeton, N.J.: Princeton University Press, 1966).

11. Folke Schmidt and Stig Strömholm, Legal Values in Modern Sweden, (Totowa, N.J.: Bedminster, 1965), p. 39. For a contrasting, negative view, see Roland Huntford, The New Totalitarians, New York, Stein and Day 1972.

12. See, for example, Bo Carlson, Trade Unions in Sweden, (Stockholm: Tiden, 1969). On white collar workers, see Arne H. Nilstein, "Sweden," White Collar Trade Unions, A. Sturmthal (ed.) (Urbana, Illinois and London: The University of Illinois Press, 1966), pp. 261-304.

13. "It is not possible to combine the demand for a fixed and planned wage policy with a decentralized system of the right of decision making." Carlson, p. 78. Since Carlson's book was published, there has been some provokation for rethinking. Wildcat strikes hit Sweden in the spring of 1970. See brief accounts in Sweden Now, March, April, and June, 1970, Hancock pp. 164-168, James Fulcher, "Class Conflict in Sweden", Sociology 7:1 (January 1973).

14. For a description of the process, see: Heckscher, pp. 166-167, and Hancock, 156-159. On the general rule in Sweden that government documents are available to the public, see Andrew Shonfield, "Sweden: the Principle of the Goldfish Bowl," Modern Capitalism. The Changing Balance of Public and Private Power (New York and London: Oxford University Press, 1965) (Royal Institute of International Affairs), pp. 399-406; Nils Herlitz, "Publicity of Documents in Sweden," Public Law, (London: Stevens, 1958).

Christian Lange comments on the variation in remiss practice: "The practice which has developed concerning what shall be sent out for comment, and which authorities shall have the right to express an opinion in this way, is different in the different Nordic countries." Nordisk offentlig samarbeid en regional integrasjonsprosess?" Internasjonal Politikk (Oslo) (hereafter IP), 1965, No. 2, p. 162.

15. Stein Rokkan, "Numerical Democracy and Corporate Pluralism," in Political Oppositions in Western Democracies, Robert A. Dahl (ed.), (New Haven and London: Yale University Press, 1966), p. 107. Also see Robert B. Kvavik, Interest Groups in Norwegian Politics, Oslo: Universitetsforlaget 1976 for a detailed study of the participation of interest groups in Norwegian politics.

16. Nils Stjernqvist, "Sweden: Stability or Deadlock?", in ibid., p. 130.

17. Arend Lijphart, The Politics of Accommodation: Pluralism and Democracy in the Netherlands (Berkeley: The University of California Press, 1968), p. 123.

18. A good source for characterizations of Nordic politicians is "Porträttet" in each issue of Nordisk kontakt (hereafter NK) a periodical distributed to members of parliament of the five countries, and reporting political news of the five individually and of their relations.

19. Compare Hugh Heclo's comment on Britain and Sweden: "Yet there is one important commonality between the two nations. In comparison with previous national policy, the nineteenth-century deliberations on poor relief in both countries exhibited a uniquely developed attention to questions of social relations, what one author [Karl Polanyi, The Great Transformation, p. 33] has called "the discovery of society". Modern Social Politics in Britain and Sweden. From Relief to Income Maintenance. New Haven and London, Yale University Press, 1974. p. 60.

20. One of the parties in the 1970 Swedish elections urged newspaper readers to "let the elections be a victory for saklighet." (Kelman, p. 41).

21. Robert Brustein, Revolution as theatre: notes on the new radical style. New York: Liveright, 1971.

22. Per Bratman discussing Alvar Alsterdal's book, Tage Erlander, in Arbeiderbladet (Oslo), No. 2641, 1968.

23. Barbara G. Haskel, "What is Innovation? Sweden's Liberals, Social Democrats, and Political Creativity." Political Studies (U.K.) XX: 3 (September 1972) pp. 306-310; Sven Anders Söderpalm, "The Crisis Agreement and the Social Democratic Road to Power" in Steven Koblick (ed.), Sweden's Development from Poverty to Affluence 1750-1970, (translated by Joanne Johnson), Minneapolis; University of Minnesota Press, 1975, pp. 258-278. (Swedish edition, Stockholm: Wahlström and Widstrand, 1973, pp. 235-257.)

24. For other suggestive characterizations of the political culture of the Scandinavian countries, see: Ulf Torgerson, "Political Institutions" in Norwegian Society, edited by Natalie Rogoff Ramsøy, Oslo: Universitetsforlaget, London: C.W. Hurst and Co., New York: Humanities Press, 1974, pp. 194-225. (Det norske samfunn, Oslo: Gyldendal Norsk Forlag, 1968, pp. 229-262). Harry Eckstein, Division and Cohesion...; Dankwart A. Rustow, The Politics of Compromise: A Study of Parties and Cabinet Government in Sweden (Princeton, N.J.: 1955); Ingemar Dörfer, "System 37 Viggen: Science, Technology, and the Domestication of Glory," Public Policy, XVII (1968), pp. 226-229; Thomas J. Anton, "Policy-Making and Political Culture in Sweden," SPS IV (1969), pp. 88-102; Donald S. Connery, The Scandinavians (New York: Simon and Schuster, 1966). On attitudes towards expertise, see Paul Britten-Austin, On Being Swedish, Reflections Towards a Better Understanding of the Swedish Character (London: Secker and Warburg, 1968), pp. 36-39. Also Tomasson, passim especially Chapter IX "Values" pp. 271-294; Hancock, passim especially Chapters 2, 3, pp. 36-88; David Jenkins, Sweden: The Progress Machine, London, Robert Hale, 1968, Chapter II, "The Practical Swede" pp. 19-36;

Joseph B. Board Jr., "Legal Culture and the Environmental Protection issue: The Swedish Experience", Albany Law Review, 37:4 (1973). 603-631.

25. Nils Andrén, "Nordic Integration - Aspects and Problems," C & C, 1967, No. 1, pp. 1-25. For a critique, see Barbara G. Haskel, "Is there an Unseen Spider? A Note on 'Nordic Integration,' "C & C, 1967, Nos. 3-4, pp. 229-234, and Andrén's reply, "A Note on a Note" in the same issue, pp. 235-237.

26. Christian Lange, "Nordiska ministermöter 1945-1965. Regjeringssamarbetet som integrerande faktor i Norden," (Stockholm: Stockholm University, 1965, mimeographed); Barbara G. Haskel, "Regional Efforts: A View from the North," Paper prepared for the Conference on Regional Integration (Madison, Wisconsin: April, 1969, mimeographed). For a brief account of the recent further institutionalization of Nordic consultation and joint efforts see Bengt Sundelius, "Nordic Cooperation: Dead or Alive?", Scandinavian Review, 64 : 2 (June 1976) pp. 46-50.

27. See: Frantz Wendt, The Nordic Council and Cooperation in Scandinavia (Copenhagen: Munksgaard, 1959) ; Olof Wallmén, Nordiska rådet och nordiskt samarbete (Stockholm: Norstedt, 1966); Stanley V. Anderson, The Nordic Council, A Study in Scandinavian Regionalism (Seattle and London: The University of Washington Press, 1967).

28. Edvard Bull, "The Labor Movement in Scandinavia," in Scandinavia Past and Present (hereafter SP & P) Vol. II (Odense: Denmark, 1959), pp. 853-63; Halvard Lange, "Internasjonale innslag i Norsk Arbeiderbevegelse i 90-årene," Festskrift til Halvdan Koht på sekstiårsdagen 7de juli 1933 i Oslo (Oslo: Aschehoug, 1933), pp. 321-329.

29. Frantz Wendt, "The Norden Association," in SP & P, Vol. III, pp. 49-54; Ole Harkjaer, Foreningen Norden, Organisation og virksomhed (Copenhagen: Foreningen Norden, 1966); Arne F. Andersson, 50 år i arbete för Norden, Föreningarna för nordiskt samarbete (Stockholm: Foreningen Norden, 1969).

30. Christian Lange, "Nordisk samarbete...," p. 163.

31. The passport union and labor market will be discussed in chapter four. On legal harmonization, see, for example: "Översikt över lagar tillkomma genom nordiskt samarbete," Nordisk udredningsserie (hereafter NU) 1965, No. 2 (Stockholm: 1966); Ivar Stahl, "Scandinavian Cooperation in the Field of Legislation," in SP & P, Vol. III, pp. 113-117; "The Scandinavian Juríst Congresses," ibid., pp. 118-121; Nils Herlitz, "Nordiskt samarbete inom offentlig rätt?" in Festskrift tillägnad Hans Excellens Riksmarskalken juris doctor Birger Ekeberg den 10. augusti 1950 (Stockholm: Norstedt, 1950), pp. 267-279.

32 For cost-benefit analysis of the conditions under which joint research institutions are likely to be desirable, see K. Stenstadvold, "Langtidsplan for Nordforsk," NU, 1968: 11, p. 25.

33. On Scandinavian cohesion in the United Nations, see: Helen Aareskjold, "Norge og Sverige i FN," unpublished M.A. dissertation, Stockholm, University of Stockholm, 1964 (mimeographed); Kurt Jacobsen, "Voting Behavior of the Nordic Countries in the General Assembly,"

C & C, 1967, Nos. 3-4, pp. 138-157; Jaakko Kalaha, "The Nordic Group in the General Assembly," ibid., pp. 158-170; Jan-Erik Lidström and Claes Wiklund, "The Nordic Countries in the General Assembly and its two Political Committees," ibid., pp. 171-187; R. Enckell, "Nordic Cooperation at the United Nations," NU, 1965:9, pp. 40-47; Per Haekkerup, "Scandinavia's Peace-Keeping Forces for the UN," Foreign Affairs, Vol. 42 (July, 1964), pp. 675-681.

On the Korean project: News of Norway, January 22, 1969, p.6; on the Tanzanian project: Kerstin Larsson, "Beslutsformerna kring en samnordisk bistandsinsats i Tanganyika," Unpublished seminar paper, Stockholm, University of Stockholm, 1965 (mimeographed); on UNCTAD, and Kennedy Round cooperation: Göran Ryding in NK, 1967, No. 1, pp. 63-67.

34. Nils Herlitz, Elements of Nordic Public Law (Stockholm: Institutet for rättsvetenskaplig forskning, LIV, 1969); Nils Andrén, "On Nordic Similarities and Differences," C & C, 1969, No. 4, pp. 309-311 (review and discussion of Herlitz).

35. Kenneth E. Miller, Government and Politics in Denmark (Boston: Houghton Mifflin, 1968), pp. 29-34.

36. Ibid., p. 34.

37. Rustow, Chapters 1-2; Elis Håstad, Sveriges historia under 1900-talet (Stockholm: Aldus/Bonniers, 1958), Part II; Stig Hadenius, Björn Molin, and Hans Wieslander, Sverige efter 1900. En modern politisk historia (Stockholm: Aldus/Bonniers, 1969). On the role of World War One in speeding political changes, see Steven Koblick, "Wartime Diplomacy and the Democratization of Sweden in September-October 1917". Journal of Modern History, Vol. 41, 1969, pp. 29-45.

38. James A. Storing, Norwegian Democracy (Oslo: Universitetsforlaget, 1963), pp. 20-30. See also Raymond E. Lindgren, Norway-Sweden, Union, Disunion, and Scandinavian Integration (Princeton, N.J.: Princeton University Press, 1959). The national holiday, May 17, is Constitution Day (not independence day).

39. Ingvar Andersson, A History of Sweden (translated from the Swedish by Carolyn Hannay), (Stockholm: Natur och Kultur, London: Weidenfeld and Nicolson, 1955), p. 317.

40. See the brilliant historical-sociological study of the Cabinet preceding the change of system: Jens Arup Seip, Et regime foran undergangen (Oslo: Gyldendal Norsk Forlag, 1965), (first published: Oslo: Johan Grundt Tanum Forlag, 1945).

41. Håstad, p. 11.

42. Rolf Danielsen, "Samlingspartiet og Unionen," Historisk tidskrift (Oslo), Vol. 41, no. 4 (1962), pp. 303-320. (English summary).

43. Nils Elvander, "Från liberal skandinavism till konservativ nationalism i Sverige," Scandia, XXVII, no. 2 (1961), pp. 366-386; for a bibliography on "Scandinavianism" see: Dansk Historisk Bibliografi, 1913-1942, Vol. I, Udgivet af Den Danske Historiske Forening ved Henry Bruun (Copenhagen: Rosenkilde og Bagger, 1966), pp. 274-277.

44. Frantz Wendt points out that for the Danes, previous unions held only proud memories. The Nordic Council..., p. 24.

45. Ibid., pp. 25-27.

46. Swedish Prime Minister Per-Albin Hansson in a speech in 1934. Johannes Lehmann (ed.), Nordisk Samarbejde, Tre taler i idraetshuset 5 december 1934 af Per Albin Hansson, Johan Nygaardsvold, Thorvald Stauning (Copenhagen: Poul Branner, 1934), p. 17.

47. Viggo Sjøqvist, Danmarks Udenrigspolitik 1933-1940, (Udgiverselskab for Danmarks nyeste Historie) Copenhagen, Gyldendal, 1966, pp. 55-63, ("the boundary of Norden" p. 58); 182-191, ("watchdog" p. 184). See also pp. 198-199 for the 1937 meeting of the Nordic Foreign Ministers, pp. 227-232 for 1938 meeting, 287-293 for Denmark's positive and Norway's and Sweden's negative responses to German offers of non-aggression pacts in 1939. Sjøqvist also mentions the contemporary evaluation of the dispute between Norway and Denmark over the ownership of Iceland (decided by the International Count in favor of Denmark) as having exascerbated feelings between the two, (pp. 59-60). See also pp. 86-92 and 265-272 for a summary of the efforts at economic and other cooperation.

48. For example: Nordiske Muligheder, Afhandlinger udgivet af Foreningen Norden, Dansk Forening for Nordisk Samarbejde (Copenhagen: 1943).

49. John H. Wuorinen, "Scandinavia and the Rise of Modern National Consciousness," in Nationalism and Internationalism, Essays inscribed to Carlton J.H. Hayes, Eric M. Earle (ed.) (New York: Columbia University Press, 1950), p. 460.

50. Karl W. Deutsch, "Communication Theory and Political Integration" The Integration of Political Communities, Philip E. Jacob and James V. Toscano (eds.), (Philadelphia & New York: Lippincott, 1964), p. 56.

51. Donald J. Puchala, "International Transactions and Regional Integration" International Organization Vol. XXIV, Nr. 4 (Autumn 1970) (Special issue "Regional Integration") p. 742. See the foundation work, Karl W. Deutsch, Nationalism and Social Communication: An Inquiry into the Foundations of Nationality (first edition, Cambridge, Mass.: MIT Press, New York, John Wiley and Sons, 1953).

52. Deutsch, "Communication Theory..." p. 53.

53. Puchala, p. 742, footnote 12.

54. Puchala, pp. 753-4.

55. Philip Selznick, Leadership in Administration. A Sociological Interpretation. New York, Harper & Row, 1957, p. 17.

56. Ernst B. Haas, The Uniting of Europe, Political, Social and Economic Forces, 1950-1957 (Stanford, California: Stanford University Press, 1958).

57. Ernst B. Haas, "Technocracy, Pluralism and the New Europe," A New Europe?, Stephen R. Graubard (ed.), (Boston: Beacon Press, 1963), pp. 62-88; Ernst B. Haas, Beyond the Nation-State, Functionalism and International Organization (Stanford, California: Stanford University Press, 1964), pp. 46, 447-458.

58. Ernst B. Haas, "International Integration. The European and the Universal Process," in International Political Communities: An Anthology (hereafter IPC), (Garden City, N.Y.: Anchor Books, 1966), pp. 93-130 (reprinted from International Organization, XV (Autumn, 1961) (hereafter IO).

59. Ernst B. Haas, "The Uniting of Europe and the Uniting of Latin America," The Journal of Common Market Studies (hereafter JCMS), V (June 1967), pp. 315-343.

60. Ernst B. Haas and Philippe Schmitter, "Ec onomics and Differential Patterns of Political Integration: Projections about Unity in Latin America," in IPC, pp. 259-300 (reprinted from IO, XVIII (Autumn 1965), pp. 870-884).

61. Mancur Olson, Jr., "Economics, Sociology, and the Best of All Possible Worlds," The Public Interest, No. 12 (Summer 1968), p. 105.

62. For examples of the literature of perception and images, see: Kenneth Boulding, The Image (Ann Arbor, Michigan: University of Michigan Press, 1956); Ole Holsti, "The Belief System and National Images: A Case Study," Journal of Conflict Resolution, VI (September 1962), pp. 245-252; Ole Holsti, "The 'Operational Code' Approach to the Study of Political Leaders: John Foster Dulles' Philosophical and Instrumental Beliefs," Canadian Journal of Political Science, III (March 1970), pp. 123-157. (Holsti, who has worked with the concepts of image and belief system for a decade, has produced progressively more sophisticated work - as he realized that the concept only partially explained outcomes); Michael Brecher, Blema Steinberg and Janice Stein, "A Framework for Research on Foreign Behavior," Journal of Conflict Resolution XIII "March 1969), pp. 75-101. See also the lucid review article on approaches to the analysis of foreign policy including the "image" approach, by Janice Gross Stein, "L'analyse de la politique étrangère: à la recherche de groupes de variables dépendentes et indépendentes," Études Internationales, Vol. II, No. 3 (September 1971), pp. 371-394.

63. R. MacGregor Dawson, "Mackenzie King as Leader," Party Politics in Canada, Second edition, edited by Hugh G. Thorburn (Scarborough, Ontario: Prentice-Hall of Canada, 1967), pp. 76-77.

64. On the "communications strategy" of the speaker, see Robert Jervis, "The Costs of the Quantitative Study of International Relations," in Contending Approaches to International Politics, edited by Klaus Knorr and James Rosenau (Princeton: Princeton University Press, 1969), p. 193. (The pitfalls involved in controlling for "communications strategy" are illustrated in the well known Yiddish tale of the meeting of two acquaintances. The first man says that he is on his way to Minsk. The second observes to himself: "He says that he is going to Minsk so that I will think that he is going to Pinsk. So I know that he is going to Minsk." The "Minsk-Pinsk effect" can often be observed in interpretations of political communications.) For an answer to Jervis, see Robert North, "Research Pluralism and the International Elephant," in ibid., pp. 218-242; on perceptions and inferences, see Robert Jervis, "Hypotheses on Misperception," World Politics (hereafter, WP), XX, No. 3 (April 1968), p. 460.

More general points may be made about the crucial importance of understanding the context for understanding the significance of the statement made. Louis Hartz argued persuasively that the _effect_ of a school of thought differs radically depending upon what other schools of thought are in the relevant context. The "meaning" of a social or philosophical position depends on to what or whom it is an "answer" or response. _The Liberal Tradition in America. An Interpretation of American Political Thought Since the Revolution_ (New York: Harcourt, Brace and Co., 1955), and _The Founding of New Societies_ (New York: Harcourt, Brace and World Inc., 1964). On the other side, the following quotation makes clear why the _intention_ (as well as the _effect_) of a statement is ambiguous without a clarification of the context in which it was made:

> There is a sense in which... the analysis of questions is logically prior to that of indicative sentences, for the meaning of an indicative sentence is often ambiguous until we know the _question_ to which it is an answer, and/or the assertation which it _excludes_. For example, the sentence S: 'I sleep in room 10' may be an answer to the question a) 'Where do you sleep?' or b) 'Do you sleep in room 10 or room 12? or c) 'Who sleeps in room 10?' or d) 'What do you use room 10 for?'...

(Donald M. Mackay, "The Informational Analysis of Questions and Commands," in _Modern Systems Research for the Behavioral Scientist: A Sourcebook_, edited by Walter F. Buckley (Chicago: Aldine Publishing Co., 1968), p. 205).

65. For example, Brecher _et al_., p. 87. This may be an instance of the more general principle that values (or imperatives) cannot logically be deduced from facts.

A further problem, not only for the analyst but also for the decision-maker is the "problem of analogies":

> ...thought depends upon classification and classification rests upon the assumption that specified analogies may, for the purposes at hand be treated as homologies... However, in all fields of thought we are faced with the problem of deciding under what circumstances characteristics can be treated as essentially the same... for certain purposes...

(Lewis A. Dexter, "Analogies for Interpreting and Studying Congress", _The Sociology and Politics of Congress_ (Chicago: Rand Mcnally, 1969), p. 185.) The decision-maker must assess the "fit" or compatibility of incoming information or impressions with the theories or beliefs or hypotheses he holds. (See Robert Jervis, "Consistency in Foreign Policy Views" _Communications in International Politics_ (Richard L. Merritt, ed.) (Urbana: The University of Illinois Press, 1972). pp. 272-294. Also Geoffrey Vickers, _The Art of Judgement_ (New York: Basic Books, 1965), pp. 50-66, chapter 3 ("Three Case Studies of Appreciation") for fascinating examples of codings which imply rules for decisions. A political cartoon also illustrated the point neatly. It showed two British senior civil servants conversing: "Is a pay rise for the royal family an inflationary demand in the public sector, or a productivity incentive for the higher echelons?" _The New Statesman_, April 23, 1971).

Foreign policy decision-makers face unusually acute problems in this regard. John Steinbruner has characterized their situation as one of "structural uncertainty" by which he means that the possible states of their world are imperfectly specified, the probability distributions attached to these are unknown, and the task involved -- unlike that in traditional rational decision-making theory -- is to establish, not just assess, the relevant parameters for the problem. Sometimes, (as Steinbruner's study of the MLF decision showed) while the beliefs of the decision-makers are only weakly supported, they are also only weakly contradicted. It can be difficult, in other words, to decide whether incoming information is either confirmation or disconfirmation. (John D. Steinbruner, "The Mind and Milieu of Policy-Makers: A Case Study of the MLF" unpublished Ph.D. dissertation, Massachusetts Institute of Technology, 1968, pp. 215-216. See also his The Cybernetic Theory of Decision. New Dimensions of Political Analysis. Princeton, N.J.: Princeton University Press, 1974.)

Essentially the same problem has arisen in experimental work bearing on decision-making and aiming to discriminate risk-prone versus conservative behavior in making choices. Discernible patterned differences emerge in the behavior over time of individuals in the experimental situation. These patterns do seem related to independently established personality characteristics. Excessively risky or excessively conservative choice patterns are "overgeneralized"; they "ignore patent differences in task properties". (Nathan Kogan and Michael A. Wallach, Risk Taking, A Study in Cognition and Personality (New York: Holt, Rinehart and Winston, 1964), p. 190.) However, to transfer this conclusion to the field of policy making (particularly foreign policy making) and to make it an operational discriminator of the appropriateness of behavior, the analyst confronts a problem not apparent in the original laboratory situation. The criterion of "task similarities" is relatively unambiguous to the laboratory experimenters; they are agreed on what are the "common structural properties" of their experiment, and what are not. In political decision-making, this is usually the crux of the issue: "what are the distinguishing or relevant characteristics of this case? Is it like others we have dealt with?" Without agreement on what are the structural properties of the situation, or on what is the relevant reality, evidence of perceptual distortion or personality-biased behavior, at any rate, cannot be decisive. Absence of adequate criteria of "fit" make perceptual accuracy (in non-trivial cases) impossible to judge.

66 An elementary text on international politics which treats rational problem-solving as well as psychological and organization influences is William D. Coplin, Introduction to International Politics. A Theoretical Overview. Chicago, Markham, 1971, (second edition, 1974).

67. This approach has been generally inspired by work of varying rigor and varying suggestiveness within broadly the "economic" or rational decision-making perspective, such as: Edward C. Banfield and Martin Meyerson, Politics, Planning, and the Public Interest, Glencoe: Free Press, 1955; Edward C. Banfield, The Moral Basis of a Backward Society, Glencoe: Free Press, 1958; Mancur Olson Jr., The Logic of Collective Action. Public Goods and the Theory of Groups, Cambridge, Mass: Harvard University Press, 1965; Mancur Olson Jr. and Richard Zeckhauser, "An Economic Theory of Alliances" Review of Economics and Statistics, 48 (1966) 266-79; N. Froelich, J.A. Oppenheimer, and O.R. Young, Political Leadership and Collective Goods, Princeton, Princeton University Press, 1971; Thomas Schelling,

The Strategy of Conflict, Cambridge, Mass: Harvard University Press, 1960; Thomas Schelling, "The Ecology of Micromotives" The Public Interest Nr. 25 (Fall 1971); Anatole Rappaport, Fights, Games, and Debates, Ann Arbor: University of Michigan Press, 1960; Richard Walton and Robert B. McKersie, A Behavioral Theory of Labor Negotiations: an Analysis of a Social Interaction System. New York: McGraw Hill, 1965; William Zartman, "The Political Analysis of Negotiation: How Who Gets What and When", World Politics 26:3 (1974) 385-399; Bruce Russett, Economic Theories of International Politics, Chicago: Markham 1968; Albert O. Hirschman, Exit, Voice, and Loyalty, Cambridge, Mass: Harvard University Press, 1970; W.H. Riker, The Theory of Political Coalitions, New Haven, Conn: Yale University Press, 1962; P.B. Clark and J.Q. Wilson, "'Incentive Systems': A Theory of Organization", Administrative Science Quarterly 6 (1961) 129-166; James Q. Wilson, "The Bureaucracy Problem", The Public Interest Nr. 6 (1967), pp. 3-9; Joseph S. Nye, Jr., "Corruption and Political Development: A Cost-Benefit Analysis", The American Political Science Review, LXI: No. 2, (1967) pp. 417-427.

Mark Sproule-Jones ("Strategic Tensions in the Scale of Political Analysis: An Essay for Philomphalasceptics", British Journal of Political Science, I, pp. 173-191, remarks that "political scientists are often engaged in disputation about various strategies of inquiry, not any logic of inquiry." (174); the differences among the strategies revolve around whether they limit the scope of analysis and leave a broad ceteris paribus assumption or whether they widen the scope of analysis and leave a narrow ceteris paribus assumption. (190). I have tried to take inspiration from works of the first type (such as those above) and combine it with my own training which is of the second type.

68. Raymond A. Bauer, "The Study of Policy Formation: An Introduction," in The Study of Policy Formation, edited by Raymond A. Bauer and Kenneth H. Gergen (New York: The Free Press, 1968), p. 5.

69. Graham T. Allison, Essence of Decision, Explaining the Cuban Missile Crisis (Boston: Little, Brown and Company, 1971). Pages 10-38 give a clear explication of the rational decision-making model. Allison compares this to two alternate models of bureaucratic bargaining and organizational process. James R. Kurth reminds us that the bureaucratic politics model is really a variant of the rational model with the locus of rationality shifted to the level of the "unitary bureau within the bureaucratic system." "A Widening Gyre: The Logic of American Weapons Procurement", Public Policy XIX No. 3 (Summer 1971) p. 378.

70. Olson, "Economics, Sociology..." pp. 106-114.

71. Nils Ørvik, (ed.) Fears and Expectations. Norwegian Attitudes toward European Integration. Oslo, Universitetsforlaget, 1972.

72. James Q. Wilson, Political Organizations, (New York: Basic Books 1973) p. 25.

See Sten Sparre Nilson's suggestive essay "Valuation: The Basis of Foreign Policy Decision-Making", Cooperation and Conflict 1969, No. 2, pp. 99-118.

73. On the distinctions between risk and uncertainty, see Ernest H. Weinwurm, "Measuring Uncertainty in Managerial Decision-Making," Management International, III, No. 4 (1963), pp. 114-122. The distinction was originally made by Frank H. Knight in Risk, Uncertainty, and Profit (Boston, 1921).

74. This paragraph follows James M. Buchanan who gives a fascinating intellectual history of the idea of cost in economic theory, in Cost and Choice, An Inquiry in Economic Theory (Chicago: Markham, 1970). Also see John C. Harsanyi, "Measurement of Social Power, Opportunity Costs, and the Theory of Two-Person Bargaining Games," Behavioral Science, VII (1962), pp. 67-80.

75. Buchanan, p. 43.
One of the implications of this change in the meaning of cost is that cost is a strictly subjective assessment; it reflects the decision-maker's own evaluation. It is in that sense "always right"; no external observer can refute it. This is, then a logical theory of how choices are made, but it is not a scientific hypothesis capable of refutation. (Buchanan, chapter 3)

76. See Nils Ørvik, "Nordic Cooperation and High Politics" International Organization 28: 1 (Winter 1974), pp. 71-73; "Integration For Whom, Against Whom?" Cooperation and Conflict 1967, No. 1, pp. 54-59.

77. Since "foresight" is "organized hindsight," tradition, habit and the ezample of others may all influence costing. On "foresight as organized hindsight," see Wroe Alderson, "Planning," in Policies, Decision, and Organization, edited by Fremont J. Lyden, et al. (New York: Appleton-Century-Croft, 1969), pp. 185-200. On the importance of "reference groups" in the diffusion of behavior patterns, see Jack L. Walker, "The Diffusion of Innovations Among the American States", "The American Political Science Review (hereafter, APSR, LXIII (September 1969), pp. 880-899; Ira Sharkansky, "Regional Patterns in the Expenditures of American States", Western Political Quarterly, XX (December 1967), pp. 955-971. Also see Arthur M. Ross, Trade Union Wage Policy (Berkeley, and Los Angeles: The University of California Press (Institute of Industrial Relations, 1950), on "equitable comparisons" which "establish the dividing line between a square deal and a raw deal," (pp. 50-51). Some comparisons are more "coercive" than others (pp. 72-74).
The notion of comparisons should be taken one step further. There may be crucial comparisons with other eras in the history of the group (golden ages, national traumas), which led to aspiring for repetition or avoidance of those situations. Likewise others in the environment may provide models or antimodels. (See for example, Lijphart, op. cit., on the memory of past religious wars, as well as the internal political strife in neighboring France, as motivations for domestic political compromise on religious and suffrage questions in the Netherlands.)

78. Vickers, pp. 41-42.

79. Roger D. Hansen explicitly raises the question of the relationship of endogenous and exogenous variables in his review and criticism of the neofunctionalists and their critics. ("Regional Integration, Reflections on a Decade of Theoretical Efforts," WP, No. 2 (January 1969), p. 249) He argues that the neofunctionalists made "no systematic attempt to locate and measure the effects of international environment changes and elite perceptions within the regional union over time". (p. 250) Hanson himself suggests a notion of differential "compellingness" of international environments (p. 264).

The first to criticize this aspect of neofunctionalist theory was Stanley Hoffmann, "The European Process at Atlantic Cross-purposes," JCMS, II, No. 2 (February 1965), pp. 85-101;"Obstinate or Obsolete? The Fate of the Nation-State and the Case of Western Europe", in International Regionalism, edited by Joseph S. Nye Jr. (Boston: Little Brown, 1968), pp. 177-230. Others have been Joseph S. Nye Jr., "Patterns and Catalysts in Regional Integration", in Nye, op. cit., pp. 333-349; Karl Kaiser, "The Interaction of Regional Subsystems: Some Preliminary Notes on Recurrent Patterns and the Role of the Superpowers", WP, XXI, No. 1 (October 1968), pp. 84-107; Barbara G. Haskel, "External Events and Internal Appraisals: A Note on the Proposed Nordic Common Market," IO, XXIII, No. 4 (March, 1969), pp. 960-968. Ernst Haas has acknowledged the problem in "The Uniting of Europe and the Uniting of Latin America", op. cit.. Amitai Etzioni also attemped to integrate the impact of the external environment into an intellectual framework by using the concept of "external elites" for the system under observation. Political Unification: A Comparative Study of Leaders and Forces (New York: Holt, Rinehart & Winston, 1965).

80. Charles Frankel, "Being In and Being Out". The Public Interest, No. 17 (Fall 1969) p. 47.

81. John C. Harsanyi, "Rational-Choice Models of Political Behavior vs. Functionalist and Conformist Theories", WP, XXI, No. 4 (July 1969), p. 527.

Chapter Two

A Critical Commitment: The Case of the Proposed Scandinavian Defense Pact

1. Philip Selznick, Leadership in Administration. A Sociological Interpretation (New York: Harper & Row, 1957), chapter 2, especially pp. 34-35. Cf. Thomas Schelling who argues that unpredictability can be useful at times. Arms and Influence (New Haven: Yale University Press, 1966), pp. 38-43.

2. See Johan Jørgen Holst, "Norwegian Security Policy," C & C, 1966, No. 2, pp. 64-79, and Nils Ørvik, "Base Policy - Theory and Practice," C & C, 1967, Nos. 3-4, pp. 198-204, for a discussion of Norwegian diplomatic efforts to retain autonomy in the interpretation of a "base policy".

3. See the experience of the Finns in the postwar years. Much Finnish attention is focused on the interpretation of the Treaty of Friendship, Cooperation and Mutual Aid (1948) with the Soviet Union. The 1961 "note crisis" revolved around this for example. The Finns maintain that they have the exclusive right under the Treaty, of initiating military consultations, and that this is the only interpretation compatible with their announced neutrality. (Kekkonen's speech, November 27. 1969, reported in NK, 1969, No. 16, pp. 1004-1005.

4. The first account of these negotiations was Lennart Hirschfeldt, <u>Skandinavien och Atlantpakten. De skandinaviska alliansforhandlingarna, 1948-1949</u>, Stockholm, 1949. Barbara G. Haskel used public sources in "The Attempt to Create a Scandinavian Defense Pact as Reflected in the Public Statements of the Swedish, Norwegian, and Danish Members of Government During 1948-1949", (Stockholm 1963 mimeographed, 70 pp.), a revised version of which appeared as "Forsøket på å skape et skandinavisk forsvarsforbund" <u>Internasjonal Politikk</u>, (Oslo) 1965, No. 2, pp. 92-131. Arne Olav Brundtland made particular use of Norwegian parliamentary records in his "Hvorfor ikke skandinavisk forsvarsforbund?" <u>Internasjonal Politikk</u> 1964, No. 3, pp. 132-150. Ingemar Dörfer deals with these years as part of his view from the Kremlin, "Stalins nordiska balans", <u>Internasjonal Politikk</u> 1965: 2, pp. 132-150.

The first "actor" to write a short version of these events was Norwegian former Foreign Minister Halvard M. Lange in <u>Norges vei til Nato</u>, Oslo, 1966. Mr. Lange was interviewed about these events by, among others, Magne Skodvin, Knut Einar Eriksen, Nils Morten Udgaard (whose work is described below) and by this writer, but his own fuller memoirs of this era were interrupted by his death in 1970.

Recent historical accounts are: Nils Morten Udgaard, <u>Great Power Politics and Norwegian Foreign Policy. A Study of Norway's Foreign Relations November 1940 - February 1948</u> Oslo, 1973. This deals with not only the wartime background but also the beginning of the defense reassessment in 1947-1948. Udgaard had access to Norwegian Labor Party archives as well as the minutes of the Labor Party's executive, and its parliamentary group, all for the period 1945-1948. Magne Skodvin, (<u>Norden eller Nato? Utenriksdepartementet og alliansespørsmålet 1947-1949</u>, Oslo, 1971), was asked by the Norwegian Foreign Office to write an account based on unlimited access to its archives. Skodvin limited his account to the role of the Foreign Office in the political reorientation in Norway. Knut Einar Eriksen, (<u>DNA og Nato. Striden om norsk Nato-medlemskap innen regjeringspartiet 1948-1949</u>. Oslo, 1972) was given access to Norwegian Labor Party archives for the period 1945-1960 including the minutes of the National Executive, other representative bodies, the parliamentary party, the Oslo Labor Party (1948-1949) and also the file on Nordic cooperation. In addition he did extensive newspaper research including in the provincial press. His book deals with the divisions within the Labor Party over the Nato decision.

In Denmark, Mary Dau of the Danish Foreign Ministry, uses principally newspaper sources in her study of Danish-Soviet relations, <u>Danmark og Sovjetunionen 1944-49</u>, Århus, 1969. Birgitte Westerholm has written a lengthy paper "Socialdemokratiet og Atlantpagten. En analyse af de faktorer, der øvede indflydelse på Socialdemokratiets stillingtagen til Danmarks optagelse i Atlantpagten i 1949", (Århus Institut for Statskundskab, 1973, 144 pp. mimeographed). Westerholm had access to the minutes of the Danish Social Democratic Party's parliamentary group, party organization minutes and other documents. She deals with the factors influencing the position of the Danish Social Domocratic Party in 1949. At the end of the 1960s, the Danish Foreign Office published the first official account in Scandinavia, its "gray book": Udenrigsministeriet, <u>Dansk Sikkerhedspolitikk 1948-1966</u>,

Volume I: Narrative, Volume II: Appendices. Copenhagen, 1968. Several important documents including the conclusions of the Scandinavian Defense Committee and some reports and assessments by the Danish Ambassador to Washington were first published here. Finally, in Sweden, Krister Wahlbäck (Norden och blockuppdelingen 1948-49, Stockholm, 1973) has reevaluated the material which was recently published and added to it based, among other things, on papers of several important figures and the minutes of the Labor Parties' Nordic Cooperation Committee for 1945-1949. In addition memoirs by Swedish former Prime Minister Tage Erlander, 1940-1949, Stockholm, 1973, and Norwegian former Prime Minister Einar Gerhardsen, Samarbeid og strid. Erindringer 1945-55 Oslo 1971 are now available.

5. See, for example: Undén, Morgon Tidningen, 31-12-47, and Lange, Stortingstidende (hereafter, Stort.),1948, nr. 8, p. 43. For Denmark, see: Udenrigsministeriet, Dansk sikkerhedspolitik 1948-1966 (hereafter DSP), (Copenhagen: 1968), I, pp. 21-23, and DSP, II, Appendices 8-10. Also Erik Reske-Nielsen and Erik Kragh, Atlantpagten og Danmark 1949-1962 (Copenhagen: 1962), p. 44; Niels Jørgen Haagerup, De Forenede Nationer og Danmarks Sikkerhed (Aarhus: Universitetsforlaget, 1956), p. 44. Denmark had even tried to buy arms from both the West and the Soviet Union, sending requests to investigate possibilities to Moscow in 1945 and 1947. In both cases the Soviet Union found it impossible to receive her. (DSP, I, pp. 21-22.)

6. Ósten Undén, Sveriges utrikespolitik (Tal i Riksdagen den 4. februar 1948), (Stockholm: Tidens forlag, pp. 29-30).

7. Hans Hedtoft, 6-2-48. Cited in Fremtiden (Copenhagen) July 1948.

8. Halvard Lange, Norsk utenrikspolitikk siden 1945 (hereafter NUS), (Foredrag og debattinnlegg), (Oslo: Johan Grundt Tanum, 1952), p. 55 (12-2-48).

9. Ibid., p. 59.

10. For the Swedish and Danish reactions, see: Svenska Dagbladet, 17-3-48, Stockholms Tidningen, 14-4-48, Rigsdagstidende Folketinget (hereafter, Folket.), 99. Samling 1947-48, nr. 172, col. 2739 (10-3-48).

For the Norwegian reaction, see: Lange, NUS, pp. 61-64. (What Lange did not include in his speech but what he noted in a review of this period after leaving office, were the Soviet demands on Norway regarding Svalbard (Spitzbergen), the island off the northern coast. Lengthy negotiations about the status of this island had gone on since 1946. Ingemar Dörfer had noted the significance of the Svalbard negotiations for Norway's attitude in "Stalins nordiska balans," IP, 1965, No. 2, pp. 132-150.)

The heart of the speech was the following:

> But in a state of such sharp opposition as we are witness to, there always lies before us the possibility that a great power can occupy a strategically important area, which is not defended or which it believes it can occupy without appreciable sacrifice, in the belief that such an occupation will not lead to war.

For my part, I lay great weight on [the hope that] as far as possible, we must reach a policy on which the three Nordic countries can stand together. There shall be weighty grounds before we choose a path which can lead us away from Denmark and Sweden or from one of them. On the other hand, we must be clear that the military-political problems and the security problems each of the three Nordic countries faces, are not identical, and that this fact can create certain difficulties in the task of finding a common solution.

11. Social Demokraten (Copenhagen), 2-5-48.

12. DSP, II, Appendix 18. Undén told this specifically to the Danish Ambassador in Stockholm, Nils Svenningsen.

13. DSP, I, p. 26.

14. Lange, NUS, p. 70.

15. DSP, II, Appendices 19, 20. Rasmus Hansen, the Danish Defense Minister told a Danish audience that Denmark had currently the weakest defense in a century, one that would take four or five years to bring up to the needed level. He repeated this shortly afterwards adding that the problem would be different depending upon whether Denmark were alone or in agreement with other Nordic countries. (TT from RB 6-6-48, and TT 20-5-48.) Utrikespolitiska Institutets Kalendarium (hereafter, Kal.), pp. 420 and 455. What is interesting is that the official statement took no cognizance of a possible Western-oriented option; no Norwegian official statement of the time would have excluded it so completely.

16. AK, 1948, No. 28, p. 9 (29-6-48).

17. Arbeiderbladet (Oslo), 7-6-49, 9-6-49 (hereafter, Arb.).

18. Lennart Hirschfeldt, Skandinavien och Atlantpakten. De skandinaviska alliansförhandlingarna, 1948-1949 (Stockholm: 1949), (Världspolitikens dagsfrägor, 1949, Nos. 4-5), p. 22. See DSP, II, Appendix 21 (Communiqué from the Foreign Ministers' meeting, September 8-9, 1948), Appendix 22 (Mandate to the Scandinavian Defense Committee, dated October 15, 1948). The Mandate specifically stipulates that the working assumption is "that the three countries, which are agreed to try to keep out of war, do not in advance make military agreements with other powers" (p. 47).

See also Skodvin, pp. 179-181 and Wahlbäck pp. 24-38.

19. "Permanence" is, of course, an exaggeration of the Swedish position; actually there is a thin line between conveying the stability of the non-alignment policy, its long history, its hold on the population on the one side, and insisting on autonomous interpretation of this policy's requirements (which implies the possibility of re-assessment) on the other.

An interesting question is the extent to which Sweden remains in control, for diplomatic purposes, of the threat to align. The theory bruited about in recent years, of a "Nordic balance" with Norway and Denmark aligned to the West, Finland with a special relationship with the Soviet Union to the East, and Sweden as the balancer, hinges on this. See, IP, 1966, No. 5 (issue on Nordic balance); Arne Olav Brundtland, "Nordic Balance," C & C, 1966, No. 2; Erik Moberg, "The 'Nordic Balance' Concept," C & C, 1968, No. 3, pp. 210-213 (a theoretical critique). For the argument that Norway, rather than Sweden, was the diplomatic activist in the 1961 Finnish-Soviet note crisis, see Tomas Torsvik, "Politisk vinter i Finland," Samtiden, Vol. 71, No. 2 (1962), pp. 63-73.

20. DSP, I, pp. 26-27.

21. Interview with Former Foreign Minister Halvard M. Lange, Oslo, 21. June 1967 (hereafter, Lange II). See Skodvin pp. 198-208.

22. Even Danish Prime Minister Hedtoft's statements were "mediatory." In November 1948 his speech sounded as if the first two sentences had been written in Norway and the last in Sweden:

> We feel ourselves most intimately bound to the world's free nations. Naturally it must be especially important for us to preserve friendship and understanding for our policy and our situation among those nations we feel our kith and kin. On the other side, I can not see any Danish or Nordic task to take any step which can raise the tension in the relations between East and West.

Social Demokraten 13-11-48 (TT, Kal., p. 901).

23. Lange II.

24 DSP, I, p. 27. Also Skodvin 209-213, especially Lange's account p. 210, and Wahlbäck, pp. 46-47.

25. On the same day a statement by Defense Minister Hauge was published stating that participation in "...a larger security system, which includes larger and richer powers, will be cheapest..." Arb. 3-1-49.

These statements were perceived in Sweden as so strong that Swedish Prime Minister Erlander asked Norwegian Prime Minister Gerhardsen whether there was any longer a point to the meeting which had been planned for two days later. (Lange, Norges vei til Nato (Oslo: Pax Forlag, 1966) (hereafter, NVN), p. 33.

26. These outlying possessions were Greenland and the Faeroes (Danish), Jan Mayen and Svalbard (Norwegian, north of Norway).

27. DSP, II, Appendix 24 (the resumé of the Karlstad negotiations), Appendix 25 (the timetable decided on at Karlstad). See also Skodvin pp. 235-244, Eriksen, pp. 149-156, Wahlbäck, pp. 49-51. See Skodvin pp. 254-255 for the development and meaning of the phrase "interested in" in Question nr. 1.

28. DSP, II, Appendix 27 (the SFK's list of tasks for the buildup of the Danish defense), and Appendix 28 (the SFK's summary concluding remarks).

The main lines could be inferred from the statements of the three Foreign Ministers to their parliaments in 1949. See Haskel, "Forsøket...," (Appendix B), 1965.

The Scandinavian Defense Committee included both politicians and military experts. The Norwegian members were Trygve Bratteli, then vice-chairman of the Labor Party (and later, Prime Minister), Dag Bryn, the undersecretary who had negotiated with both London and Washington about arms in the spring of 1948, W. Munthe Kaas who was military attaché in the US and Canada during 1948, and Ole Berge, also an officer in the defense establishment. Secretary to the committee on the Norwegian side was Arne Gunneng, who had been in the Norwegian Embassy in Washington until July 1948, and who was one of the three to accompany Lange on his trip to Washington in February 1949. (Gunneng later became Ambassador to Washington).

Among the Swedish members were two members of parliament, Elon Andersson, a Liberal, and Sven Andersson, a Social Democrat (later Defense Minister), Carl Hamilton, a career diplomat, and a general, Nils Swedlund. The Swedish secretary was Sverker Åström, later Sweden's Ambassador to the United Nations.

Denmark's members also included two members of parliament, Poul Hansen, a Liberal, and Harald Peterson, an Agrarian (both of whom were ministers of Defense in different Danish governments), Frantz Hvass, Permanent Undersecretary in the Foreign Office, and Vice Admiral A.H. Vedel, retired Chief of Defense, and spokesman on defense for the Social Democrats.

While this was not a Governments' negotiating team, it was more than an expert committee.

29. DSP, II, Appendix 28. "...til en vis grad at virke praeventivt og udgøre en vis garanti mod saeraktioner." (p. 55)

30. Ibid. Tim Grève (Norway and Nato, (Oslo: Oslo University Press, 1959, pp. 10-11) stated this in 1959 but for understandable reasons this was never stated officially by any of the parties. (At the time he wrote the account, Grève was Lange's secretary.)

Cf. DSP, II, Appendix 34, a dispatch from Danish Foreign Minister Rasmussen to Danish Ambassador in Washington, Henrik Kauffmann, just after the defense pact negotiations (2-2-49). Kauffmann was instructed to inform the American authorities that the proposed pact would not be able to withstand a Great Power attack "in the long run" ("i laengden") but would need outside aid.

31. DSP, II, Appendix 28.

32. Ibid. See Skodvin pp. 31, 105 for the history and significance of this phrase.

33. Skodvin's account cites also a weighing of the probability of attack on Denmark versus other scenarios in which Denmark would not be such a liability. p. 250.

34. DSP, II, Appendix 28.

35. The New York Times, 15-1-49 (James Reston's column).

For two interesting and contrasting discussions of the US Government's attitude toward Scandinavia in or out of Nato, see Reston's analyses February 11 and February 20, 1949. In the first of these he notes that the question of a neutral Scandinavian bloc versus (part of) Scandinavia in Nato, had been considered by the National Security Council which, according to Reston, had concluded that "...the North Atlantic Pact would definitely be weakened, in strategic and psychological terms, if Norway and Denmark did not join with the United States, Canada, and the Brussels treaty powers." In the second article Reston discusses what he calls "two concepts" of the proposed Atlantic Pact, wonders whether the "military" conception was not overweighted in the NSC in comparison to the "political" conception, and relates this to Washington's position on Scandinavia.

36. Morgon Tidningen (Stockholm), 19-1-49, Kal. p. 44.

37. Lange II.

38. "There was no way of agreeing on the form and content of a common approach to investigate whether the three countries in such a union could count on the delivery of materiel in peacetime, which was a mutual prerequisite for the alliance to become a reality." (Lange to the Storting, 3-2-49.)

"On the Norwegian side, in connection with the planned approach to the United States and England about the question of war matériel, they wanted to take up for consideration with the Western Powers, the question of their attitude toward the Scandinavian countries in event of a conflict, [the question] of the help which they could count on, etc." "Freedom from alliances, thus, according to the Swedish conception, ought to exclude military cooperation with states outside [the alliance], and not only be interpreted to mean avoidance of mutual commitments." (Undén to the Riksdag, 9-2-49.) See Skodvin pp. 265-278 for a detailed account.

39. DSP, II, Appendix 30, Communiqué from the Oslo meeting, 29-30 January 1949.

40. Viktige storpolitiske dokumenter (hereafter, VSD), pp. 118-119. Soviet note of 29 January.

41. VSD, pp. 119-120. Norwegian answer of 1 February.

One effect of the Scandinavian negotiations was to make the Norwegian government aware of the Swedish (and indirectly, the Finnish) evaluation of the effects of foreign military bases in Scandinavia.

On Danish Foreign Minister Rasmussen's trip to Washington in late March 1949 he was assured that no bases in Denmark proper would be requested either (DSP, II, Appendix 56).

See Holst, op. cit., and Ørvik, op. cit., on developments in the 1950s.

42. Cf. Dean Acheson's account of his interview with Lange on 7 February, his vignettes of Lange, Norwegian Ambassador Morgenstierne, and of Rasmussen. Acheson says that his impression was that both Lange and Morgenstierne favored the Nato option. Present at the Creation, My Years in the State Department (New York: Norton, 1969), pp. 278-279.

Acheson also notes that the French tried to make Norway's acceptance conditional upon the acceptance of Italy into the pact. (There is some poetic justice in this since the Norwegians were distinctly unenthusiastic about joining in a pact which might include Italy. However, Lange says that his trip revealed that the matter was all decided. Cf. Acheson (p. 278), who says that, "I reported to the ambassadors at our meeting on March 1 -- [i.e., a few weeks after the Norwegian visit] -- that our Government, while open-minded about Italy, was united in requesting that we accept Norway at that meeting

See Skodvin, 288-96; cf Eriksen and Wahlbäck 52-53 on the detailed instructions and the "addendum to the instructions" given the Lange delegation. The instructions concerned questions about Nato and the addendum the advantages of a Nordic pact. Eriksen argues that the addendum was added by Gerhardsen in order to obtain agreement to the mission. Wahlbäck believes the Norwegians softened their requirement that aid from the West be "prepared" in advance ("with military staff discussions").

43. VSD, pp. 120-122. Soviet note of 5 February 1949. Note that the idea of a non-aggression pact had been rejected by Lange in his 19 April 1948 speech. Wahlbäck (p. 24) notes that while the content was not surprising, for a small power to state publicly its reserved relations with one big power without having decided its relations with other big powers, was.

44. Lange, NVN, p. 47; cf Acheson, p. 278; see Skodvin, pp. 296-304 for an account based on and quoting from stenographic references.

45. Per Haekkerup, "Nordic Cooperation and the World Around Us", NU, 1965, No. 9 ("Nordic Cooperation"), pp. 24-28.

46. Nils Ørvik, "Integration for Whom, Against Whom?", C & C, 1967, No. 1, p. 56. Ørvik's argument was a general one about trends in Scandinavia rather than a particular explanation of the defense pact case per se.

Ørvik has used here Karl Deutsch's concept of "core area". Karl Deutsch, Political Community and the North Atlantic Area.

47. Nils Morten Udgaard, Great Power Politics and Norwegian Foreign Policy. A Study of Norway's Foreign Relations November 1940 - February 1948. Oslo, Universitetsforlaget 1973. See also review by Olav Riste in Historisk tidskrift (Oslo) September 1973.

Riste (in a personal communication to this writer, 4-9-73) has remarked that the Soviet's differentiation of Eastern and Western Scandinavia was partly self-evident, based on relative propinguity, and partly due to the strategic situation at the time. The point here is, however, not why they made the distinction but whether they did. If the concept of spheres of influence is to have any utility it must be presumed to be relatively permanent.

48. See Ny Tid (the publication of the Swedish Communist Party,) 3-10-48, cited by Grève, p. 11. See also 59-61. See also Udgaard, pp. 150-153 and Skodvin, pp. 59-61.

49. Olav Riste, London-regjeringa. Norge i krigsalliansen 1940-45 bd I (Utgitt av Forsvarets Krigshistoriske avdeling.) Oslo: Det norske samlaget, 1973.

50. Konrad Nordahl, Minner og meninger Oslo: Tiden Norsk Forlag, 1967, p. 113.

51. Udgaard. Walter Lippmann in his 1948 U.S. Foreign Policy, Shield of the Republic, warned that "...no spheres of influence can be defined

which do not overlap, which would not therefore bring the great powers into conflict... On which side would the Scandinavian countries lie?" (New York: Pocket Books, 1943, p. 125).

52. Wahlbäck, p. 32.

53. DSP, II, Appendix 50, p. 100.

54. Greve, op. cit., pp. 6-7; Tomas Torsvik, 15 ars i Nato (Oslo: Forsvarets Pressetjeneste, 1964). For analogous interpretations with respect to Denmark, see Norman J. Padelford, "Regional Cooperation in Scandinavia, "International Organization, XI (1957), and also an article by H.C. Hansen (who was in the Danish government from 1947) in which he mentions "...the occupation which ended this country's neutral foreign policy and led to the Atlantic Pact and the defense buildup which followed from it." "Socialdemokratiets formaend", Idé og Arbejde (Copenhagen, 1953), p. 29. Cf. Sven Henningsen, "The Foreign Policy of Denmark", Foreign Policies in a World of Change, edited by Joseph E. Black and Kenneth W. Thompson (New York: Harper & Row, 1963), p. 107.

55. Philip M. Burgess, Elite Images and Foreign Policy Outcomes, A Study of Norway (The Ohio State University Press, 1968). (See also Barbara G. Haskel, "A Mirror for Princes? Elite Images," C & C, 1968, No. 4, pp. 240-246, for a critical view of Burgess' treatment and its application to the defense pact case.)

56. Erlander, 20-2-49 (TT from NTB & MT, 21-2-49, Kal., p. 137).

57. Nils Ørvik, Trends in Norwegian Foreign Policy (Oslo: Institute of International Affairs, 1962), p. 23. Also see Ørvik's The Decline of Neutrality, 1914-1941 (Oslo: Johan Grundt Tanum Forlag, 1953).

58. There is an interesting parallel in Denmark. From Birgitte Westerholm's work one can note that although several of those making decisions in the 1940s had been decision makers in the 1930s and thus felt personal responsibility not to leave Denmark undefended once again (p. 103), the "9 April" argument -- We must not be defenseless and unprepared as we were on 9 April 1940. -- seems to have been used only after the fact, in justifying the Atlantic decision. It discriminated only between isolation and cooperation but not between the alternative forms of cooperation. "Socialdemokratiet og Atlantpagten. En analyse af de faktorer, der øvede indflydelse pa Socialdemokratiets stillingtagen til Danmarks optagelse i Atlantpagten i 1949" Institut for Statskundskab, Århus Universitet, 1973, pp. 91-92, p. 103.

59. Udgaard, chapter 12 "The Policy of Bridge-building".

60. Johan Jørgen Holst, "Surprise, Signals and Reaction. The Attack on Norway April 9, 1940", C & C, 1966, No. 1, pp. 29-45.

61. Riste op. cit., argues that Koht was not passive nor legalistic but that his position was one of realpolitik. He did not want to bind Norway's policy after the war particularly because he was concerned to have good neighborly relations with the Soviet Union. See Skodvin's review of Riste in Aftenposten, 26 March 1974.

62. Trygve Lie, Hjemover (Oslo: Tiden, 1968), pp. 57-59. This North Atlantic grouping was to include the United States, Canada, Great Britain, Iceland, Denmark, The Netherlands, Belgium, and Ireland.

63. Regjeringen og Hjemmefronten, Aktstykker utgitt av Stortinget (Oslo: Aschehoug, 1948), Document 21, pp. 102-103. Those who were consulted in the formation of this reply are listed on pp. 27-28. There were some tensions between the London Government and the Home Front (Hjemmefronten), but basically the relationship, in contrast with that in other countries, was very good.

64. Lange's father, Christian Lange, had been the Secretary-General of the Interparliamentary Union, As a boy, Lange lived in Brussels for several years and from that time spoke fluent French. Thereafter, he lived for a few years in Geneva, spent a year in Italy (during the rise of Fascism) and several years in England, as well as traveling elsewhere in Europe. His reaction of disappointment to the Versailles Treaty strengthened the liberal-pacifism of his home milieu. But from the age of 20, he belonged to the social democratic movement. Cf. Trygve Bull, Mot Dag og Erling Falk (Oslo: Cappelen, 3rd revised edition, 1968), p. 98.

65. Arne Ording, "Norwegian Foreign Policy", The Norseman, March-April 1953, pp. 73-76, here p. 73. (This was, however, written several years later, and after Lange had been subject to attack from some quarters for his Nato decision.)

66. Udgaard, passim.

67. Egil Helle interview with Gerhardsen, Arb., 28-5-69. Trygve Lie's preference was for Finn Moe, who from then on was a member of the Storting's Foreign Affairs Committee. (Udgaard from the memoirs of Konrad Nordahl, the head of the Trade Union Confederation, LO.)

68. Cited by Udgaard in "Utenrikspolitikk og Forestillingsverden" (a review of Burgess), Aftenposten, Oslo, 7-1-69, from "Gjenreisningsarbeidet og den økonomiske politikken i Norge etter krigen," Veien fram, No. 1, 1945, dated 14-5-45.

69. Arb., 1947-48 passim, especially foreign affairs and economics commentators "J.S." and "Økonom."

70. The resolution stated, "The initiative the British Labor Government has taken for broader economic and political cooperation must also have our adherence." (Arb., 4-2-48).

The editor of Arbeiderbladet, Olav Larsen, was concerned with a Nordic, not Atlantic, orientation, and this treatment was deliberate policy. A speech of Lange's in April was also played as if its main emphasis were to soften, instead of underline, the increasing tensions.

Cf. Wahlbäck's interpretation (p. 19) that the resolution was mainly about Nordic cooperation.

71. "J.S." (John Sanness) in Arb., 7-6-48.

72. Interview with Ambassador Arne Skaug, Oslo, 5 July 1967. See also Lange's report to the Storting about the Marshall Plan, 7-2-48. In general there was fear that full participation would inhibit the national economic planning Norway had embarked on. See Chapter

Three below and also Udgaard (pp. 217-218) and Eriksen (p. 293, footnote 42) on the reaction of Erik Brofoss, the chief economic planner.

Gunnar Myrdal headed the Economic Commission for Europe. For his conception of the ECE as a European integrative force, see Jean Siotis, "The Secretariat of the United Nations Economic Commission for Europe and European Integration: The First Ten Years", IO, XIX, No. 2 (Spring 1965), pp. 177-202.

73. Skodvin, p. 51.

74. Burgess. pp. 75-77.

75. Udgaard shows, with materials from several polls, the persistent pattern of difference between parts of the Labor Party and the majority of Norwegians on East-West orientation. He also has interesting material on the discrepancies between what the Government wanted for its defense budget from 1946 on and what passed in parliament where Labor was in the majority (pp. 202,203, 239, 264-266).

Christian Lange noted that, in the mid-1930s, the isolation of defense policy from foreign policy in general was symbolized by the fact that the two could not be debated together in a closed Storting meeting. "Nöytralitet eller kollektiv sikkerhet. Det norske Arbeiderparti og Folkeforbundet 1935-36", Oslo, University of Oslo, unpublished Magister thesis, 1958, typed, p. 58.

76. Skodvin, p. 31. This does not determine aid from whom, however.

77. Skodvin, pp. 33-34.

78. Skodvin says that Hauge was alert and interpreting the effect of world events on Norway from at least 1947 on. He and a staff of "young intellectuals" whom he had recruited to the Defense Departement met daily for discussions. He kept up a stream of memos to the Prime Minister. Interviews, Professor Skodvin, Oslo, 8-8-73, 14-8-73.

79. Lange II.

80. Lange, NVN, p. 18. On the visit, which took place in May 1948, see Skodvin, pp. 160-162.

81. Udgaard, p. 187.

82. Riste agrees that the policy was conditional but believes continuity to be great; in his view both prewar and postwar policy built on "common great power interest with anglo-saxon protection as the fall-back position. The important difference... was a realisation that this fall-back position was no longer automatic...and therefore would have to be specified or eleborated." (Olav Riste, personal communication to the author, 4 September 1973) Perhaps it is due to the different propensities of a political scientist compared to an historian, but this seems to me to exaggerate the degree and kind of continuity very much.

83. Lange, NVN, pp. 50-51. Acheson, pp. 276-8. For an example of Morgenstierne's tone, see "The Atlantic Pact: A Norwegian Point of View," Proceedings of the Academy of Political Science, XXIII, No. 3 (May 1949).

84. Edvard Bull, "The Labor Movement in Scandinavia," Scandinavia Past and Present, Vol. II, 1959, pp. 853-863. There were Scandinavian labor congresses from the 1890s on, interrupted when the Norwegian party, newly radicalized, joined the Third International for a few years. The Nordic Cooperation Committee of 1934 reestablished the formal ties. The Norwegian LO joined the International Labor Congress in 1936, and finally the Norwegian Labor Party joined the Second International in 1938.

85. Arne Olav Brundtland, "Hvorfor ikke skandinavisk forsvarsforbund?", IP, 1964, No. 3, pp. 179-198, footnote 7.

86.

87. Brundtland, op. cit., "Hvorfor...," pp. 192-193.

88. Skodvin, cited p. 29. This was one of Hauge's formulations.

89. Haskel 1963, 1965.

90. Undén "Pressdebatt om utrikespolitiken," Tiden (Stockholm), May 1948, p. 271: "And in the end, it is peace we believe and consider to be the most likely course of development in the nearest future."

91. Excerpt from the Oslo Labor Party report in Knut Einar Eriksen and Geir Lundestad, (eds.) Norsk utenrikspolitikk (Kilder til moderne historie: I) Oslo, Universitetsforlaget, 1972, pp. 44-45.
Also Eriksen, p. 34. Haakon Lie, however, may also have been opting for cooperation with the United States. See Eriksen, pp. 41-43.

92. For Tranmael see the excerpt from the Nordic Social Democratic Cooperation Committee meeting of 7-8 February 1948, in Eriksen and Lundestad, I, pp. 45-48. For Lange, see Skodvin, p. 99 (Lange's conversation with U.S. Ambassador Bay), and Wahlbäck, pp. 20-23.

93. Udgaard, pp. 230-235.

94. William T.R. Fox, "American Foreign Policy and the Western European Rimlands", American Academy of Political Science, XXII, No. 4. (January 1948), pp. 431-438.

95. Skodvin, p. 91. Compare Wahlbäck, who reviews the Swedish-Norwegian contacts on defense from 1945 on, and points out that there were feelers on the Swedish side for a Scandinavian pact -- a neutral one -- from immediately after the war, much earlier than suspected. (pp. 15-17).

96. On the rumors and diplomatic reports, Lange NVN p. 19; Skodvin 97-98.
Ingemar Dörfer, in his article on Soviet policy toward Scandinavia in this period, notes that The New York Times of February 29 showed a map with Finland as part of the Soviet bloc. ("Stalins nordiska balans," IP, 1965, No. 2, p. 148, footnote 21.) Dörfer also argues that much Scandinavian reaction was stimulated by Western Great Power reaction.

97. Skodvin pp. 96-103. Torolf Elster wrote in 1951 that Norway had tried to feel out the possibilities for a British-Norwegian pact. "Norges Utenrikspolitiske Stilling," Økonomi og Politik (Copenhagen), XXV, Nos. 2-3 (1951), p. 127.

98. Already in December 1947 Marshall had suggested that the General Staffs of England, France and the United States plan for the defense of Europe. They began to consult. On January 13 Bevin notified Washington of coming talks with France and Benelux and asked about the United States attitude. Truman and Marshall told Bevin the need was urgent and the United States would do all possible to assist. On March 4, Bidault suggested collaboration in the political and military area in a message to Marshall. Herbert Feis, From Trust to Terror. The Onset of the Cold War, 1945-1950 (New York: W.W. Norton, 1970), pp. 286, 295. (See also Eriksen, chapter 2, footnote 16 cited from Theodore White, Fire in the Ashes.).

    Returning on the boat after the breakdown of the London conference on Germany, Marshall oriented Dulles (his Republican adviser) and Hickerson. There were talks with Vandenberg as early as January 1948. The British proposed secret talks at the end of March or early April, and there were in fact secret military talks among the British, Americans and Canadians about the same time. (Interviews with John Hickerson and Theodore Achilles by T.A. Hockin and G.C.V. Wright for the York University Oral History Project on Canada. These were kindly made available by the interviewers.)

    By March 8 Arbeiderbladet (Oslo) was reporting that Robert Lovett had said that the United States was ready to give a guarantee to the Western Union.

    Van der Beugel called the United States reaction to Bevin an immediate endorsement and said that it was accompanied by no specific immediate plan because of the absolute priority given to getting the Europen Recovery Program through Congress (pp. 122-123).

    Norway would not have known this so early, however. (Lange II).

99. Skodvin pp. 103-106.

100. Lange II. Lange had been skeptical of American understanding of the social and economic aspirations of the socialists. (Udgaard from the private papers of Kaare Fostervoll, and a Lange memo of 12-1-48. Fostervoll was a member of the Labor Government and sympathetic to the Nordic orientation.)

101. Skodvin, Interview II; also see Skodvin, p. 112.

102. Feis, op. cit., p. 309.

103. Lange II. Norway kept oriented on the summer discussions. Henry Villard of the American Embassy in Oslo was authorized to speak more freely than usual.

104. Stanley Hoffmann, Gulliver's Troubles. The Setting of American Foreign Policy (New York: McGraw Hill, 1968), pp. 103-107.

105. Joseph M. Jones, The Fifteen Weeks (February 21 - June 5, 1947), (New York: Viking Press, 1955).

106. George F. Kennan, Memoirs 1925-1950 (Boston: Little, Brown, 1967), chapter 17.

107. Harry S. Truman, Memoirs, Vol. II ("Years of Trial and Hope, 1946-1952"), (1956) Signet, 1965, p. 282.

Truman reports that Robert Lovett, addressing the National Security Council on May 20, 1948, argued: "First, we wanted to get away from the one-way arrangements in which we did something for foreign countries without receiving anything in return, ... second, we did not want any automatic, unlimited engagements under our constitutional system. We could not agree upon anything amounting to a guarantee." George Kennan says that these two stipulations were the result of the Lovett-Vandenberg negotiations, and calls them "two principles on which, I gather, Senator Vandenberg had insisted." (Kennan, p. 406).

John Hickerson who headed the European office, asserted that the change from Dunkirk-type to Rio-type had been his idea, and was introduced because he recognized immediately that ultimately Germany, would have to be brought into the alliance; the Dunkirk model had been a thinly disguised treaty against Germany. Moreover, both Vandenburg and Connolly, whom the State Department were very eager to win over, had been active in drawing up the Rio Pact. (Interviews with Mr. John Hickerson and Mr. Theodore Achilles by Professors T.A. Hockin and G.C.V. Wright of York University, Toronto, Ontario, Canada for the York University Oral History Project on Canada and the Origins of Nato).

108. Hickerson interview above.

109. Achilles interview above.

110. Feis, op. cit., p. 305.

111. See Truman, op. cit., II, p. 28, on the preoccupation to avoid Wilson's mistakes. On "oversell" see Theodore J. Lowi, "Making Democracy Safe for the World: National Politics and Foreign Policy," in Domestic Sources of Foreign Policy, edited by James Rosenau, (New York: The Free Press, 1967), pp. 314-323.

112. Ernst H. van der Beugel, From Marshall Aid to Atlantic Partnership. European Integration as a Concern of American Foreign Policy (Amsterdam, London, New York: Elsevier Publishing Co., 1966), pp. 65-66.

113. Ibid., p. 83. Colbjørnson was co-author with Axel Sømme of En norsk tre-års plan (Oslo: Det norske Arbeiderpartis forlag, 1933), the first attempt at a comprehensive sketch for an economic plan.

114. Jones, op. cit., p. 226.

115. Fox, op. cit., pp. 433-435.

116. The New York Herald Tribune, January 3, 1949.

117. Ibid., January 15, 1949.

118. Skodvin infers from Lippmann's writings that Lippmann had assumed participation in Nato meant Nato bases in Scandinavia. (p. 262).

For a while it was thought in Norway that Dulles also held these views, but it turned out not to be so. ("J.S." in Arb. 23-2-49.) Lange says that this was checked out (Lange II).

Danish Ambassador Henrik Kauffmann reported on 14 February 1949 that Dulles, along with Lippmann, was a supporter of the principle behind the Danish position. (DSP, II, Appendix 37, p. 76.)

119. Another major figure whose views were close to Lippmann's, and who was high inside the State Departement at the time, was George Kennan. For years Kennan has been associated with his famous "Mr. X." article and the foreign policy initiatives, including Nato, which seemed to flow from it. However, in his Memoirs, published in 1967, he revealed that while he approved the idea of a major American commitment to Europe, he rejected the concept of mutual commitment and the formalism associated with the new pact. His view was conditioned by his analysis of the likely extent of Communist spread in Europe, his estimate of the needs of Western Europe, and his understanding of American politics. Already in 1945 he had appraised the effects of the war and the likely consequences for the countries in Central Europe (Appendix B). He viewed the events in Czechoslovakia in 1948 as having been what he had predicted (pp. 378-379), and the strikes in France and Italy and the obstruction in Berlin as what Trotsky had called "slamming the door so that all Europe would shake" (pp. 424-426). Because he believed the Russians could not extend themselves further, he saw all these as reactions to the success of the Marshall Plan initiatives, rather than a preview of what was to come. Hence military defenses were not what were needed in Western Europe.

> I regarded the anxieties of the European as a little silly; this was not, it seemed to me the time to start talking about military defenses and preparations. I agreed that they needed some sort of reassurance, but I saw dangers in any form of such reassurance that would encourage them in their military preoccupations (p. 399).

In his eyes if European leaders had a proper view of their own problems and of American policy, they would not really have needed such reassurance:

> The suggestion, constantly heard from the European side, that an alliance was needed to assure the participation of the United States in the cause of Western Europe's defense, in the event of an attack against it, only filled me with impatience. What in the world did they think we had been doing in Europe these last four or five years? (p. 408).

Finally his view of State Department-Congressional relations was resentment that State had to "lobby" Congress to obtain what should be in their joint interest, and that diplomats should have to spend great lengths of time educating Congressmen on foreign policy. The Vandenberg Resolution struck him as "arid legalism and semantic pretentiousness" and the struggles of State Department colleagues over it evoked "amused contempt" (p. 409). Neither domestic nor foreign political leaders understood their true interests in the situation.

Kennan's comment, "what in the world did they think we had been doing in Europe these last four or five years?" is interesting since Kennan is usually such a good historian. The Europeans remembered vividly that the United States had been deeply involved in the First World War only to return to isolation -- after intervening in many decisive ways in the postwar settlement with which the Europeans had to live.

120. This represents a revision of my views of 1965. Cf. Haskel, "Forsöket...," pp. 19-20, and 26.

121. The tradition of the professional diplomat tends to underestimate this dimension.

In 1965 I noted that the policy of aid to an independent pact might have had disincentive effects on other potential pact members (ibid., footnote 85). I would still maintain this but would now emphasize the problem of winning Congressional support even more.

122. DSP, II. Appendix 37, p. 79.

123. Lange, NVN, p. 36. Lange argued that Norway perceived this as information. Also Skodvin passim. See David Baldwin's acute discussion of "non-aid" as a diplomatic instrument: "Foreign Aid, Intervention, and Influence," WP, XXI, No. 3 (April 1969), pp. 429-432.

124. Radar, for example, has come from the West.

125. DSP, II, Appendix 28: "allerede i indledende fase."

126. Interview with former ambassador Erik Boheman, Stockholm, 30 May, 1967. Boheman, who had been ambassador to the United States in the defense pact period, said that he believed that "after a year or two" members of a Scandinavian pact would have been able to buy what they needed. Sweden, he said, has had "the best possibilities" to do so in the years since.

Skodvin cites the Swedish view that "a new situation would be created" (ett nytt läge inträtt). (p. 243 and pp. 242-243.)

127. DSP, II, Appendix 50 (22 February, 1949). No dispatches from Kauffman from before February 1949 are included in DSP.

128. Ibid., Quotation p. 97. Kauffmann mentioned agreement in principle on a currency union, a customs union, a free labor market, etc. (p. 96) (See Chapters Three and Four for the problems which these faced.)

129. Norwegian Ambassador Wilhelm Morgenstierne told Kauffmann that it had been a decision by both Lange and Acheson not to say anything in their joint communiqué which would indicate that the Scandinavian pact option had not been given up by Norway. (DSP, II, Appendix 37, p. 75 (14 February, 1949). There was a different emphasis for the Norwegian public.

130. DSP, II. Appendix 37, p. 78. Kauffmann saw Acheson as opposed to the Scandinavian plan on grounds that under Swedish leadership it might be too accommodating to the Soviet Union (p. 76).

There is material which if it does not confirm this, is at least compatible with it. Stenographic report of Acheson's remarks to Lange in February 1949. Skodvin p. 322.

131. Foreign Minister Lange did phrase his analysis at various times in terms of a strategic and undefended area constituting a power vacuum tempting preemption, even though no Power desired war. But Lange's statements are also consistent with a style of non-provocation. Burgess' interpretation is too literal.

132. Udgaard (Chapter 15 "Towards a Balance of Power Policy") was interested in distinguishing wartime from postwar Norwegian foreign policy, not Norwegian from Swedish foreign policy.

133. Ernst B. Haas, "The Balance of Power as a Guide to Policy Making," The Journal of Politics, XV (August 1953); Inis L. Claude Jr., Power and International Relations (New York: Random House, 1962), chapters 2-3.

134. This use of optimization and suboptimization applied to foreign policy is taken from Ingemar Dörfer (System 37: Viggen, (1973) p. 227), who applied it to Swedish defense policy.

135. Glenn H. Snyder, Deterrence and Defense. Toward a Theory of National Security (Princeton University Press, 1961), pp. 9-15.

136. Svenska Dagbladet, 30-5-49.

137. Lange, NUS, pp. 61-62.

138. Ibid., p. 95 (27-1-49).

139. Det Norske Arbeiderparti Protokoll over forhandlingene på det 33.ordinaere landsmøte 17.-20. februar 1949 i Oslo (hereafter DNA Protokoll), pp. 132-133.

There is now evidence for my inferences made originally from the fragmentary public data available to me in 1963. In his book Skodvin cites Lange's notes for his presentation at the Copenhagen negotiations. The preference for an acknowledged connection with the West--which by this time had been decided within Norway--was attributed to the following:

> "Such a policy can:
> a) contribute to decrease in tension because cooperation within such a [Western] security system fills the military and power political vacuum Norway today represents -- and thereby eliminates a disturbing factor
> b) secure us against isolated attack by making it clear that an attack on a Nordic Country is a casus belli for the U.S.A.
> c) give us the possibility for effective help if we are attacked during a general war -- help which can be effective because it has been prepared
> d) make it possible for us to obtain military materiel with high priority as to time and on reasonable economic conditions." (quoted pp. 269-270)

The first point would be relevant both to considerations of deterrence and defense, the second is clearly about deterrence; the third is about defense, the fourth about supplies. Thus all three issues were addressed in a quite self-conscious manner.

140. Folketinget, 100. Sam. nr. 165, col. 2631 (Rasmussen, 9-2-49).

141. J. David Singer, "Inter-Nation Influence: A Formal Model," APSR, LVII (1963), pp. 420-430; Thomas Schelling, Arms and Influence, passim.

142. Rasmussen, 9-2-49.
See Johan Jørgen Holst, "Norwegian Security Policy," (C & C, 1966, No. 2, pp. 64-79), for a discussion of the deterrence-reassurance dialectic in Norwegian base policy.

143. Fremtiden, (Copenhagen, July 1948), quoting New Times, December 1, 1948.
Traditional Czarist Russian foreign policy had been to oppose any plans toward Scandinavian union. Thus they looked favorably on Norway's breakaway from Sweden in 1905. After the Winter War in 1939-40 the Soviet Union opposed a Scandinavian pact including Finland. In the postwar years, the Soviets opposed any type of Nordic cooperation.
Ingemar Dörfer argues that they used the criterion of countries which joined the Marshall Plan as their operational definition of "Western." Dörfer, ("Stalins nordiska balans") p. 135.

144. For the "mediator" characterization, see Hedtoft (5-11-48) in Folketinget.

145. On Sweden's official position, see DSP, II, Appendix 18 (Denmark's Ambassador to Sweden, Nils Svenningsen, reporting a conversation with Undén: "If it should turn out that Norway will not go along with cooperation along the lines proposed by the Swedish government, well, then there was nothing to be done.") After a Danish request Erlander took up the matter once more with other party leaders, none of whom would recommend a strictly Swedish-Danish pact. Erlander told the Danish Ambassador that he himself did not judge the risk to be so great but foresaw no political possibility of pushing it through and did not want to encourage Denmark to start up a blind alley. It would not be very surprising to Sweden should Denmark choose to follow Norway (DSP, II, Appendix 39).
For some unofficial statements contemplating a Swedish-Norwegian pact, see Arb., 3-5-48 (Chairman of the Norwegian Foreign Affairs Committee, Terje Wold) and (separately) Swedish Liberal Party leader, Bertil Ohlin. See also Skodvin, pp. 147-154.

146. Skodvin, pp. 96-103, Wahlbäck, p. 25.

147. Skodvin, Interview II, Wahlbäck, p. 36.

148. Skodvin, p. 209, Eriksen, pp. 150-151.

149. Skodvin, p. 91.

150. Interview, Professor Troels Fink, Copenhagen, 24 July 1973.

152. Johan Jørgen Holst, "Surprise, Signals and Reaction. The Attack on Norway, April 9, 1940." Cooperation and Conflict 1966, No. 1, pp. 29-45.

152. See Chapter I above and also: Troels Fink, Otte foredrag om Danmarks krise 1863-64. Aarhus, Universitetsforlaget i Aarhus, 1964; Ustabil balanse. Dansk udenrigs- og forsvarspolitik 1894-1905, Aarhus, Universitetsforlaget i Aarhus, 1961; Viggo Sjøqvist, Danmarks Udenrigspolitik 1933-1940, (Udgiverselskab for Danmarks nyeste Historie) Copenhagen, Gyldendal, 1966.

153. Dau, p. 197.

154. "...partly -- and this is quite important -- is the question of whether Denmark really could choose to join the West." Dau, p. 197.

155. DSP, II, Appendix 50, p. 101. Also see the editorial in Social Demokraten (Copenhagen), 27-1-49, discussed in Haagerup, pp. 67-68.

156. DSP, II, Appendix 28, p. 55. Norwegian Defense Minister Jens Chr. Hauge, told the Labour Party Congress in 1949 that what the Swedes had to gain from the plan was:

> ...very simply this, that their prospects for getting aid in the event of an attack will be greater if they are not isolated...if an attack on Sweden will, because of the defense pact, actually imply an attack upon the Norwegian Atlantic coast and upon Denmark which occupies [sic] Greenland.

(DNA Protokoll, p. 156.)

157. One expression of this cross-party cooperation is the good communication of party leaderships in the field of foreign policy. In Sweden since 1921 there has been an Advisory Council on Foreign Affairs which is identical in membership to the Standing Committee on Foreign Affairs of the Riksdag, and which is informed and consulted on important matters of foreign policy. The Danes have had an equivalent body since 1928.

The Norwegians have the tradition of holding closed Storting meetings. (See Udgaard, Appendix III, "Secret Sessions of the Storting" for a list of the twelve undisclosed Storting sessions between the end of the war and February 1948. Material on several other important sessions in the period involved here, is in Skodvin.) Not even the fact of such closed meetings -- of one hundred and fifty Stortingsmen! -- is public. What is fascinating is that such secrets are impeccably kept. Sensitive issues, for example German reparations (1946), participation in the occupation of Germany (1946), the Svalbard negotiations with the Soviet Union (1947), relations with Spain (1947), changing evaluations of the international environment (28 October 1947, 8 April 1948), were discussed in such closed sessions. Skodvin compared the text of Lange's address to the closed Storting (8 April 1948) with the text of his public address at the Oslo Military Society (19 April). (pp. 117-123)

One of the repercussions of the Czech coup was the establishment of an "extended foreign affairs and constitution committee" of the Storting. (This has sometimes been called the Special Committee or the Preparedness Committee.) Its purpose was to create a confidential, cross-party forum for orientation and discussion about foreign affairs, which excluded Communist membership. Communist Stortingsmen were present at the closed full, Storting sessions discribed above.

158. See Herbert Tingsten, Mitt liv. 1946-52 (Stockholm: Bonniers, 1963). Tredje Standpunkten - En Orimlighet (Stockholm: Bonniers, 1951) was a brochure Tingsten wrote against the Swedish neutrality policy.

159. DNA Protokoll, p. 175. There was much confusion about this afterwards. See Haskel, "Forsöket...," footnote 74; cf. Johanne Amlid, Ut av kurs (Oslo: Pax, 1966).

160. Troels Fink, Ustabil balans, p. 25 citing Hørup 1883.

161. Harald Westergård Andersen, Dansk Politik i Går og i Dag 1920-66 (Copenhagen: Fremads Focusbøger, 1966) and Miller, op. cit.

162. Haagerup, op. cit., p. 76. Birgitte Westerholm argues that the Socialists and Radicals had parallel traditions rather than that the latter influenced the former. (p. 90)

The Radicals actually split, with the parliamentary majority opposed to Nato and the parliamentary group thus voting against it. Their major newspaper, Politiken, however, argued for the Nato solution.

163. Erik Eriksen (Liberal), and Ole Bjørn Kraft (Conservative) in parliament, November 5, 1948. Cited in Haagerup.

164. Arne-Olav Brundtland. Also see Skodvin, pp. 80-84.

165. Knut Einar Eriksen, DNA og Nato. Striden om norsk NATO-medlemskap innen regjeringspartiet 1948-49, Oslo, Gyldendal Norsk Forlag, 1972, p. 182. Also pp. 118-123, 139-140, 180-186.

166. Eriksen, p. 170.

167. Udgaard, p. 241.

168. Eriksen, pp. 106-109. See passim for Oksvik's role within the Labour Party.

169. Lange, NVN, pp. 53-56. See also Olav Larsson, Den langsomme revolusjonen Oslo, Aschehoug, 1973, p. 93.

170. Eriksen, p. 173.

171. Eriksen, p. 252 and passim.

172. Gerhardsen says that he heard this was the opinion of Dag Bryn, who, as Undersecretary in the Defense Department, in 1953 wrote an account of the 1948-49 negotiations. Gerhardsen adds "Perhaps there is something in that." Einar Gerhardsen, Samarbeid og strid. Erindringer 1945-55. Oslo, Tiden Norsk forlag, 1971, p. 217. (See pp. 190-226 for Gerhardsen's account.)

173. Eriksen, pp. 39-43.

174. Skodvin, pp. 135-6.

175. Udgaard, pp. 226-7, also p. 244. On which trade unions Skodvin, Interview I.

Lange had worked for the Trade Union Federation, LO, after the war until February 1946 when he became Foreign Minister. The background on this issue also includes friction between the Communists and the Home Front which had individual membership but would not permit organizations as such, for example the Communist Party, to join.

176. Sosialistisk Perspektiv No. 2, 1967, Utgitt av Det norske Arbeiderparti, p. 29.

177. Lange, NVN, pp. 36-37. Also Eriksen, p. 156 and, on Torp's various roles, passim.

178. Lange II. This answers the question Haskel raised in 1965 (pp. 19-20): "What would have been lost for Norway by trying the joint démarche strategy?"

179. Lange II.

180. The Foreign and Defense Ministers had been skeptical of it at the time. "I had many compunctions about agreeing to such a conclusion." Lange, NVN, p. 35. Also Wahlbäck, p. 49, and Eriksen, pp. 151-152.

181. For a different line of reasoning, see Eriksen, pp. 156-158. Eriksen argues that Gerhardsen chose the little risk of a split within the Labor Party over a bigger risk of a fight in the parliament, possibly also an electoral fight, with the non-socialist opposition, which might have led to Labor defections as well.

182. There were problems with it even as a theory of defense, because the question of how effective aid would be if not prepared in advance, was a real one. It was not only believed necessary by the Western powers but had also been Norway's experience in 1940 that the aid from Britain was of little use unprepared. (On this theme see Skodvin passim.)

183. It is possible to accept the critical mass theory of defense but still believe that to bargain for the needed weapons on the basis of the fait accompli strategy would fail.

184. Eriksen, p. 152.

185. Lange, NVN, p. 41.

Mary Dau notes the contacts which Danish Prime Minister Hans Hedtoft had with Scandinavian Social Democratic movements. Many have testified to Hedtoft's Nordic orientation. This may be seen as an additional force in the same direction, but does not help us clearly differentiate Denmark from Norway where for example the same can be and has been said about Gerhardsen. Dau p. 198; on Gerhardsen, Eriksen p. 155.

Eriksen says he finds Denmark's preference for a Nordic pact difficult to account for. The factors he adduces include: the stronger influence of the Communist movement within the Danish Resistance (therefore leaving it less Western-oriented), the preference of Hedtoft, and possibly also strategic considerations. With respect to the last he argues that perhaps the Danes felt less need of an American guarantee so long as there were American occupation troops in Germany immediately to its south (pp. 154-155).

186. Birgitte Westerholm, "Socialdemokratiet og Atlantpagten. En analyse at de faktorer, der øvede indflydelse pa Social demokratiets stillingtagen til Danmarks optagelse i Atlantpagten i 1949," (Institut for Statskundskab Aarhus Universitet, 1973, mimeographed, 144 pps), pp. 87-92.

187. Dau, p. 209. Only after the Oslo meeting did the Radicals give unambiguous support to the Nordic plan. In January 1948 their youth wing had vetoed the idea of a defense union.

188. Westerholm p. 41.

189. Westergård-Anderson, Table 1, p. 244.

An Associated Press article dated 4 March, 1949 from Kirkenes (The New York Times 5-3-49) quoted the editor of the only newspaper (a Communist one) in that area of Finnmark close to the Soviet border, as saying: "I cannot say yet whether the Soviet Union will consider itself seriously endangered by American intrigue in Norway and act accordingly as it did when Finnish reactionaries built the Mannerheim line." For the Danish Communist Party's approval of Thorez's spring 1948 declaration that the French Party would not oppose the Red Army, see Dau p. 226.

190. May Dau comments that when Denmark received an invitation to join the Atlantic Pact (early 1949) "it was more than anything else on account of Greenland" (p. 200).

191. Lange, NVN pp. 51-54. See also Udgaard's comment on Gerhardsen's January 1948 early backing of the Bevin plan: "Almost every speech on foreign policy and defense now contained a reference to 1940. To Gerhardsen, the need for a decision also seems to have been of a psychological nature: he maintained that after the German attack he had observed that many people had become calm when they had made their choice, even if it entailed dangers, and he asked whether the situation was not the same today" (p. 245).

Gerhardsen himself attributed his speed to his early experience with the Communists: "Another consideration was also involved. From 1923 until the war we in the Labor Party had fought with the Communists, them against us and us against them. We knew them well. So long as a difficult and controversial matter was undecided, they kept up resolutions, and denunciations in every single trade union and in every single work place where they had members. The moment a matter had been finally resolved, they cut it out. With regard to these experiences among other reasons the [Labor Party] Executive considered it an advantage that the decision be taken as quickly as possible." Samarbeid og strid. Erindringer 1945-55. Oslo, Tiden Norsk Forlag, 1971, pp. 208-209.

Chapter Three

Changing Opportunity Costs: The Proposed Scandinavian Common Market, 1947-1959

1. The committee of experts was agreed upon at the semiannual meeting of the Nordic Foreign Ministers, 27-28 August, 1947 but was not established until their next meeting 23-24 February, 1948 and did not begin work until April.

The committee was called the Joint Nordic Committee for Economic Cooperation and shall hereafter be referred to as "the Committee" or "NECC". Both the Foreign Ministers' meetings and the Committee included Icelandic, but not Finnish members. (The Icelandic members acted as observers.) "Beretning fra Det Faelles nordiske udvalg for økonomisk samarbejde, afgivet pa udvalgets møde i Oslo den 16.-17. januar 1953," Appendix 3, Nordisk råd, 1st session. February 1953, cols, 799-802 (hereafter, "Beretning..." and NR). The mandate of the Committee is cited in the "Beretning," p. 726. The Committee could call on experts.

The Committee's chairman was C.V. Bramsnaes, a Danish Social Democratic member of the Folketing who was a long time advocate of a Scandinavian customs union, labor market, and other allied measures. (See NK, 1957, No. 9, pp. 51-52, for a vignette of Bramsnaes.)

For a brief discussion of the Norwegian-Swedish customs union of the late nineteenth century, see pp. 163-177 ("The History of Norway's Commercial Policy and the Customs Union of the Second Half of the Nineteenth Century") in Sara Lieberman, The Industrialization of Norway, 1800-1920, Oslo, Universitetsforlaget, 1970. For the economic efforts at Nordic cooperation in the 1930s, see Viggo Sjöqvist, Danmarks Udenrigspolitik 1933-1940, Copenhagen, Gyldendal (Udgiverselskab for Danmarks nyeste historie) 1966, pp. 86-92, 268-272.

2. The full text of the 1950 report is in "Nordisk Økonomisk Samarbeid. Foreløpig rapport til regjeringene i Danmark, Island, Norge og Sverige fra Det faelles nordiske utvalg for økonomisk samarbeid," 3 January 1950, Oslo, Appendix 2 to Stortingsmelding, nr. 87, 1954, Stort. 1954 (hereafter, "NØS"). A concise summary by Lars Frisk can be found in "Beretning..."

3. Et faelles nordisk marked. Rapport til regeringerne i Danmark, Island, Norge og Sverige fra Det Faelles Nordiske Udvalg for Økonomisk Samarbejde (Copenhagen: J.H. Schultz A/S, 1954), p.5 (hereafter Et faelles nordisk marked).

There were some suggestions of a Swedish-Danish market, but they were not pursued.

Both before and after the Foreign Ministers' meeting, Bertel Dahlgaard, a member of the Radical Left party in the Folketing, and one of the main supporters of a Scandinavian customs union, suggested that "one country" opposed should not hinder the other two from going ahead. Folket., Vol. 102 (1950-1951), cols. 3783-3784, 2468, 3406-3407, 3459. Finance Minister Hansen hinted that if the discussions failed, "it might be possible to take up the question on a more limited basis" (cols. 2464-2465).

Paul Gersmann, a member of the Committee, said years later that the question of a Swedish-Danish market had been raised in the Committee, but had not been taken seriously. He thought it would have been politically unacceptable to isolate Norway. (Interview, Departementschef Paul Gersmann, Department of customs and sales taxes, Copenhagen 22 May 1967.)

4. "Beretning...," NR, 1. session (Februar 1953), Sag nr. 9. cols. 726-735, plus appendices 737-814. "Redegørelse vedrørende det nordiske økonomiske samarbejde siden 1945- udarbejdet af Utenriksdepartementet, Oslo," Sag. nr. 12, cols. 707-724. Norwegian report, Appendix 2; Swedish-Danish report, Appendix 3.

5. NR, 1st session, February 14, 18, 20, 1953, cols. 203-217, 1155-1158, 380-410.

6. Et faelles marked, pp. 167-168. Thus none of the industrial sectors had been eliminated, nor any packages suggested.

7. Et faelles marked, p. 163.

8. "Om økonomisk samarbeid mellom de nordiske lande", (Tilråding fra UD 18 juni 1954 and Appendix, "Utredning om et naermere økonomisk samarbeid i Norden, utarbeidet av Handelsdepartementet i samarbeid med de interesserte departementer", Stortingsmelding, nr. 87 (1954).

9. NR, 2nd session, 17 August 1954, pp. 156-159. In the Economic Committee of the Nordic Council Lange said that Norway would prefer cooperation in new areas of production first, but was willing to proceed along other lines of cooperation. A comprehensive market would take time. (See Aftenposten (Oslo), 12 August 1954, p. 1. and p. 9.)

10. For the Nordic Council resolution, see NR, 2nd session, 17 August 1954, pp. 152-153. (English translation in Nordic Economic Cooperation. Report by The Nordic Economic Cooperation Committee, General Part, Copenhagen, 1958 (translation of the first part of the five part report, Nordisk Økonomisk Samarbeid, Rapport fra det Nordiske Økonomiske Samarbeidsutvalg, Oslo 1957) (hereafter, NEC), pp. 11, 12.

11. (Organizationally, this was a Danish plan for designated Ministers to be responsible; the Norwegians had proposed more ad hoc arrangements.) Given the total opposition of its non-socialist parties, the Norwegian Government made no binding commitments - even in principle.

For the communiqué from the Harpsund conference, see, NEC, pp. 12-13. For a list of the participants, see Stortingsmelding nr. 106, Stort. (1954). On the Danish organizational ideas see Svenska Dagbladet, 28-10-54, 30-10-54; on the Norwegian proposals, Notat, Utenriksdepartementet, Oslo, 29 oktober 1954, "Organiseringen av det nordiske økonomiske samarbeid," mimeographed, 3 pp.

12. Nordisk Samhandel, (Copenhagen: Nielsen and Lydiche, June 1955). A summary is contained in "Beretning fra det nordiske økonomiske

samarbejdsutvalg til Nordisk Råds session januar-februar 1956 i København," 12 December 1955.

The Swedish secretary on the NECC (from 1955 on) said later that there had been no "political evaluation" until 1958. (Interview, Departementsråd Åke Englund, Handelsdepartementet, Stockholm 2 June 1967.)

13. NEC. The report was supplemented in the fall of 1958 with a plan for the remaining 20% of intra-Nordic trade. See NR, 6th session (1958).

14. NEC, pp. 131-139 ("Draft Agreement for the Nordic Investment Bank"), pp. 99-105 for the explanation of it (from which the quotations are taken), and pp. 140-143. The Bank was said to have been modeled on features from IBRD, IFC "and the proposed European Investment Bank" (p. 99).

15. The Nordic Ministers of Cooperation met the following number of times between the Harpsund decision (30-31 October 1954) and Kungälv (11-12 July 1959): 1954-1; 1955-3; 1956-3; 1957-8; 1958-4; 1959-3. The NECC met the following number of times in the same period: 1955-5; 1956-5; 1957-9; 1958-11; 1959-7. (List compiled by Christian Lange from Nordisk Tidskrift and other sources.) In addition, there were subcommittee and secretariat meetings, for example between February 1957 and November 1958, 65 of the former and 30 of the latter. See "PM angående nordiska ekonomiska samarbetsutskottets verksamhet," NR, 7th session (1958), Sak D 16, pp. 1255-1260.

16. "NØS," p. 3.

17. William Clayton was extremely influential in arguing the case within the United States government for an extraordinary program of aid to Europe in the spring of 1947. In June he conferred with Bevin. Clayton came to the sixteen nation conference in late July and then again in late August. Between these two visits there seemed to be a change, more emphasis was laid on a customs union as well as on a permanent organization outside the UN to administer the forthcoming aid. Van der Beugel, pp. 61, 78-80.

18. Lange to the Storting, 7 February, 1948. Lange told the Storting that more than "a summary of the lists of needs and national production programs" would be required by the United States. "Something more and different will be needed, something which can appeal to the imagination of the Americans, and give expression to a new will to cooperation among the participating countries." NUS, p. 40.

"NØS" (3 January 1950, pp. 20-21) placed the Scandinavian negotiations in the context of the Marshall Plan agreement's promise to investigate customs unions and noted that the Committee had sent a report to the OEEC for use in its first interim report to the ECA. The Committee report itself stated: "The Governments of all four countries are extremely interested in the development of economic co-operation between their countries," cited work begun on standardization of customs nomenclature as a prelude to discussions on a customs union, cited the establisment of SAS with the remark "northern co-operation along similar lines might be possible inside other branches of transport," etc. (Det faelles nordiske udvalg for økonomisk samarbejde, "Memorandum concerning co-operation between the northern countries", November 1948, 2 pp. mimeographed.)

19. The proposal at the July 1947 Ministerial meeting was for "joint planned investment." This most likely meant more than coordination. It fits well with the aims and economic philosophy of the Norwegian Finance Minister at the time, Erik Brofoss. He recalls that he was preoccupied with the problem of exploiting Norway's plentiful water resources.(Interview with Erik Brofoss, Director of The Bank of Norway, Oslo, 20 June 1967.) One of his Cabinet colleagues of the time remembers him as having been eager not only for a planned Norway, but a planned Scandinavia.

20. Per-Olaf Jonsson argued (in "The Projected Scandinavian Customs Union, 1945-1959," Florida State University, unpublished Ph. D. dissertation, 1964) that the negotiations were begun in response to the proposed Marshall Plan with its insistence on the reduction of European trade barriers. He adduces as evidence 1) known American policy, 2) the timing of the meetings discussed above, in relation to the ongoing Marshall Plan discussions (as well as the timing of further Scandinavian moves in the 1949-50 period in their relation to the OEEC), and 3) contemporary comments (p. 523 and *passim*).

In the opinion of the writer, he is correct -- and there is more evidence for his position in the Scandinavian documents -- but only partially correct. Jonsson argues, for instance, that the 9 July 1947 Norwegian proposal was motivated by anticipation of the forthcoming 12 July European meeting to which the Scandinavian countries and others had been invited by England and France, and by the fear that the organization to be formed from this conference would be dominated by the Great Powers (pp. 83-84, 90),

It seems unlikely that this explanation is correct. First of all, if the purpose of the proposal were diplomatic leverage, the communiqué from the meeting would at least have revealed the proposal and would probably have expanded on it. In this case there was no public mention of it until 1950. (Of course, the primary purpose of the meeting was to try to agree on a joint position for the Paris meeting. (The Communiqué. Also Lange, cited in *Arbeiderbladet*, 10 July 1947, p.1.) There *was* probably fear of Great Power influence.(See van der Beugel.) And there is no doubt that the Scandinavians persisted in supporting the ECE plan long after the Americans and other Europeans had given it up. It makes sense to interpret the *August* ministerial meeting as a response to pressures for a wider market. But according to van der Beugel, in July the American emphasis at the conference was on presenting a four year plan to Congress; it was not until Clayton came to Europe the second time in late August that there was more stress on a customs union and an organization outside the ECE (pp. 78-80). It seems unlikely, then, that the Norwegian July proposal was made for diplomatic purposes.

Jonsson's view on this topic is related to his insufficient differentiation of the Norwegian from the Swedish and Danish viewpoints. Although he notes the terms of the Norwegian proposal (p. 85), he tends to treat the Customs Union as central, and everything else as peripheral. There were, right from the beginning, *two* issues: 1) the view that what was central and desirable was joint planned investment (Norway), and 2) the view that what was crucial was the freeing of inter-Scandinavian trade through a common market (Sweden and Denmark). The Scandinavian habit of speaking of "Nordic economic cooperation" obscures this.

This having been said, I thing it is nevertheless evident that by late August the diplomatic possibilities of the situation had been realized and acted upon accordingly.

Gunnar Preben Nielsson ("Denmark and European Integration: a Small Country at the Crossroads," University of of California at Los Angeles, unpublished Ph. D. dissertation, 1966) also cites the relationship between the Marshall plan and these early Scandinavian proposals, apparently on the basis of the Jonsson thesis. Nielsson qualifies Jonsson by saying that Norway was genuinely interested in a division of labor in investments (VII-18) and summarizes the Danish-Swedish versus the Norwegian view as being a "customs union" versus an "economic union" (VII-25).

21. The New York Times, 1 November 1949, text of the speech, p. 22.

22. Interview with Foreign Minister Halvard Lange, New York, 3 November 1966. (This was generally the position of the British Labour Government. On November 1, Cripps gave a speech to the OEEC group, sharply limiting the extent of the proposed cooperative measures. The New York Times, 2 November 1949, p. 1.)

23. Ibid. Horace Callender cited Lange as saying that regional trade was dependent on productive investments, which indeed was the Norwegian position, although its significance was obscured by the context.

24. Callender in The New York Times, 4 November 1949. As Diebold noted, this must have been an "oversimplified" account. (William Diebold Jr., Trade and Payments in Western Europe. A Study in Economic Cooperation 1947-1951 (New York: Harper & Row, 1952), p. 378.

25. Paul Hoffman, "Trade Restrictions...and Peace", Proceedings of the Academy of Political Science, XXIII, No. 4 (January 1950), p. 464. (Speech to the Academy, 10 November 1949.)

26. See Lange, NUS, pp. 153-154 (6-2-50). Lange had given a lengthy discussion of the shift in American policy toward "liberalization of trade for its own sake" as he saw it (p. 146), and the developments in OEEC and EPU. He explicitly linked UNISCAN which had been suggested by the British in December 1949 and signed in January 1950, to the OEEC resolution of 2 November 1949 stressing regional cooperation (p. 152).

However, the OEEC report to ERP in February 1950 mentioned under "regional arrangements" UNISCAN among others, but not any Scandinavian plan. European Recovery Program, Second Report of the Organization for European Economic Cooperation, Paris, February 1950, pp. 241-245. (The first report, a year earlier, had mentioned the recent beginning of Scandinavian negotiations on a customs union. European Recovery Program, A Report on Recovery Program and United States Aid, ECA, February 1949, p. 17.)

Both Jonsson. *op, cit*., and G. St.-J. Barclay ("Background to EFTA: An Episode in Anglo-Scandinavian Relations", *The Australian Journal of Politics and History*. XI (2), August 1965, pp. 185-197) link UNISCAN and the Nordic proposal to the OEEC meeting in October-November 1949.

Lange himself mentioned the possibility that this "relance" of the negotiations might have been partially in response to the 1949 failure of the defense pact negotiations, to show that Norway did not reject cooperation in all areas. (Interview, 3 November 1966.)

27. Richard E. Walton, and Robert B. McKersie, *A Behavioral Theory of Labor Negotiations. An Analysis of a Social Interaction System* (New York: McGraw Hill, 1965), p. 5.

28. These pages on game theory and the implications of the two strategies described here follow Walton and McKersie. I have made one terminological change. Walton and McKersie use the terms "issue" and "problem" for the styles of bargaining giving priority to dividing, respectively enlarging, the joint pie. These terms proved confusing to my readers and I have substituted "distributive" versus "expansive" bargaining orientations. The latter term was suggested to me by Dr. Donald L. Horowitz.

29. Walton and McKersie, p. 165.

30. For suggested dynamics underlying this hypothesis, see Barbara G. Haskel, "Disparities, Strategies, and Opportunity Costs: The Example of Scandinavian Economic Market Negotiations in the 1950s and 1960s", *International Studies Quarterly* 18, 1 (March 1974), pp. 3-30.

31. The Norwegian members of the Committee had concluded that the plan would be a net gain for Norway only "if special measures to balance the development within the customs union area were first taken" (p. 107 above). The whole Committee then concluded that there was no basis for agreement at the time unless "special measures to overcome the difficulties" could be taken.

32. Paul Gersmann was a leading Danish civil servant and a member of the Committee. (*Forhandlinger ved Det Nordiske Nasjonaløkonomiske Møte i Oslo den 19.-21. juni 1952*, pp. 141-142.)

An example of the liberal conception was the comment of Swedish Prime Minister Tage Erlander: "A Nordic market will also in my understanding, more or less automatically lead to mutual adaptation (*indbyrdes tilpasning*) of investment activities." "Muligheder og Begraensninger i Nordisk Politik", *Idé og Arbejde. En Bog til Hans Hedtoft på 50-årsdagen* (København: Forlaget Fremad, 1953), p. 13.

33. See Axel Sømme, *A Geography of Norden: Denmark, Finland, Iceland, Norway, Sweden* (Oslo: 1960, London: 1961); Sven Groennings, *Scandinavia in Social Science Literature. An English Language Bibliography* (Bloomington and London: Indiana University Press (for the International Affairs Center) 1970), especially pp. 1-4 introducing the literature on economics.

34. Odd Aukrust, Norges ekonomi etter krigen. The Norwegian Post-War Economy (Oslo: Statistisk Sentralbyrå, 1965)
Special help had been given Northern Norway which had suffered a "scorched-earth" policy as the Germans retreated. In 1952 the "North Norway Fund" was established to develop the sparsely settled and economically marginal northernmost reaches of the country. In 1960 the question of regional planning was met more generally by The Fund for Regional Development (Distriktenes utbyggingsfund). "Vart går den norska landsbygden?", Industria (Stockholm), July-August 1966, pp. 63-118. For a polemic against the attempt to build up industries viable according to the usual economic criteria, see Ottar Brox, Hva skjer i Nord-Norge? En studie i norsk utkants-politikk (Oslo: Pax 1966).

35. Nils Ørvik makes a very interesting argument that historically Sweden's extra-regional losses (as a Great Power) were balanced by intra-regional gains (Norway) leaving its self-esteem intact, while Denmark's losses were on both fronts (on the south to Germany, on the east to Sweden) leaving what Ørvik terms defeatism, (low self-esteem). See "Nordic Cooperation and High Politics" International Organization 28:1 (Winter 1974) pp. 61-88.

36. Lange I (3 November 1966).

37. Norway's gross domestic investment as a % of its gross domestic product was 35-38% after 1950, just under 37% from 1955-1958. Statistiska Sentralbyrå, Norges ekonomi etter krigen (The Norwegian Postwar Economy), Samfunnsøkonomiske studier 12, Oslo, 1965, p. 120. Its gross fixed capital formation as a % of GNP in current prices was 30% in 1953 and 28% in 1956. That of Sweden was 21% and 20% respectively, and of Denmark 17% in both years. Ibid., p. 123, Table 26.
Import surpluses financed about half Norway's investments. Alice Bourneuf, Norway, The Planned Revival (Cambridge, Mass.: Harvard University Press. 1958). p. 38. Also see P.J. Bjerve, Planning in Norway, 1947-1956 (Contributions to Economic Analysis, 16) (Amsterdam: 1959).

38. An interesting index of this are the accounts of prewar and postwar student politics which is quite central throughout Norwegian history. The leaders of the "Student Society" in Oslo, (which was until recently the only University), almost always were prominent in the following years. Many political competitors as well as associates have known each other much of their lives. See Det Norske Studentersamfund gjennom 150 år, 1813-2. oktober 1953 (Oslo: Aschehoug, 1963).

39. Bourneuf, op. cit., pp. 15-17.
In the fall of 1944, the Home Front (the Resistance coordinating organization in Norway, recognized by the legal Government in London) asked the representatives of the four big parties ("bourgeois" and socialist) to prepare a joint program for the period immediately following liberation. The first coalition government of June 1945 was headed by Gerhardsen, who then in September headed a Labor Party Government based on a majority in the newly elected Storting. Summary account in Chr. A.R. Christensen, "Norge i 1945",

Nordisk Tidsskrift, 1946, pp. 60-74. For a detailed account of the politics of the coalition government's formation, see Wyller, Frigjøringspolitik.... Brofoss headed the new Ministry of Trade from its establishment in 1947. It was, in fact, the center of the Government's economic planning together with the Central Bureau of Statistics. Brofoss himself was chairman of the "Council for questions relating to the European Recovery Program in Norway", a body with representatives from many Government departments as well as from industry, labor, commerce, fishing.

41. James Reston in The New York Times, 5 August 1949; George Soloveytschik, in The Norsemen, XLII (June 1954).

42. Compare the tone of the Norwegians with that of Swedes writing in Industria, the organ of the Swedish Federation of Industries, between 1945 and 1949 for example. Also Leif Lewin, "The Debate on Economic Planning in Sweden" in Koblick, (ed.), Sweden's Development ... pp. 282-302.

43. Forhandlingar vid XV Nordisk nationalekonomiska mötet i Helsingfors 20. - 21. juni 1955, pp. 11-41.

44. Frantz Wendt, Danmarks historia, edited by John Danstrup and Hal Koch, vol. XIV ("Besaettelse og Atomtid 1939-1965"), (Copenhagen: Politikens forlag, 1966), p. 345.

45. On the significance of an organizational (membership) versus electoral focus, see Ulf Torgersen, "Landsmøtet i norsk partistruktur 1884-1940", (Oslo: Institutt for samfunnsforskning, 1966), mimeographed, 109 pp. On the development and ideology of the Norwegian Labor Party, see: Aksel Zachariassen, Fra Marcus Thrane til Martin Tranmael, (Oslo: 1962), and the selected bibliography in Norsk sosialisme. En dokumentasjon, edited by Einhart Lorenz (Oslo: Pax Forlag, 1970), pp. 156-158; on the entry and exit from Comintern, see Knut Langfeldt, Moskva-tesene i norsk politikk (Oslo: Universitetsforlaget, 1961); for divergent theses on the radicalization of the Labor Party in the post-World War I era compare Edvard Bull's rapid industrialization hypothesis, (Edvard Bull, Arbeiderklassen: Norsk Historie (Oslo: Tiden Norsk Forlag, 1948), and Ulf Torgersen's organizational structure hypothesis, ("Landsmötet...," pp. 35-42). See also William M. Lafferty, Economic Development and the Response of Labour in Scandinavia. A Multi-level Analysis, Oslo: Universitetsforlaget, 1971.

46. The discrepancy between the majority of the Storting and the majority of the voters represents the bias of the electoral system toward the larger parties. In 1952 Norway had changed its method of proportional representation, lessening but not eliminating this bias. See Henry Valen and Daniel Katz, Political Parties in Norway. A Community Study (Oslo: Universitetsforlaget, 1964), p. 20.

47. Conversation with Professor John Sanness, Oslo, August 1974.

48. On the early liberalization of Swedish socialism, see Herbert Tingsten, The Swedish Social Democrats: Their Ideological Development. Totowa, N.J.: Bedminster, 1973. (Translation of Den Svenska socialdemokratiens idéutvikling (Stockholm: 1941)); also David J. Thomas, "Swedish Social

Democracy 1932-1960: A Study of Ideology," unpublished Ph. D. dissertation, Harvard University, November 1967. For a discussion of Swedish Social Democratic views on planning, see Leif Lewin, Planhushållningsdebatten (Skrifter utgivna av Statsvetenskapliga föreningen i Uppsala, XLVI) (Stockholm: Almqvist and Wiksell, 1967), and Diane Sainsvury, "A Critique of Leif Lewin's Planhushållningsdebatten," Statsvetenskaplig tidskrift (Stockholm), 1968, No. 2, pp. 109-125.

49. My reading that there was a change in the Norwegian position in the spring of 1954 was based on:
1) the differences between the statements of the Norwegian members of the Nordic committee in the report of March 1954, and the report of the Government to the Storting of 18 June (Stortingsmelding, nr. 87 (1954), "Om økonomisk samarbeid mellom de nordiske lande," (Tilråding fra UD, 18 June 1954.),
2) other Storting documents and debates (e.g., Dokument nr. 8 (6 April 1954) and Stort. 28 May 1954, pp. 1492-1539),
3) the debates of the Nordic Council's second session, August 1954.
This thesis has now been confirmed by Brofoss who said that the Cabinet discussed the issue. Dagfinn Juel of the Ministry was told to write the statement. It was toned down because of divergent views. (Interview with Brofoss, Montreal, 23 october 1973. Hereafter, Brofoss II).

The reasoning in the 18 June Government statement is worth citing in detail. The introductory Foreign Ministry statement accompanying the documents noted a need for "decisions on principles to serve as guidelines" (prinsipielle retningslinjer), indicating that this report itself could not be considered to be those guidelines. However, the attached report written by Juel argued: 1) that there is a need for larger markets (cf. US market), that OEEC has helped via liberalization measures but that these were only partial, and by themselves, too slow. It is quicker and more effective to influence the structure of industry by "a direct coordination of investment to further a rational development of production" (p. 7). (This was the old Norwegian position now argued to be serving more "liberal" ends.) 2) Scandinavia must be aware of its position vis-á-vis developing blocs such as Benelux, the Commonwealth and the Schuman plan. A particular consideration is that Scandinavia has had trade deficits with Germany and surpluses with England. When full convertibility is attained, this may create problems. 3) There had been objections to a customs union in 1949-50 because Norway had had to give priority to some industries, and this had unduly handicapped others. But that argument was "valid only for a limited time period" (p. 9). 4) "The Government has thus not turned down the suggestion of a customs union or a free trade area as a long range policy," although other kinds of cooperation were stressed "in the first instance" (p. 9). 5) A possible customs union must "be prepared for by investments to increase competitive ability and to ease structural adjustments" (p. 11). 6) There followed a host of suggestions on possible fields for negotiations.

To summarize the change: until the spring of 1954 the Norwegian Government thought of concrete projects and common investments as an alternative to the common market (although the possibility of a package was never excluded); thereafter, they were persuaded to regard the prospect of a common market as something positive, even if it required certain economic and especially political preconditions and therefore had to be approached gradually.

Compare Frantz Wendt, who calls the 18 June Norwegian Government statement "an entirely new co-operation programme, which virtually set aside the Norwegian part of the Committee's report," (The Nordic Council..., p. 171) and Stanley V. Anderson who says of the same statement: "the Norwegian position was restated and alternative areas of cooperation--other than a common market--were suggested" (op.cit., p. 127). Wendt does not attempt to explain why this change took place. When Wendt was interviewed many years later, he said that Bramsnaes, the Committee Chairman, had decided that rather than have a compromise report (for March 1954), he would have the Norwegians write their own conclusions separately, which they did. According to Wendt, the Ministry of Commerce statement of 18 June was due to the fact that "Norway couldn't stand to be isolated." Anderson does not have to explain a change, because he believes none took place.

Both Jonsson and Nielsson (op. cit., VII-36) attribute the 1954 change in Labor Party attitude to the change in economic conditions in Norway.

50. On the temporary nature of the original Norwegian argument, see Brofoss to a closed session of the Storting, 6 April 1954, Stort. Dok. nr. 8 (1954), p. 3 and Stortingsmelding nr. 87 (18 June 1954), p. 9.

51. Brofoss, Interview, Oslo, 20 June 1967. (Hereafter, Brofoss I).

52. The following all stressed the effect of participation in the OEEC on Norwegian economic thinking and self-confidence: Direktør Knut Getz-Wold, who was Brofoss' second in command at The Bank of Norway, and involved all through the 1950s in the Nordic negotiations (Interview, Oslo 21 June 1967), Ambassador Arne Skaug, who had been involved in both Marshall Plan and Nordic negotiations in a variety of Governmental and civil servant capacities (Interview, Oslo, 5 July 1967), and Swedish Landshövding Gustav Cederwall, who negotiated on the common market question from the Swedish side (Interview, Västeras, Sweden, 13 June 1967).

53. Communication from Förstearkivar Erik-Wilhelm Norman, Det Kgl. Utenriksdepartementet, Oslo, 12 March 1969. The Committee was the so-called Temporary Council Committee set up by the NATO Council in September 1951 to conduct a coordinated analysis of NATO's defense plans. It had twelve members and met from October to December under Averell Harriman' chairmanship. Also, Brofoss II. The Committee reported to the NATO Council Meeting at Lisbon, 1952.

54. Brofoss I.

Both Prime Minister Torp (Prime Minister from 1951 to 1955 between two Gerhardsen periods) and Brofoss emphasized to the closed session of the Storting that the advantages of Scandinavian economic cooperation were "first and foremost... to strengthen the Nordic countries' commercial (handelspolitiske) position." Gerhardsen added that such cooperation would be "to remedy the common weaknesses in Scandinavia's position vis-á-vis the rest of the world." (Stort. 28 May 1954, pp. 1504, 1495).

There was also an internal Foreign Office "note" which made clear that it was the Ministry of Trade (which Brofoss headed), which was pressing for an early evaluation of the issue. Another such note asked whether the Nordic issue should not be considered against the background of the current Schuman plan and other international groupongs such as the Commonwealth; thus the idea had some currency. ("Notat" 24 April 1954, Utenriksdepartementet, file 25-3/33).

Ambassador Arne Skaug, who followed Brofoss as Minister of Trade, remembered Brofoss' viewpoint as having been that the three countries could do better in European cooperation if they were together in a customs union. (Interview, Ambassadør Arne Skaug, Oslo, 5 July 1967.) On the other hand, it is interesting that one of Brofoss' closest professional (as opposed to Party) colleagues, Knut Getz-Wold (who had followed Brofoss from the Ministry of Commerce to the Bank of Norway, and who had been Brofoss' choice to head the higher level Nordic investigations in 1954) stressed only the realization of the need for liberalization, and the positive experience Norway had had in the liberalization, measures required by OEEC. (Interview, Direktør Knut Getz-Wold, Oslo, 21 June 1967.) Likewise Odd Gøthe, who had been an L.O. economist, then deputy minister (statssekretaer) in the Ministry of Industry, thought Brofoss' arguments were mostly economic. (Interview, Ekspedisjonssjef Odd Gøthe, Industridepartementet, Oslo, 28 June 1967.)

There was a Swedish economist whose view on the possibilities for and the political-economic prerequisites for a Nordic customs union came close to that of Brofoss. Professor Ingvar Svennilson presented a broad series of interconnected measures in a speech early in 1954. He set them against the background of the relative autarchy of the large countries, and the rise of an economic bloc in Europe, of which he saw the Schuman Plan as the first step. See a summary of his speech in Industria (Stockholm), vol. 50, No. 3 (1954), p. 13. Professor Svennilson remembers Brofoss' attitude to have been that a customs union would "make us independent of Germany." (Interview, Professor Ingvar Svennilson, Stockholm, September 1, 1967.)

55. Brofoss, I. (See H.J. Arndt, The Economic Lessons of the Nineteen Thirties, The Royal Institute of International Affairs (Oxford: Oxford University Press. 1944), pp. 112-113). Arndt says that Great Britain was able to extract great concessions from several small countries whose exports to Britain were greater than their imports from Britain and/or who specialized in exports to the British market. He mentioned Argentina, the Scandinavian countries, the Baltic countries, Poland, and Russia, and says that Argentina and Denmark were worst hurt.)

56. On currency problem argumentation see Ingeborg Lie, "Forhandlingene om Nordisk Tollunion/Nordisk Fellesmarked 1954-1956".

Hovedfagsoppgave i historie, Oslo University, spring 1973, unpublished, pp. 36-38.

57. Brofoss II (23 October 1973). See also Olav Larssen, Den langsomme revolusjonen, (Oslo: Aschehoug, 1973), pp. 123-125 on the discontent within the Labor Party Storting group, and p. 131 on Lange's emphasis on this in internal party discussions. (Larssen was the editor of Arbeiderbladet, the Labor Party's Oslo newspaper and main organ.)

58. Arb. 28-6-71. Landshövding Gustav Cederwall's explanation for the 1954 shift was that Brofoss had won over Gerhardsen to his view. (Interview, Västeras, Sweden, 3 June 1967.) See also Gerhardsen's affectionate sketch of Brofoss in his memoirs. Einar Gerhardsen, Samarbeid og strid. Erindringer 1945-55, (Oslo: Tiden norsk forlag, 1971), pp. 124-126.

59. A summary of Nordens Bondeorganisationers Centralråd, "Landbruket och en nordisk tullunion," (April 1951) is included in Et faelles nordisk marked, pp. 8-12.

There were fears in Norway that the Danes would press for the inclusion of agriculture, or at least concessions to agriculture, should an industrial common market once be agreed upon.

The relative size of the agricultural interest group and the profitability of agriculture in the economy is indicated by the following figures:

		D	F	N-S
1950	population in agriculture	22%	39%	18%
	contribution of the GNP	20%	15%	7-8%

Source: NEC, Copenhagen, 1958, p. 22.

60. The three trade union federations (hereafter, each cited as LO), critical of the negative inter-governmental report of January 1950, established their own inter-Scandinavian committee, which issued a joint report in September 1951. (Nordisk økonomisk samarbejde, utgivet af De samvirkende fagforbund i Danmark, 22 September 1951; hereafter, "LO's report".) See also Nils Kellgren's statement to the Swedish Social Democratic Congress: Sveriges socialdemokratiska arbetarepartis 19: de kongress i Stockholm, 2. - 7. juni 1952, Protokoll, p. 133.

Odd Gøthe, the Norwegian LO economist who was on the committee of three which wrote the report, said that the question of the size of the investment bank in relation to the extent of the tariff reductions, had not been discussed, although he characterized the bank as a "prerequisite" for such reductions. (Interview, Gøthe, Oslo, 26 June 1967.)

61. What happened to this report? The Nordic conference of LOs which had commissioned it, discussed it and decided to publish it. It was described in a couple of articles in the Swedish trade union organ, Fackföreningsrörelse, once in a column-long announcement which warned against exaggerated expectations (A. L-m, "Nordiskt ekonomiskt samarbete," Fackföreningsrörelse, 1951, No. 44, p. 419), and once in a long article by Kellgren, the Swedish trade union economist on

the committee (Nils Kellgren, "Nordiskt ekonomiskt samarbete," ibid., 1951, No. 47, pp. 468-473).

In Norway, the LO magazine, Fri Fagbevegelse, had up to 1954 a single article, translated from the Swedish newspaper Göteborgs Handels- og Sjöfartstidende, which had interpreted the report in accordance with its liberal view, and which was reprinted without comment ("Ökonomisk samarbeid i Skandinavien," Fri Fagbevegelse, 1952, pp. 200-201). Likewise, in Denmark, one article appeared in 1951 describing the report, noting that both Denmark and Norway would have difficulties maintaining full and productive employment because of balance of payments difficulties, and noting that the bank and customs union were the most important parts of the plan. ("Nordisk økonomisk samarbejde" (editorial), Arbejderen, Meddelsesblad for de Samvirkende fagforbund i Danmark, 1951 (vol. 47), pp. 173-175).

62. Interview, Gøthe, Oslo, 26 June 1967.

63. Interview, Riksdagsman Nils Kellgren, Stockholm, 12 June 1967. (Kellgren had been the Swedish LO economist involved in the report, and is also an enthusiastic proponent of Nordic cooperation.) In February 1956 Foreign Minister Osten Undén warned the Nordic Council not to take Kellgren's views as typical for Sweden. ("Anförande av utrikesministern i Nordiska rådet den 3 februari," Utrikesfragor 1956, p. 12.)

Several interviewed in Sweden and Norway mentioned Swedish Finance Minister Per-Edvin Skiöld as being particularly unyielding in Nordic issues.

The Nordic inter-governmental report explored Norwegian labor hesitation about economic cooperation--at this point, 1953, a "partial free trade area" was what was being discussed-- but the joint statement of the three labor confederations remained positive. (Et faelles nordisk marked, pp. 135-142)

64. Industriforbundets uttalelse (the statement of the Norwegian Federation of Industry) of 15 December 1949 is given in extenso in Norges Industri XXXV, No. 19 (9 October 1954), pp. 376-379.

Industriforbundet rejected in advance a change in its position based on either changes which could be effected by the Government (desired changes in regulations) or changes which could develop over a period of time (strengthening the home industries as recovery eased the stringent channeling of scarce capital).

Asked about the validity of the argument that involvement in a Nordic customs union would invite reprisals, Roem-Nielsen, the head of the Norwegian Federation of Industries noted that that was part of Industriforbundet's "argumentation". (Interview with Direktør Roem-Nielsen, Norges Industriforbund, Oslo 30 June 1967.)

One observer believes Norwegian industry's fear to have been that in a Nordic (rather than a larger) market, Swedish industry would "concentrate" on the Norwegian market, and that this, rather than the "reprisals" argument was central. (Interview, Gøthe, Oslo, 28 June 1967.)

65. Industriforbundets uttalelse, 15 December 1949.

The following "home" industries had not been permitted foreign exchange to modernize: clothing and woven goods, plant oils, soap, and cleaning stuff, furniture. Norges Utenrikshandel (published by Norges Exportråd), 1954, p. 97.

66. Stort. (27 October 1954), p. 2432. (The October debate in the Storting lasted nine and a half hours.)

When asked whether Norwegian industry did not think it could obtain some liberalization from the Government as a result of the Nordic market, Direktør Roem-Nielsen of Industriforbundet said that Swedish industrial colleagues had used that argument, but without success (Interview, Oslo, 30 June 1967).

67. See Stein Rokkan, "Geography, Religion, and Social Class: Cross-cutting Cleavages in Norwegian Politics," in Lipset and Rokkan, eds., op. cit., pp. 367-444, especially pp. 375-379.

T.K. Derry has a brief account in English of the consolidation of Venstre around the concession laws: A History of Modern Norway, Oxford, Clarendon Press, 1973, pp. 196-200. Also Arthur Stonehill, Foreign Ownership in Norwegian Enterprises (Oslo: Statistisk Sentralbyrå (Samfunnsøkonomiske studier nr. 14) 1965). Concession laws were passed in 1883 but especially between 1910-1920. In the 1914-1919 period there was a policy of "repatriation," of buying back foreign-held stock in Norwegian firms.

(In the nineteenth century, the Storting had been so chary of foreign control that it had adopted a policy of approving railroad construction only where the major part of the costs were raised through popular subscriptions. (Vincent H. Malmström "The Norwegian State Railroads, 1854-1954," The American-Scandinavian Review, XLII, No. 3 (September 1954), p. 225.)

68. Stort. 28 May 1954, pp. 1500-1502; NR, 2nd session (1954), p. 167.

69. Brofoss, II.

70. Stort. 38 May 1954, p. 1502. It would be erroneous to say that these were Venstre's arguments alone. Christian Holm, a Conservative, argued very sharply in the same vein (Stort. 27 October 1954, pp. 2441-2442). Representatives of the Agrarian Party emphasized this too (Stort. 27 October 1954, p. 2471 (Frogner).

71. St. forh. 27 October 1954. p. 2477. Evensen had been Minister of Trade 1945-7, and Minister of Industry 1947-1953. It was he who had pushed for earlier electricity negotiations which had not succeeded. In the May Storting debate he said that his view had not changed from 1950: cooperation (i.e., the sale of Norwegian electricity) would have been beneficial for all then too. (St. forh. 28 May 1954, pp. 1510-1511)

72. NR, 2nd session, pp. 197-203; citation, p. 200.

73. See Stein Rokkan and Henry Valen, "Regional Contrasts in Norwegian Politics" in Erik Allardt and Yrjo Littunen, eds., Cleavages,

Ideologies, and Party Systems (Helsinki: Westermarck Society, 1964), pp. 162-238.

74. Knut Getz-Wold, "Økonomisk samarbeid i Norden," Samtiden, Vol. 64, No. 2 (1956), pp. 88-102, especially pp. 91, 97-99.

75. Aftenposten, 13-1-56, p. 7. This was a speech (12 January) by Getz-Wold to Oslo's Handelsstands Forening (The Oslo Trade Association).

76. Interview, Gøthe, Oslo, 26 June 1967. On Evensen, Brofoss, II. Brofoss called Evensen the principal "skeptic".

77. Samuel H. Beer, British Politics in the Collectivist Age (New York: Alfred P. Knopf, 1965), chapter III, "The New Group Politics," particularly pp. 325-329 on "acquiescence". Stein Rokkan, "Norway: Numerical Democracy and Corporate Pluralism", in Robert A. Dahl, ed., Political Oppositions in Western Democracies (New Haven and London: Yale University Press, 1966), pp. 70-115, especially pp. 105-110, "Votes Count but Resources Decide".

78. Interview, Oslo, 1967.

79. Interview, Stortingsmann Einar Gerhardsen (former Norwegian Prime Minister), Oslo, 22 June 1967.

80. Interview, Gustaf Cederwall, Västeras, Sweden, 13 June 1967. Cederwall gave as examples a large joint aluminum or steel project. This would have required a more radical policy than Sweden was conducting domestically, said Cederwall. Similarly the Norwegian Government never seemed to have considered seriously a change in taxation as the price of opposition adherence to the market. It would have meant too crucial a change in economic policy. (Interview, Ambassador Arne Skaug, Oslo, 5 July 1967.) The major lines of economic policy are seen here as constraints in the negotiations both domestically and with the other countries. These major policies can, of course, be related back to the relative strength of the Government parties in their respective political systems.

In Norway, both Roem-Nielsen and Getz-Wold felt that significant concessions came too late to be effective. Roem-Nielsen felt that the transition measures which eventually were offered might have split the Industriforbund. (Interview, Oslo, June 1967.) Getz-Wold said that he had tried to convince the Swedish negotiators that a hard position was reasonable only where both sides knew they had to reach an agreement, whereas this was not the case here. He felt that in the end (1959) the concessions by Sweden had been "large, one-sided, and favorable" to Norway. (Interview, Oslo, June 21, 1967.)

That this might well have become an electoral issue is indicated by the fact that in June 1956 Venstre's national convention entertained a resolution to make the Nordic market an electoral issue and to oppose "statements and suggestions which have come from different places about a Nordic state (unionstat) as a goal for Nordic coopera-tion". ("Meddelande från Nordisk råd," nr. 6 (1956), 19-6-56. Nordisk råds arkiv, Copenhagen, file 6B 1/c1.)

81. Udgaard, chapter 13, especially pp. 208-9, 216-18. "Indefensible", Brofoss I. See also David L. Larsen, "Marshallplanen og Norge",

Internasjonal Politikk 1972:2 pp. 251-275 particularly pp. 266-9 for the contemporary press debate.

82. See Knut Einar Eriksen, footnote 37, p. 292 and footnote 42, p. 293.

83. On the changes in Norwegian leaders' images of the international environment see Philip M. Burgess, Elite Images and Foreign Policy Outcomes. A Study of Norway. (Columbus, Ohio, The Ohio State University Press, 1968).

84. Impression from Brofoss II interview.

85. The Norwegian experience paralleled and was, perhaps, related to the British. See H.M. Lange, "European Union: False Hopes and Realities", Foreign Affairs, 23 (April 1950), pp. 441-450.

86. The concept of a "privileged means" is taken from David J. Thomas' concept "ideologically privileged means" in "Swedish Social Democracy 1932-1960: A Study of Ideology" unpublished Ph. D. dissertation, Harvard University 1967, pp. 274-5.

87. Brofoss II. Getz-Wold mentioned that there was irritation in the Foreign Office at the major role of the Ministry of Trade in this issue. Getz-Wold II.

88. Brofoss II.

89. Robert J. Lieber, British Politics and European Unity: Parties, Elites, and Pressure Groups (Berkeley: University of California Press, 1970). I am following Lieber's use of the term politicization.

90. Brofoss II. Also see Olav Larssen's account of the discontent within the Party leadership with Torp's leadership and of the change of Government around Christmas 1954. "No bed of roses for Oscar Torp", in Den langsomme revolusjonen, pp. 120-134.

91. Interview, Englund, Stockholm 2 June 1967. (Englund had been the Swedish secretary on the NECC from 1955 on.)

92. Jonsson, op, cit., pp. 536-538. He sees the governments as having been "overresponsive" to interest groups (pp. 126-127).

The process of Government-industry consultation has been described as follows:

> The contact with industry is carried out in this way: first preliminary comments are solicited from a representative circle of firms, after which the Danish civil servants meet with their Norwegian and Swedish colleagues for a discussion which results in a concrete suggestion for a common Nordic market for the goods (vareområde) concerned. This suggestion is thereafter presented to the interested branches and firms for comment (udtalelse).

Tidskrift for industri, No. 24, 1955, reprinted in Norges industri, vol. 38, no. 1 (14 January 1956), p. 9.

This does not mean that industries were always satisfied even with this arrangement. The same article complained that industries were allowed too little time to investigate and weigh implications (p. 10). Jernindustri, the organ of Mekaniske Verksteders Landsforening (the Engineering Industries' organization of Norway) complained that the NECC's report to the Council's 4th session tried to cover over the disagreements which had been revealed at the "hearings" held by the Committee, and that they had not mentioned the Norwegian objections. Both the NECC and the Ministry of Trade had been worried about this. (Aftenposten and Norges Handel- og Sjøfartstidende, 9 March 1956.)

93. See Theodore J. Lowi, "American Business, Public Policy, Case-Studies, and Political Theory," WP, XVI (July 1964), pp. 682-683, for the significance of competition over the "definition" to be applied to foreign policy.

> The outcome depended not upon compromise between the two sides in Congress but upon whose definition of the situation prevailed. If tariff is an instrument of foreign policy and general regulation for international purposes, the anti-protectionists win; if the traditional definition of tariff as an aid to 100,000 individual firms prevails, then the protectionists win.
> (emphasis in the original)

Lowi is describing a highly politicized versus an unpoliticized (or low politicized) issue.

94. Discussion between Aksel Larsen (Danish Communist Party) and Jens Otto Krag (S.D.) in reference to a speech by Krag at Strömstad in Sweden, 17 June 1956. Folket. 1955-56 (vol. 107), cols. 5440, 5502-5506 (22 June 1956). Also Sydsjaellands Social-Democrat editorial 20 June 1956 in "Meddelande från Nordisk råd," nr. 6 (1956), 19-6-56.

Krag stated that Denmark had held off joining the ECSC to see whether the Scandinavian Common Market would be established.

What is interesting, however, is that Krag was speaking in terms of a two year timetable.

95. Bent Røiseland (Venstre's parliamentary group leader), in NR, 5th session, 19 February 1957, p. 97. Erling Petersen (Conservative) also thought this might be an incentive to wrong investments (p. 105).

96. On the external strength issue, see Stort., 28 January 1957, pp. 254-309, where Norwegian Government spokesmen focused on bloc developments in Europe, and the "impact" of a unified Scandinavia. In this debate Skaug stressed that he personally was for the Nordic market (p. 297). On possible leverage for insisting on a Nordic plan within EFTA, interview Getz-Wold, above.

97. Interview, Skaug, above. Odd Gøthe (interview above) noted that Maudling had had trouble as it was, getting EFTA through the British Cabinet. Bertil Ohlin, leader of the Swedish Liberal Party, also thought there would have been a possibility for a Nordic group within EFTA, but stressed that it was not the British who prevented this; no plan was ever presented to them. (Interview, Professor Bertil Ohlin, Stockholm, 30 May 1967.)

98. An interesting indication that the negotiations were not pro forma is that in June 1959, just before they ended, Swedish Minister of Trade Gunnar Lange reassured the Soviets, in trade negotiations, that if either a Scandinavian market or the European Free Trade Area were to be formed, Sweden would apply the most favored nation clause to the Soviet Union in the same way as to members of GATT. (Interview, Cederwall, above. Cederwall accompanied Gunnar Lange on the trip to the Soviet Union.)

The concessions were, in the end, significant ones. The final proposal has been characterized this way in a study published by the Central Bureau of Statistics in Norway in 1965:

> For individual disadvantaged sectors there was the condition that especially Finland and Norway would have transition measures of up to twelve years. In several especially important areas (among them machinery, iron and metal goods, textile wares and ready made clothing) these transition measures would be exclusive, meaning that as soon as the Common Market went into effect, Norway and Finland would meet no duties in Sweden, and for the most part also Denmark, while those two countries' goods would only gradually in the course of the transition perion receive equivalent treatment in Norway and Finland. Sweden would for her part receive very few transition arrangements. The concessions which Sweden and Denmark in this way gave Norway and Finland were quite significant.

Norges ekonomi etter Krigen, p. 182.

A Swedish economist has pointed out that while the Nordic scheme contained no "escape clause" for the difficulties of an economic activity or region, the transition measures specified were closely adapted to special needs. He used this as an example of "the substitutional character of different means of dealing with transitional difficulties". Hans O. Lundström, Capital Movements and Economic Integration (Leyden: A.W. Sijthoff, 1967), p. 159.

99. Interviews, Englund, Stockholm, 2 June 1967, and Cederwall, Västeras, Sweden, 13 June 1967.

Finland and EFTA eventually formed FINEFTA, which formally has separate council. In fact, decisions are made in that council and the EFTA council has become pro forma.

100. "Kommuniké från regeringsmötet i Kungsälv den 12 juli", Utrikesfrågor 1959, pp. 70-71. Also, NR, 7th session, Sak D63. Axel Waldemarsson ("Norden och de yttre sju", Svenska Dagbladets årsbok 1959 (Stockholm: 1960), pp. 73-6) says that at the Kungsälv meeting, Finland thought the Scandinavian solution best, but "hinted" that it could be interested in the seven state arrangement.

101. See Waldermarsson, op. cit., and Barclay, op. cit., for the significant concessions which Norway and Denmark received from EFTA.

102. Mark W. Leiserson, "A Brief Interpretive Survey of Wage-Price Problems in Europe", Study Paper no. 11, Joint Economic Committee,

Congress of the United States, 86th Congress, 1st Session, Washington, D.C., p. 51.

103. Statement from H. Abenius and Axel Iveroth on behalf of Sveriges Industriförbund to the Minister of Trade, 6 February 1958, 6 pp. with appended statements from each industrial sector's organization (mimeographed). See pp. 4-5 where the organization opposes the suggestion of a joint investment bank on the grounds that: 1) it will be used to support uneconomic investments for the purpose of maintaining employment, 2) that the division of costs was "somewhat one-sided," and 3) that the directing of capital investment out of social considerations would restrict "the Nordic economies' (näringslivets) natural expansion."

Although Svenska Dagbladet noted, just before Harpsund (30 October 1954), that it was "incontrovertible" that Norway as the least developed industrially would run greater risks than the others at first, it never suggested any meliorative or compensatory measures.

Cf. Ingvar Svennilson, (the Swedish economist who sat on the joint Committee), in Industria, L. No. 3 (1954), p. 13. Svennilson emphasized that in order for Norway to be able to agree to a common market she must be permitted some "infant industries" and must be given long term capital transfers of significant amount. When interviewed many years later, Svennilson said that he had been thinking of something like half a million crowns. (Interview, Professor Ingvar Svennilson, Stockholm, 3 September 1967).

104. "Address by the Prime Minister to the Foreign Press Association in Stockholm, 1st June 1954," Documents on Swedish Foreign Policy 1954, Stockholm, 1955, p. 35.

105. NR, 4th session, 27 January 1956, p. 193.

106. Svenska Dagbladet, 23 February 1956, p. 1 and editorial "Progress requires capital," p. 4. On the Wallenberg banking family's influence, see "New Paths for Sweden. A Special Survey," The Economist (London), 28 October - 3 November 1967, especially pp. XVI-XXII. For a polemical treatment, see Åke Ortmark, Maktspelet i Sverige. Ett samhällsreportage (Stockholm: Widstrand, 1967), pp. 155-186. The implications of the Chamber of Commerce conference for the capability of Sweden to give investment funds to others was underlined in Norway. (Norges Handels- og Sjøfartstidende, editorial 28 March 1956.)

107. Nielsen, op. cit., pp. vii-29.

108. Interview, Bertil Ohlin, Stockholm, 30 May 1967.

109. Amitai Etzioni, Political Unification. A Comparative Study of Leaders and Forces (New York: Holt, Rinehart, and Winston, 1965), pp. 315-316.

110. Ambassador Arne Skaug maintains that the Bank was never formulated as a price for Norwegian cooperation because the Norwegians were doubtful about being able to get the market plan through. (Interview, Oslo, 5 July 1967.) This would support Ohlin's contention that the Norwegians never stipulated conditions of acceptance. (Interview, Stockholm, 30 May 1967.)

This is probably, literally speaking, true. However, note the following: 1) Skaug noted to the Storting (23 January 1957) that the possibilities of obtaining capital "must play a decisive role for Norway's attitude toward the Nordic cooperation plan". (Stort., 1954, pp. 169-170.) 2) Tor Stokke, who was Trade Advisor (Handelsråd) in the Norwegian Embassy in Stockholm from 1952 to 1956 (although never part of the NECC itself), says that in negotiations one looks for a gesture, but that "it never came... it was run as a pure business negotiation". (Interview, Ekspeditionssjef Tor Stokke, Handelsdepartementet, Oslo, 16 June 1967.)

111. Jonsson argues that "Denmark alone seemed to take the idea of a Scandinavian customs union seriously," (op. cit., p. 528). Unless one measures this by sheer popularity (for example, favorable general mention in newspapers), it is difficult to assess this statement. Tyge Dahlgaard, who had been the Danish secretary on the Nordic committees, maintained (years later) that pro-Scandinavian feelings influenced the Danish position in the following ways: The Danes were willing to accept:

1) a common external tariff, for example, on iron (to protect Norway),
2) leaving agriculture out, for the most part,
3) a net capital transfer via the Investment Bank, although this would be more from Sweden, than from Denmark. (Interview, Handelsminister Tyge Dahlgaard, Copenhagen, 22 May 1967.)

As early as the summer of 1954 a Danish agricultural economist had written that capital from Sweden and Denmark could counterbalance the (expected) negative impact of a customs union on Norwegian industry. However, he thought any large scale flow of capital unlikely, although he did not specify why. Frank Meissner, "Scandinavian Customs Union," The Norseman, July-August 1954, pp. 246-254.

112. Interview, Departementschef Erik Ib Schmidt, Finansdepartementet, Copenhagen, 18 May 1967.

Denmark's own economic policy was not to import capital for development (to the point of prohibiting the selling of Danish shares and bonds on foreign -- including other Scandinavian -- markets). Thus it was not interested in obtaining funds. As the second wealthiest it feared that it might be asked to pay Norway. Presumably this economic policy and its Nordic effects was related to the relatively weak position of the Social Democrats and their need for coalition support.

113. Percentage of import-controlled commodities in imports of common market industrial products from the other three countries (excluding food products and ships) in 1955: Denmark - 14.6, Finland - 23.8, Norway - 9.2, Sweden - 0.3. (Source: Table III, p. 32, Nordic Economic Cooperation, Supplementary Report by The Nordic Economic Cooperation Committee, General Part, Copenhagen, 1959.)

Some people interviewed maintained that Danish industry was far more protectionist than was commonly understood.

The 1955 Danish Federation of Industries statement had been -- in contrast to the position of its Nordic counterparts -- that it had no position of its own but would present the views of different branches and firms to the government. It noted, however, that Denmark imports all raw materials, and it also urged the government not to bee too sparing with transitional agreements. (Reprinted from the (Danish) Industriraadet's organ, Tidsskrift for industri, 1955, No. 24, in Norges Industri XXXVIII, No. 1 (14 January 1956), p. 10.) Industriraadet sent no statements to the Government before 1958.

For Many examples of interest group statements from all four countries, but mostly from 1957 and 1958, see Jonssen, op. cit., passim.

114. Anderson, The Nordic Council,,,, p. 122.

115. See footnote 86 above.

116. Jonsson, op. cit., p. 425, from Mogens Korst in Göteborgs Handels- och Sjöfartstidning. 6 February 1957.

The fact that (until the mid 1960s) Denmark's main export was agricultural products, which the Nordic proposals had no intention of including in any significant way, led Denmark to focus on the EEC, which did indeed propose to include agriculture.

117. For the characterization in Norges ekonomi etter krigen, see footnote 90. Interview, Getz-Wold, Oslo, 21 June 1967.

There were significant agreements in the iron and steel area. The importance of this sector went back to the early years of the discussions when Lars Evensen, then Norwegian Minister of Industry, supported cooperation in production and investment in these industries, and an investment bank as "an apparatus for this." (Interviews, Gøthe, Oslo, 26 June 1967, and 28 June 1967). By 1957 this was clearly not practical politics, but the Norwegians considered it very desirable that the plan included an arrangement in which private industry was willing to participate voluntarily. (Interviews, Gøthe.)

It had been agreed as well that contingent upon agreements in other areas, there would be a 5-7% duty on iron and steel, a compromise between the 6-8% desired by Sweden and the free trade position of Denmark. (This supports Tyge Dahlgaard's assertion. See footnote 104.) Norwegian industry wanted free trade for iron, while the Norwegian government wanted protection for the state iron works. (Interview, Stokke, Oslo, 16 June 1967.) See "Forslag til vedtekter for de nordiske jern- og stål produsenters samarbeids-organisjon," Appendix , pp. 68-71 to Nordisk Økonomisk Samarbeid, Spesiell del, Oslo, 1957.

118. Brofoss said of the Norwegian industrial organization, "they terrorized" those industries which showed some interest in the Nordic proposals. (Brofoss, I)

119. See Barbara G. Haskel, "External Events...," International Organization, XXIII, No. 4 (1969), pp. 960-968, from which this account is taken. See also: Internasjonal Politikk, 1968, No. 1 (Whole issue: "En nordisk økonomisk alterativ?"); Valter Angell, "Norway and Scandinavian Entry into the Common Market without

Great Britain?", C & C, 1969, No. 2, pp. 73-98 (translated from I.P., 1968, No. 5); IP, 1969, No. 6 ("Scandinavia i EEC uten Storbritannia?"), pp. 761-776, articles replying to Angell; Claes Wiklund, "The Zig-Zag Course of the Nordek Negotiations," SPS, 1970, No. 5, pp. 307-335.

120. Norges industriforbundets uttalelse, 1949. See footnote 59, Also Roem-Nielsen, Interview, Oslo, 30 June 1967.
It was for this reason, the statement had concluded, that even if other objections were assuaged, the Federation of Industry would continue to oppose the Nordic market.

121. Interview, Cederwall, Västeras, Sweden, 13 June 1967. The secret meeting of the UNISCAN countries plus Switzerland was on 21 February 1959 near Oslo, and EFTA negotiations were agreed upon there.

122. Brofoss, I.

123. Svenska Dagbladet, 31 December 1968, 16 January 1969; Dagens Nyheter, 19 January 1969. Cf. footnote 96 above for their positions in the 1950s.

124. Svenska Dagbladet, 24 April 1969.

125. "UD-informasjon" (Oslo), 18 January 1969 from the Swedish television statement of 15 January 1969.

126. Dagens Nyheter, 18 July 1969.

127. What finally jettisoned the proposal was the withdrawal of Finland which felt -- more correctly, whose President, Kekkonen, felt -- that it could not get Soviet sympathy for its interpretation that a connection between a Nordic group and the EEC -- clearly the aim of Denmark and in varying degrees, Norway and Sweden -- would be compatible with Finland's special policy of non-alignment.

Chapter Four

Reducing Costs: The Nordic Parliamentary Committee for Freer Communication, Etc.

1. Joseph S. Nye Jr., lectures, Harvard University 1968.

2. Nils Andrén "Nordic Integration - Aspects and Problems" Cooperation and Conflict 1 (1967) 1-25.

3. There was a lack of Governmental level contacts in the 1950-1954 period. Christian Lange, "Nordiska ministermöter 1945-1965," (mimeographed) p. 6.

4. Rolf Edberg, "Osynliga gränser i Norden" (Invisible borders in Norden), Nordisk tidskrift, 1954, p. 198.

5. Rolf Edberg, I morgon, Norden, Stockholm, 1944.

6. Edberg.

7. Edberg, Öppna grindarna, (Open the Gates.) (Stockholm: KF:s forlag 1952) p. 12.

8. Edberg, "Osynliga gränser...," pp. 206-207.

9. Letter from Ambassador Rolf Edberg, 24 November 1965. See AK/23/1951 (11-4-51), the interpellation of Hedtoft in the Folketing (24-1-51), and the report from the presidents of the Storting ("Meddelande från stortingets presidium, 26-4-51) for Sweden, Denmark, and Norway respectively.

10. Erlander and Undén had suggested that the discussion of a "passport union" (passunion) should be avoided so as not to create difficulties for Finland. A phrase such as "easing inter-Nordic communication" ("lättnader i den internordiska samfärdseln") was suggested in lieu of "passport and customs relaxations" (pass- og tullättnader). (Letter from Rolf Edberg to Hans Hedtoft 6-12-52. NR arkiv, Copenhagen, 6. B.2).

11. Interview, Consul-General Sten Aminoff, 24 October 1974, Montreal. Aminoff had been the Swedish Secretary of the original Committee.

12. Statens offentliga utredningar 1952:4, "Nordisk passfrihet" (del.1 Passfriheten för nordbor), Betänkande nr. 1 avgivet av Nordiska parlamentariska kommittén för friare samfärdsel m.m., Stockholm, 1952 (hereafter, SOU). The Committee had met three times in plenum and in several smaller sessions.

13. Interview, Ambassador Rolf Edberg, Oslo, 16 June 1967.

14. Edberg, Öppna grindarna, p. 16.

15. Ibid., p. 17.

16. Letter from Ambassador Rolf Edberg, 24 November 1965.

17. See Thomas Hammar, Sverige åt svenskarna. Invandringspolitik, utlänningskontroll och asylrätt 1900-1932, Stockholm, 1965, pp. 183-187, 213, 219-223 (English summary, pp. 385-400). For a parallel story of the origins of United States passport regulations, see The New York Times, 6 June 1976, travel section, p. 1.

18. Edberg, Öppna grindarna, p. 18.

19. First they treated passports for Scandinavian inhabitants, then the need for permission to remain in a country for longer than three months, and finally regulations for non-Scandinavians.

    Denmark had originally proposed creating a passport union in one step. Denmark's policing of passport regulations relied less on border checks and more on internal checking. Thus such a move would have been simpler for it. Interview, Consul-General Sten Aminoff, 24 October 1974, Montreal.)

20. The governments reduced currency checks to random sampling, although not that first summer when they liberalized passport procedures for Nordic citizens. (NR, 1st session 1953, col. 199 (Edberg)). As late as 1956 Norwegian citizens had to present a passport to buy foreign currency for travel abroad, and have the

amount stamped on it, even for Scandinavian travel. (SOU, 1956:45, "Slutbetänkande," pp. 44-46.)

On motor vehicle restrictions: "Lättnader i fråga om tullbehandling m.m. av motorfordon i trafiken mellan de nordiska länderna," Betänkande, nr. 5, SOU, 1953:5 (9 January 1953); "Nordiska rådets verksamhet 1952-1961, "NU, 1962:8 pp. 263-264. See Recommendation 165 (1958) unanimously passed by the Council of Europe's Consultative Assembly.

21. "Nordiska post- och teletaxor," Betänkande, nr. 7 & 8, 22 May 1954, SOU, 1954:20; NU, 1962:8, pp. 237-238; see also "Samarbeid på post-telegraf- og telefonvesenets område, "Melding fra den danske, den norske og den svenske regjering", NR, 2nd session (1954), pp. 561-563.

22. "Nordiska vägtrafikbestämmelser m.m.", (9 September 1955), SOU 1955:33, p. 133.

See NR rek. nr. 16/1955. This Nordic Council recommendation passed with two of the sixteen Swedish members abstaining, Oscar Werner (SD) and Erik Fast (Agrarian). Since negative votes are extremely rare, an abstention is somewhat stronger than might appear. (See Anderson, op. cit., p. 92ff.)

23. The second consultative referendum in Swedish history -- the first one was on prohibition in 1922 -- was held on October 16, 1955. Turnout was 53% (as compared with the usual 80% in parliamentary or provincial elections) and the measure was defeated by more than five to one. The Government accepted this decision. (Nils Andrén, "Sverige 1955," Nordisk tidskrift, XXXII (1956), pp. 176-177.) (In 1963 Swedish political party leaders without any further referenda, agreed to the change, which was fully implemented in 1967.)

24. SOU, 1956:45, p. 37.

25. NR, 9th session (1961), Sak A 13 and pp. 124-125.

Cf. Sletten, Five Northern Countries Pull Together, p. 51: "One important result of Northern cooperation is Sweden's decision to go over to right-hand driving on roads...."

26. Proposals about Communications matters - broadly conceived - are now dealt with by the standing Traffic Committee of the Nordic Council, established in 1956 when Finland joined the Council and its Committees. The Council Committees are composed of parliamentarians. Moves to retain a separate Nordic civil servants committee on communications matters were opposed by the governments. The Traffic Committee may consult experts and some of the same civil servants who worked with the original Committee now work with the Traffic Committee. One of the Governments' arguments was that there were already joint administrative meetings on customs, air transport and passports. (Interview, Konsulent Axel Gormsen, Handelsdepartementet, 25 May 1967.)

27. Ernst B. Haas, "International Integration," p. 96.

28. Edberg, "Osynliga gränser...," p. 199.

29. Ibid., p. 201.

30. Ibid., p. 202, and Edberg to the Swedish parliament (AK, 27 April 1955, pp. 99-102). For a picture of the two door system, see Wendt, The Nordic Council, facing p. 160.

    Note that Edberg said the same thing to the Swedish Social Democratic Party Congress in June of 1952, i.e., before the Committee's suggestion had been implemented. (Sveriges social-demokratiska partiets 19: de kongress, 2.7. juni 1952, Protokoll, pp. 134-135.

31. Rolf Edberg "Folkliga kontakter i Norden," Norden i världen (Speeches at Foreningen Norden's second congress, Stockholm 1959), (Stockholm: Rabén & Sjögren, 1960). Also "Osynliga gränser...," 1954, p. 201.

32. Erik Eriksen of Denmark made this point to the Nordic Council. NR, 4th session (1956), col. 5388.

33. There are regular conferences of Scandinavian police chiefs (p. 124), and some efforts to exchange personnel, and on a more symbolic level to standardize police uniforms, such efforts being "partially successful."

    Nils Lüning (Commissioner of Police, Stockholm), "Police Systems in the Scandinavian Countries," SP & P, 1959, III, pp. 122-124.

34. NR, 6th session (1958), p. 244.

35. Professor Bruno Suviranta of Finland proposed identity cards for both Nordic and non-Nordic citizens because the elimination of any check on Nordic citizens "would lead to the check on other foreigners being dependent upon their voluntary identification of themselves to the authorities." Two of the Norwegian MPs considered the Committee's mandate to concern restrictions on Nordic citizens only. (SOU, 1952:4, p. 36.)

36. The Committee's Report nr. 3 (SOU, 1952:16-17) and Report nr. 12 (SOU, 1956:45), as well as the Nordic Council recommendations based on them (nr. 9/1953, nr. 11/1957, nr. 3/1960) all called upon the Norwegian government to do away with this system It was finally agreed to as of January 1961. (NU, 1962:8, pp. 280-281.)

37. Ernst B. Haas to the Western European Seminar, Harvard University, 8 December 1967; Albert Hirschman, "The Principle of the Hiding Hand," The Public Interest, No. 6 (Winter 1967), pp. 10-23.

    There was some effort to expand the scope of the Committee's activities. The Nordic Council was used to widen the Committee's mandate. It sent postal and telegraph matters to the Committee. (NR, 1st session (1953), Recommendation nr. 9.) This proposal was checked with the Governments. (Letter from Rolf Edberg to Danish Prime Minister Hedtoft, 6-12-52, where Edberg reports having spoken to Swedish Prime Minister Erlander and Foreign Minister Undén who approved. NR, arkiv, Copenhagen, file 6.B.21.) Edberg was probably the prime mover of the Council recommendation. (Letter from Edberg to Hedtoft asking for Danish signatures, 20-12-52, NR arkiv, Copenhagen, file 6.B.2[1]) See also letter from the Secretary-General to the Danish Delegation to the Nordic Council. Frantz Wendt suggested to his Norwegian and Swedish counterparts that the successes of the Committee indicate it might be given more tasks. (Letter 23-3-54 to Erik Nord and Gustav Petrén, NR arkiv, Copenhagen, file 6.B.2c).

38. Interviews, Edberg, Oslo, 22 June 1967; Gormsen, Copenhagen, 25 May 1967.

39. Interview, Aminoff, Montreal, 24 October 1974.

40. Ernst B. Haas, "The Challenge of Regionalism," IO, XII, No. 4 (Autumn 1958), p. 451.

41. Edberg, "Osynliga gränser...," p. 199. Cf. NR arkiv, Copenhagen, 6.B.2.

42. Reports nr. 4 and nr. 5 were submitted to the Governments on 9 January 1953. The Nordic Council's first session was 12-22 February 1952.

> If the Council should find that it cannot venture to adopt any recommendation-- and there are of course the cautious--the calculated profit can become the opposite.

Edberg added that he had no clear feeling of the atmosphere. (Letter from Rolf Edberg to Hans Hedtoft, 30-12-52.) Also letter from Frantz Wendt to Hans Hedtoft, 3-1-53. NR arkiv, 6.B.2[1]. Cf. NR rek. 9/1953.

43. Edberg's statement to the first session of the Nordic Council, that there had been objections from "police sources" (NR, 1st session (1953), col. 198.) The phrase "crime market" (brottsmarknad) is found in the report of the Council's Legal nine-man committee, NR, 6th session (1958), p. 242. Also Interview, Edberg, Oslo, 16 June 1967.)

44. On military objections: "Doubts about free travel." The Norseman, May-June 1953, pp. 165-166; Ragnar Lassinantti of the criminal police in Norrbotten (northern Sweden, with a fifty-five mile border with Finland) argued that he did not fear criminals, but "a couple of thousand skogsgardister (forest wardens)" "who in a given situation would be prepared to act very violently against Swedish democracy" should not be permitted in. (Sveriges socialdemokratiska arbetarepartis 19:de Kongress, 2. - 7. juni 1953, Protokoll, pp. 135-136, in answer to Edberg.)

On provincial authorities: Göteborgs Posten (29 September 1956) reports that, "Even such a strongly Nordic minded man as the provincial governor of Malmöhus province [southern Sweden, near Denmark] turned down the elimination of passports, maintaining that there would be enormous risks (of spies)." (NR, arkiv, Copenhagen, 6.B.2c). The Provincial Governor was Arthur Thomsom, who told Edberg that he would take the matter to the Cabinet. The Provincial Governor of Västermanland, Per Conrad Jonsson, was also opposed (Interview, Edberg, Oslo, 16 June 1967.)

Sten Aminoff confirmed particularly the fear of spies. He himself thought the police could have bargained for more money for internal policing - but they did not. (Interview 24 October 1974, Montreal).

45. "Doubts about free travel," The Norseman, May-June, 1953.
The Aliens Commission objected to stage two being put through in Sweden by administrative directive, and requested that the matter be brought before the Riksdag. (SOU, 1953:4.)

46. Edberg maintained that there was opposition from the military, police, and aliens authorities in all three countries. (Interview, Oslo, 16 June 1967.)

47. Helge Seip, "Social and Economic Problems in Connection with the Nordic Labour Market," NU, 1968:9, p. 46. (Issue on "Nordic Economic and Social Cooperation.")

48. SOU, 1952:16, p. 17.

49. SOU, 1954:20, p. 13.

50. SOU, 1952:16, p. 20

51. SOU, 1956:45, p. 21.

52. NR, rek. 9/1953, points 5,6,7.

53. Letter from Erik Brofoss to the Foreign Ministry, 15 May 1953 (file 25 3/31). The Ministry of Trade's viewpoint did not always win out. The same letter advised against raising the permissible value of goods brought back by Norwegians from the prevailing 100 kroner to the Committee's suggested 350 kronor. Nevertheless the increase went through. See NR, 2nd session (1954), "Beretning fra den Nordiske parlementariske samferdsels komité m.m.," p. 566.

54. NR, 2nd session (1954), "Friere samferdsel mellom de nordiske land. Melding fra den danske, den norske og den svenske regjering," pp. 613-614.
The Nordic Council's Committee which reviewed the government's report decided to put the matter aside; its spokesman, Kaj Bundvad (also a member of the Communications Committee), called the matter "an internal Norwegian matter" and noted that permission to use an expired passport lessened inconvenience. (NR, 2nd session (1954), "Den socialpolitiske innstilling nr. 4" and p. 111). The Parliamentary Communications Committee repeated its own proposal in its Final Report, however (SOU, 1956:45, p. 46). The Final Report did not acknowledge that expired passports were permitted. Note that the Council of Europe also met its Waterloo on currency controls and decided to concentrate on passports, visas, customs, etc. (See Document 345, 1955).

55. Interview, Edberg, 16 June 1967.

56. SOU, 1952:4, p. 21; "Osynliga gränser," p. 200.

57. SOU, 1952:4, pp. 23-24.

58. AK, 27 April 1955, p. 100 (Edberg). The two-door system had been used at Øresund between Denmark and Sweden in the 1930s for travelers visiting for up to two weeks. (Hammar, op. cit., p. 223; Sveriges socialdemokratiska..., Protokoll, pp. 134-135.

59. SOU, 1956:45, p. 14.

60. Edberg, Öppna grindarna, p. 48.

61. Ingemar Dörfer, "System 37 Viggen: Science, Technology, and the Domestication of Glory", Public Policy XVII (1968) pp. 216-217.

62. SOU, 1952:4, p. 17.

63. Ibid., p. 23. Also Edberg, Öppna grindarna., p. 21.

64. SOU, 1952:4, p. 17.

65. Einar Løchen, "Mål och medel i nordiskt samarbete," NK, 1967, No. 1, pp. 3-4. Joseph S. Nye has pointed out that Bela Belassa's five levels of economic integration imply that the "higher" levels (for example, free flow of factors) succeed the "lower" levels (for example, a common market). Nye questions whether the order need hold, and this Scandinavian case supports his point. (See, "Comparative Regional Integration", IO, XXII, No. 4 (Autumn 1968), pp. 860-861.)

66. There were 60,000 non-Swedes in Sweden at the end of the war, of whom more than 60% were from Norway. Seip, op. cit., p. 46.

67. This applied to Danes, Finns, Icelandic citizens, Norwegians, Swedish speaking Estonians (Estlandssvenskarna) and was later extended to citizens and now stateless people from Estonia, Latvia and Lithuania. Edberg, Den öppna..., p. 7.

68. The Riksdag motion (AK, 238/1944) was initiated by Rolf Edberg and and others. The introduction to the Swedish Social Democrats' Postwar Program had two pages on Nordic economic cooperation, looking forward to aiding in reconstruction, to greater bargaining power through a common trade stance, to a Nordic labor market as a way of "evening out and limiting" the risk of unemployment. (Arbetarrörelsens efterkrigsprogram, Stockholm, 1946, pp. 65-66.)
    During the war there had been a renaissance of Nordic aspirations in Sweden. (Harald Runblom, "Nordens enhet i den svenska debatten under andra världskriget," seminar paper, University of Stockholm, Department of Political Science, Spring 1963.)

69. Nordisk tidskrift, XXI (1945).

70. The meeting of the Ministers of Social Affairs of the five Nordic countries (from Sweden, Gustav Möller, from Denmark, Hedtoft, from Norway, Oftedal) took place 10-12 September 1945. This account of it is from Berger Ulsaker, "Det Nordiske Arbeidsmarkedsutvalg," Arbeidsmarkedet, Utgitt av Arbeidsdirektoratet, September 1960, pp. 3-5, and an interview with Ekspedisjonssjef Ulsaker, Kommunal- og arbeidsdepartementet, Oslo. (Interview, Oslo, 3 July 1967. Ulsaker was one of the civil servants at that meeting.)

71. Ulsaker, Interview, Oslo, 3 July 1967. The matter was also discussed at the Nordic Foreign Ministers' meeting, 28 March 1946. ("Notat. 21.4.53," Norwegian Ministry of Foreign Affairs, Utenriksdepartementet, hereafter UD, File 25. 3/31.)

72. Foreningen Norden continued efforts for a more limited objective, organized labor exchanges, as in the prewar years. Edberg, Den öppna..., p. 9.

73. The Ministry of Municipal and Labor Affairs procrastinated in giving its opinion on the possibility of a labor market agreement, and

finally in February 1953 advised that the matter needed a new and time consuming study. ("Notat. 21.4.53," Oslo, UD, File 25, 3/21.)

74. Seip, op. cit., p. 46. This was specifically the fear of The Ministry of Trade in 1953. ("Notat. 28.8.53," Oslo, UD, File 25. 3/31.)
Figures from the Statistical Yearbook, United Nations, Prepared by the Statistical Office of the United Nations, Department of Economic Affairs, show the following comparison in unemployment figures:

Unemployment (%) 1945 1953*

	Source (Yearbook	Pages)	Year	Norway	Sweden	Denmark
	1948	84-5	1945	1.6	4.5	8.2
	"	"	1946	2.0	3.2	4.7
	"	"	1947	1.2	2.8	4.9
	"	"	1948	1.2	2.8	4.7
D&S	1949-50	90-1	1949	0.8	2.7	9.6
N	1954	59				
D&S	1951	80-1	1950	0.9	2.2	8.7
N	1954	59				
D&S	1952	51-2	1951	1.1	1.8	9.7
N	1954	59				
D&S	1953	51-2	1952	1.2	2.3	12.5
N	1954	59				
D&S	1954	58.9	1953	1.5	2.8	9.2

* There were no % figures given for Finland.

75. Edberg, Den öppna..., pp. 10-11.

76. Ulsaker, op. cit., p. 3; Stortingsproposisjon nr. 96 (1954).

77. "Notat. 21.4.53." Oslo, UD.

78. Ibid.

79. Anderson, op. cit., p. 119.

80. This is to assume that the Foreign Ministry's assessment was decisive. The Foreign Ministry's note is dated 21 April, and in June Sweden invited the others to discussions. In all probability Sweden was unofficially informed of the shift in Norwegian attitude. At the negotiations, a draft was discussed. Norway's representatives to the meeting, were, however, from the Ministry of Municipal and Labor Affairs and from the Ministry of Justice. They had reservations and suggested an "escape clause" for the possible difficulties in maintaining employment; the others found this unacceptable. Thereafter the Foreign Ministry pressed the first department to meet with several other departments so that the Nordic negotiations could be continued early in the fall. ("Notat. 28 August 1953"). There were, apparently, delays, because the further negotiations took place instead in January and March 1954, and the convention was finally signed 22 May 1954, to go into effect 1 July 1954. When the convention came up for ratification in the Storting, 28 May 1954, 12 members voted against it. (Seip, p. 40.)

There is also another kind of evidence against the argument that the abolition of the labor permit was a result of the difficulties of maintaining the system in the absence of passport control. There are other sets of countries which do not require passports for travel between them, but which simultaneously maintain a system of labor permits: e.g., France and Belgium.

81. It is the unclear what the operational meaning of this stipulation was - unless inserted as a possible future ground for withdrawal - since the Danish unemployment rate continued to be quite high: 1954 - 8.0%, 1955 - 9.7%, 1956 - 11.1%, 1957 - 10.2%, after which it declined, particularly in the 1960s. (UN Statistical Yearbook, 1966.)

82. St. prop. nr. 96 (1954). The committee, the Nordic Labor Market Committee (Nordisk Arbeidsmarkedsutvalg) was included upon Norwegian initiative. (Seip, op. cit., p. 50.)

83. NØS, 1957, p. 22; Seip, p. 46.

84. Sweden, – Number of foreigners on the labor rolls (arbetsanmälda) by nationality, in thousands

	1950	1953	1957	...1966
Finns	16.1	32.0	49.6	70.4
Danes	17.0	20.0	24.8	19.2
Norw.	12.6	12.6	12.4	12.9
Others	41.3	47.7	50.5	59.7
Sum	87.0	112.3	137.3	162.2
Nordic %	50.9%	57.4%	63.0%	63.0%

Source: Tomas Hammar, "Den svenska utlänningspolitiken," in Schwartz, op. cit., p. 15 (excerpts of Table 15). Nordic percents calculated by this writer; percent for 1966 calculated by Hammar. Note that the number of Norwegian workers in Sweden before and after agreement of 1954 is practically static.

85. See NR, 1958, "Berättelse från Nordiska arbedsmarknadsutskott," Sak C8, pp. 1068-1070. This was the first report of the Committee to the Nordic Council; reports followed most years thereafter.

86. See, NR, 1960, Sak C2, pp. 328-329.

87. Seip, p. 49.

88. Rolf Edberg, "Folkliga kontakter i Norden," Norden i världen, (Speeches at Foreningen Norden's second congress, Stockholm 1959), (Stockholm: Rabén & Sjögren, 1960), p. 75.

89. Richard E. Neustadt, Alliance Politics (New York: Columbia University Press, 1970).

90. The possibilities and limitations of the Scandinavian model of reform in this area is revealed by a comparison with the efforts of the Council of Europe. Rolf Edberg himself was chairman of the relevant subcommittee of the C of E's Assembly from 1951-1953;

his subcommittee attempted to use the Scandinavian methods. One major problem was its lack of authority to gather evidence or call on experts. It tried to use evidence from Scandinavia and from the English-Irish passport union as proxies. The "reasonable proportion" argument was tried, as was the small-steps-to-the-goal tactic. The subcommittee proposed the elimination of passports in favor of identity cards (a even smaller step then the first one within Scandinavia).

Nevertheless the Council of Ministers (governmental representatives) of the CofE rejected the proposals in 1955, saying that the Scandinavian data were "too rosy" to be useful (i.e. implying that the homogeneity of the area made analogies from it irrelevant). The Assembly angrily asked the Ministers for a discussion of the proposals "from the point of view of their general desirability on political grounds". Only after a political mandate had been obtained--particularly through efforts within the French and German legislatures, pressuring their own governments-- and Ministers set up a committee of civil servants headed by a Minister and with a specific mandate for particular, defined reforms, was there progress. That is to say, the principles were decided on Ministerial level.

As of 1971, nine of the countries (and none of the Scandinavian countries) had ratified the European Convention on Movement of Persons which permits visits in Member countries for up to three months without a passport but with a specified identity card. Once this Convention had been achieved, the Ministers reduced the meetings of the special committee, and did not expand its mandate; all investigations, reports, proposals remained at the descretion of the Governments.
(Sources: "European Agreement on regulations governing the movement of persons between member states of the Council of Europe", European Treaty Series, Nr. 25, Council of Europe, Consultative Assembly, Documents, Strasbourg. Quotations: Doc. 346 (18-5-55, 7th Ordinary Session). Communication from the Committee of Ministers on the simplification of frontier formalities, Doc. 436. See also Barbara G. Haskel, "The Scandinavian Option: Opportunities and Opportunity Costs in Postwar Scandinavian Foreign Policies", Unpublished Ph.D. dissertation, Harvard University, 1972, pp. 210-218 and footnotes 89-102.)

It was Ernst Haas who first suggested the model of a "transnational pressure group", which is the way he characterized the Assembly of the Council of Europe. It gives impetus to Ministers in areas "where the governments are not seriously divided over the merits of the issues at stake". Consensus Formation in the Council of Europe (London: Stevens and Sons Limited, 1960) pp. 69-70. Haas thus disagrees with A.H. Robertson (The Council of Europe. Its Structure, Functions, and Achievements. (London: Stevens and Sons Limited, 1961) who argued that the Council's conventions could have been drafted without the Assembly. Haas maintains that although this is possible, they would not have been drafted without Assembly prodding. (p. 21)

Chapter Five

The Costing Perspective

1. Amitai Etzioni, "European Unification. A Strategy of Change", in IPC, pp. 188-193. (Reprinted from WP, XVI (October, 1963), pp. 32-51); Karl Deutsch, excerpt from Political Community in the North Atlantic Area, in IPC, pp. 1-91.
2. NR, 2nd session, 1953, p. 289. (The Norwegian was Stortingsmann Finn Moe.)
3. On the formation and early experience of the Scandinavian Airlines System (SAS) see: Robert A. Nelson, "Scandinavian Airlines System: Cooperation in the Air." Journal of Air Law and Commerce, XX (1963), pp. 178-196; Nils Horney, "Så föddes SAS", Industria, (1966), pp. 68-112; Thomas S. Falck, Jr., "Hvordan SAS ble til", SAS informationsmöte for skandinavisk press i Oslo, den 18-19 oktober 1966 (mimeographed).

BIBLIOGRAPHY

PRIMARY SOURCES

Unpublished

"Aktuell debatt", Norsk Rikskringkasting, 28 October 1966. (Radio program on the February 19, 1949 Norwegian Labor Party Congress discussion on security problems. Participants: Gerhardsen, Lange, Wyller, Åmlid.)

Press-Museet, Stockholm.

Nordisk råds arkiv, Copenhagen (File 6.B.2).

Utenriksdepartementet. Det faelles nordiske udvalg for økonomisk samarbejde. "Memorandum concerning co-operation between the northern countries", November 1948 (mimeo, 2 pp.).

Utenriksdepartementet. "Felles skandinavisk arbeidsmarked". P. Jebsen. 21 April 1953. (File 25 3/31.)

Utenriksdepartementet. "Notat. Det Felles Nordiske Utvalg for Økonomisk Samarbeid. Rapport til Det Nordiske Råd." P. Jebsen, 27 April 1953. (File 25 3/31.)

Utenriksdepartementet. "Det Nordiske Råd. Tilråding angående friere samferdsel mellom de nordiske folk." Erik Brofoss, 15 May 1953. (File 25 3/31.)

Utenriksdepartementet. "Felles nordisk arbeidskraftmarked." Kjell Christiansen, 28 August 1953. (File 25 3/31.)

Utenriksdepartementet. Det Felles Nordiske utvalg for Økonomisk Samarbeid, "Notat", Kjell Christiansen, 24 April 1954. (File 25 3/31.)

Utenriksdepartementet. "Notat. Organiseringen av det nordiske økonomiske samarbeid." 29 October 1954.

Published

Arbetarrörelsens efterkrigsprogram [published by the Swedish Social Democratic Party and L.O.], Stockholm 1946.

Colbjørnsen, Ole og Axel Somme. En norsk 3-årsplan. Veien frem til en socialistisk planøkonomi i Norge. Oslo: Det Norske Arbeiderpartis forlag, 1933.

Council of Europe, Consultative Assembly, Documents, Strasbourg.

Det Norske Arbeiderparti Protokoll over forhandlingene på det 33. ordinaere landsmøte 17.-20. februar 1949 i Oslo.

"European Agreement on regulations governing the movement of persons between member states of the Council of Europe." European Treaty Series, Nr. 25.

European Recovery Program. A Report on Recovery Progress and United States Aid, ECA, February 1949.

European Recovery Program. Second Report of the Organization for European Economic Cooperation. Paris: February 1950.

Folketingstidende. Folketingets forhandlinger. (1953 on)

Forhandlinger ved Det Nordiske Nasjonaløkonomiske Møte i Oslo den 19.-21. juni 1952.

Forhandlinger vid XV Nordisk nationalekonomiska mötet i Helsingfors 2.-21. juni 1955.

(Official Reports on the Scandinavian Common Market Negotiations. Chronologically.)

"Nordisk Økonomisk Samarbeid. Foreløpig rapport til regjeringene i Danmark, Island, Norge og Sverige fra Det faelles nordiske utvalg for økonomisk samarbeid," 3 januar 1950, Oslo, Appendix 2 to Stortingsmelding nr. 87, 1954, Stort.1954.

"Beretning fra Det faelles nordisk udvalg for økonomisk samarbejde, afgivet på udvalgets møde i Oslo den 16.-17. januar 1953." Nordisk råd, 1st session (February 1953), Appendix 3, pp. 799-802.

Et faelles nordisk marked, Rapport til regeringerne i Danmark, Island, Norge, og Sverige fra Det Faelles Nordiske Udvalg for Økonomisk Samarbejde. Copenhagen: J.H. Schultz A/S, [March] 1954.

Stortingsmelding nr. 87 (1954), "Om økonomisk samarbeid mellom de nordiske lande." (Tilråding fra UD 18. juni 1954 and Appendix, "Utredning om et naermere økonomisk samarbeid i Norden, utarbeidet av Handelsdepartementet i samarbeid med de interesserte departementer".)

Nordisk Samhandel, Copenhagen: Nielsen & Lydiche, June 1955.

Nordic Economic Cooperation, Report by the Nordic Economic Cooperation Committee, General Part, Copenhagen, 1958. (Translation of the first part of the five part report, Nordisk Økonomisk Samarbeid, Rapport fra det Nordiske Økonomiske Samarbeidsutvalg, Oslo, 1957.) (Also printed as Statens offentliga utredningar 1957:95 in Sweden.)

Utvidet Nordisk Økonomisk Samarbejde, Rapport fra det Nordiske embedsmandsudvalg, Copenhagen, July 1969 (99 pp. mimeographed).

Nordisk råd, 1953-1969.

Regjeringen og Hjemmefronten. Aktstykker utgitt av Stortinget. Oslo: Aschehoug, 1948.

Riksdagens protokoll (Andra kammaren).

Rigsdagstidende. Folketingets forhandlinger. (to 1953).

Statens offentliga utredningar (SOU), Stockholm. "Nordisk passfrihet. (Del. 1 Passfriheten for nordbor)." 1952, No. 4.

Statens offentliga utredningar (SOU). "Nordisk passfrihet. (Del. 2. Fullständig passfrihet för nordbor samt upphävande av bestämmelserna om arbets- och uppenhållstillstånd för nordbor vid vistelse i annat nordiskt land." 1953, No. 4.

Statens offentliga utredningar (SOU). "Lättnader i fråga om tullbehandling m.m. av motorfordon i trafiken mellan de nordiska länderna." 1953, No. 5.

Statens offentliga utredningar (SOU). "Nordisk passfrihet. (Del. 3 upphävande av all passkontroll vid gränserna mellan de nordiska länderna)." 1954, No. 7.

Statens offentliga utredningar (SOU). "Portosatser i den internordiska brevväkslingen." 1954, No. 20.

Statens offentliga utredningar (SOU). "Internordiska korsbandstaxor." 1955, Nos. 3-4.

Statens offentliga utredningar (SOU). "Nordiska Vägtrafikbestämmelser m.m." 1955, No. 33.

Statens offentliga utredningar (SOU). "Slutbetänkande." 1956, No. 45.

"Stortingets behandling av innstilling fra Spesialkomiteen for saerlige utenrikspolitiske spørsmål og beredskapssaker angående utenriks- og sikkerhetspolitikken (inst. S. nr. 43 for 1949)," Stortingstidende, Dokument nr. 4 (1963-64). (Minutes of the closed meeting of the Storting 3 March 1949.)

Stortingstidende.

Sveriges socialdemokratiska arbetarpartis 19:de kongress i Stockholm, 2.-7. juni 1952, Protokoll.

The Royal Ministry of Foreign Affairs, Documents on Swedish Foreign Policy. Stockholm, annually since 1951. (Translation of Utrikesfrågor, also annual.)

Udenrigsministeriet, Dansk sikkerhedspolitik 1948-1966. 3 vols. Copenhagen: 1968. (Vol. 1. Fremstilling (Narrative); Vol. II, Bilag (Appendices)).

United Nations, Statistical Yearbook. Prepared by the Statistical Office of the United Nations, Department of Economic Affairs, 1967.

Viktige storpolitiske dokumenter 1945-50. (Verdenspolitikken dokumenter, nr. 6). Utgitt av Chr. Michelsens Institutt for Videnskap og Åndsfrihet, Bergen, Norway, 1950.

Newspapers and Periodicals

Aftenposten (Oslo) (independent Conservative).

The American-Scandinavian Review.

Arbeiderbladet (Oslo) (Labor)

Arbejderen. Meddelseblad for de Samvirkende fagforbund i Danmark.

Dagens Nyheter (Stockholm) (Liberal).

Fackföreningsrörelse, Landsorganisasionen i Sverige (1947-1959).

Fri Fagbevegelse, Landsorganisasjonen i Norge (1947-1959).

Industria (The Federation of Industries and The Export Association of Sweden.)

The New York Times.

Nordisk Kontakt. Parlamentarisk orientering. Stockholm.

Norges Industri, Organ of the Norwegian Federation of Industries (Norges Industriforbund).

The Norseman.

The Norwegian Information Service, Washington, D.C. News of Norway.

Social Demokraten (Copenhagen) (Social Democratic).

Svenska Dagbladet (Stockholm) (Conservative).

Sweden Now. Stockholm: Industria-Press, Näringslivets Förlags AB established by the Swedish Employers' Confederation, the General Exports Association of Sweden, and the Federation of Swedish Industries.

Utrikespolitiska Institutets Kalendarium. 1947, 1948, 1949. Edited by Lennart Hirschfeldt in cooperation with Chr. Michelsens Institutt, Bergen. Stockholm.

Interviews

Danish

Handelsminister Tyge Dahlgaard, Ministry of Trade, Copenhagen, 22 May 1967.

Professor Troels Fink, Copenhagen, 24 July 1973.

Departementschef Paul Gersmann, Department of Customs and Sales Taxes, Copenhagen, 22 May 1967.

Konsulent Axel Gormsen, Ministry of Trade, Copenhagen, 25 May 1967.

Departementschef Erik Ib Schmitt, Ministry of Finance, Copenhagen, 18 May 1967.

Generalsekretær Frantz Wendt, Nordisk råd, Copenhagen, 23 May 1967.

Norwegian

Direktør Erik Brofoss, The Bank of Norway, Oslo, 20 June 1967. (Brofoss I); Montreal, 23 October 1973 (Brofoss II).

Stortingsmann (and former Prime Minister) Einar Gerhardsen, The Storting, Oslo, 22 June 1967.

Direktør Knut Getz-Wold, The Bank of Norway, Oslo, 21 June 1967. (Getz-Wold I); Oslo, 13 August 1973 (Getz-Wold II).

Ekspedisjonssjef Odd Gøthe, Ministry of Industry, Oslo, 26 June 1967, and 28 June 1967.

Ambassadør Arne Gunneng, The Royal Norwegian Embassy, Washington, D.C., 9 September 1968.

Utredningssjef Per Kleppe, Oslo, 3 August 1973.

Stortingsmann (and former Foreign Minister) Halvard M. Lange, New York, 3 November 1966 (Lange I); Oslo, 21 June 1967, (Lange II).

Stortingsmann Jon Leirfall, The Storting, Oslo, 6 July 1967.

Generalsekretaer Håkon Lie, The Norwegian Labor Party, 6 July 1967.

Stortingsmann Finn Moe, The Storting, Oslo, 16 June 1967.

Direktør Rolf Roem-Nielsen, The Norwegian Federation of Industries, Oslo, 30 June 1967.

Ambassadør Arne Skaug, The Foreign Office, Oslo, 5 July 1967.

Professor Magne Skodvin, The University of Oslo, Oslo, 8 July 1973, 14 August 1973.

Handelsråd Olav Solli, The Royal Norwegian Embassy, Washington, D.C., 6 September, 1968.

Ekspedisjonssjef Tor Stokke, The Ministry of Trade, Oslo, 16 June 1967.

Ekspedisjonssjef Berger Ulsaker, Municipal and Labor Department, Oslo, 3 July 1967.

Swedish

Generalkonsulent Sten Aminoff, The Royal Consulate of Sweden, Montreal, 24 October 1974.

Ambassadör Hugo de Besche, The Royal Swedish Embassy, Washington, D.C., 9 September 1968.

Förste kammarens talman, Ambassadör Erik Bohemann, The Riksdag, Stockholm, 30 May 1967.

Landshövding Gustav Cederwall, Västerås, 13 June 1967.

Ambassadör Rolf Edberg, The Royal Swedish Embassy, Oslo, 16 June 1967 and 22 June 1967.

Departementsråd Åke Englund, The Ministry of Trade, Stockholm, 2 June 1967.

Riksdagsman Nils Kellgren, The Riksdag, Stockholm, 13 June 1967.

Professor Karin Kock, Stockholm, 31 May 1967.

Riksdagsman, Professor Bertil Ohlin, The Riksdag, Stockholm, 30 May 1967.

Professor Ingvar Svennilson, Stockholm, June 1967.

SECONDARY SOURCES

Unpublished

Aareskjold, Helen. "Norge og Sverige i FN." Unpublished M.A. thesis, Stockholm, University of Stockholm, 1964 (mimeographed).

Einhorn, Eric Stanley. "Security Policy and Internal Politics in a Small State: The Case of Denmark, 1945-1960". Harvard University, PhD thesis, 1971.

Falck, Thomas S. Jr. "Hvordan SAS ble til." SAS informationsmøte for skandinavisk press i Oslo, den 18.-19. oktober 1966 (mimeographed).

Haskel, Barbara G. "The Attempt to Create a Scandinavian Defense Pact as Reflected in the Public Statements of the Swedish, Norwegian, and Danish Members of Government During 1948-1949." Stockholm, mimeographed, 70 pps., 1963.

Haskel, Barbara G. "Regional Efforts: A View from the North." Paper prepared for The Conference on Regional Integration, Madison, Wisconsin, April 1969.

Johnsson, Per-Olaf. "The Projected Scandinavian Customs Union, 1945-1959." Ph.D. dissertation, Florida State University, 1964.

Lange, Christian. "Nöytralitet eller kollektiv sikkerhet. Den norske Arbeiderparti og Folkeforbundet 1935-36." Oslo: University of Oslo, Magister thesis, 1958, (typed).

Lange, Christian. "Nordiska ministermöter 1945-1965. Regeringssamarbetet som en integrerande faktor i Norden." Stockholm, Stockholm University, 1965 (mimeographed).

Larsson, Kerstin. "Beslutsformerna kring en samnordisk bistandsinsats i Tanganyika. Seminar paper. Stockholm: University of Stockholm, 1965 (mimeographed).

Lie, Ingeborg. "Forhandlingene om Nordisk Tollunion/Nordisk Fellesmarked 1954-1956", Hovedfagsoppgave i historie våren 1973 i Oslo.

Lijphart, Arend. "Cultural Diversity and Theories of Political Integration." Prepared for Presentation at the Colloquium on "Integration and Disintegration in the Canadian Political System", organized by The Canadian Political Science Association and the Société Canadienne de Science Politique at Laval University, Québec City, October 17-18, 1970.

Nielsson, Gunnar Preben. "Denmark and European Integration: a Small Country at the Crossroads." Ph.D. dissertation, The University of California at Los Angeles, 1966.

Runblom, Harald. "Nordens enhet i den svenska debatten under andra världskriget." Seminar paper, University of Stochholm, Department of Political Science, Spring 1963.

Sandhaug, Sverre. "Forsvarspolitisk strid i D.N.A." History Faculty, University of Oslo, spring 1973, (mimeographed).

Schive, Jens Petter Sooth. "Sovjetunionens stilling til planer på et nordisk forsvarsforbund 1949." Stockholm: Institutionen for statskunskap, December 1961, (mimeographed).

Selleck, Roberta G. "The Language Issue in Finnish Political Discussion: 1809-1863." Ph.D. dissertation, Radcliffe College, Harvard University, 1961

Steinbruner, John D. "The Mind and Milieu of Policy-Makers: A Case Study of the MLF." Ph.D. dissertation, Massachusetts Institute of Technology, 1968.

Thomas, David J. "Swedish Social Democracy 1932-1960: A Study of Ideology." Ph.D. dissertation, Harvard University, November 1967.

Torgersen, Ulf. "Landsmøtet i norsk partistruktur 1884-1940." Oslo: Institutt for samfunnsforskning, 1966, (mimeographed), 109 pp.

Westerholm, Birgitte, "Socialdemokratiet og Atlantpagten. En analyse av de faktorer, der øvede indflydelse på Socialdemokratiets stillingtagen til Danmarks optagelse i Atlantpagten i 1949", Århus Universitet, Institut for Statskundskab, 1973.

Published

Acheson, Dean. Present at the Creation. My Years in the State Department. New York: Norton, 1969.

Alderson, Wroe. "Planning," in Policies, Decisions, and Organization. Edited by Fremont J. Lyden et al. New York: Appleton-Century-Croft, 1969, pp. 185-200.

Allison, Graham T. "Conceptual Models and the Cuban Missile Crisis." The American Political Science Review, LXIII (September 1969), pp. 689-718.

Allison, Graham T. Essence of Decision. Explaining the Cuban Missile Crisis. Boston: Little, Brown and Co. 1971.

Alstad, Bjørn (Ed.). Norske meninger 1. Norge, nordmenn og verden. Oslo, Pax, 1969.

Åmlid, Johanne. Ut av kurs. Oslo: Pax Forlag, 1966.

Anderson, Gidske. "Halvard Lange forlater Akershus-benken." Arbeiderbladet, 5 July 1969.

Anderson, Stanley, V. The Nordic Council, A Study in Scandinavian Regionalism. Seattle and London: The University of Washington Press, 1967.

Andersson, Arne F. 50 år i arbete för Norden. Foreningarna för nordiskt samarbete. Stockholm: Foreningen Norden, 1969.

Andersson, Ingvar. A History of Sweden. (Translated from the Swedish by Carolyn Hannay.) Stockholm: Natur och Kultur, London: Weidenfeld and Nicolson, 1955.

Andrén, Nils. "Sverige i 1955." Nordisk tidsskrift, XXXII (1956).

Andrén, Nils. "Nordic Integration-Aspects and Problems." Cooperation and Conflict, 1967, pp. 1-25.

Andrén, Nils. "A Note on a Note." Cooperation and Conflict, 1967, Nos. 3-4, pp. 235-237.

Andrén, Nils. "On Nordic Similarities and Differences." (Review of Herlitz, Elements.) Cooperation and Conflict, 1969, No. 4, pp. 309-311.

Andrén, Nils and Åke Landqvist. Svensk utrikespolitik efter 1945. Stockholm: Almqvist & Wiksell, 1965.

Anton, Thomas J. "Policy-Making and Political Culture in Sweden." Scandinavian Political Studies, IV (1969), pp. 88-102.

Arndt, H.J. The Economic Lessons of the Nineteen Thirties. (The Royal Institute of International Affairs.) Oxford: Oxford University Press, 1944.

Aukrust, Odd. Norges ekonomi etter krigen. The Norwegian Postwar Economy. Oslo: Statistisk Sentralbyrå, 1965.

Baldwin, David. "Foreign Aid, Intervention and Influence." World Politics, XXI, No. 3 (April 1969), pp. 429-432.

Banfield, Edward C. The Moral Basis of a Backward Society, Glencoe: Free Press, 1958.

Banfield, Edward C. and Martin Meyerson, Politics, Planning, and the Public Interest, Glencoe: Free Press, 1955.

Barclay, G. St. J. "Background to EFTA: An Episode in Anglo-Scandinavian Relations." The Australian Journal of Politics and History, XI, No. 2 (August 1964), pp. 185-197.

Bauer, Raymond A. "The Study of Policy Formation: An Introduction." The Study of Policy Formation. Edited by Raymond A. Bauer and Kenneth J. Gergen. New York: Free Press, 1968.

Benum, Edgeir, Maktsentra og opposisjon. Spaniasaken i Norge 1946 og 1947. Oslo: Universitetsforlaget, 1969.

Bergqvist, Mats, Sverige och EEC. En statsvetenskaplig studie av fyra åsiktsriktningars syn på svensk marknadspolitik 1961-1962. (Lund: Political Studies) Stockholm: P.A. Norstedt & Soner-forlag, 1970.

Bergqvist, Mats. "Sweden and the EEC: A Study of Four Schools of Thought and their Views on Swedish Common Market Policy in 1961-1962". Cooperation and Conflict ,VI, No. 1 (1971), pp. 39-56.

Beugel, Ernst van der. From Marshall Aid to Atlantic Partnership, European Integration as a Concern of American Foreign Policy. Amsterdam: Elsevier Publishing Co., 1966.

Beukel, Erik. Socialdemokratiet og stationeringsproblemet 1952-53. En sikkerhedspolitisk beslutning. Odense, Odense University Press, (Odense University Studies in History and Social Science 15) 1974.

Bjerve, P.J. Planning in Norway, 1947-1957 (Contributions to Economic Analysis, 16). Amsterdam: 1959.

Bjøl, Erling. "Foreign Policy-making in Denmark." Cooperation and Conflict, 1966, pp. 1-17.

Board, Joseph B.Jr. "Legal Culture and the Environmental Protection, Issue: The Swedish Experience", Albany Law Review 37:4 (1973) pp. 603-631.

Boulding, Kenneth. The Image. Ann Arbor, Michigan: University of Michigan, Press, 1956.

Bourneuf, Alice. Norway, The Planned Revival. Cambridge, Mass.: Harvard University Press, 1958.

Brecher, Michael, Blema Steinberg, and Janice Stein. "A Framework for Research on Foreign Policy Behavior." Journal of Conflict Resolution, XIII (March 1969), pp. 75-101.

Brenner, Hans. Småstat mellan stormagter. Beslutningen om mineudlaegning, augusti 1914. Århus, Munksgaard, (Dansk udenrigspolitisk institutets skrifter 5) 19

Britten-Austin, Paul. On Being Swedish. Reflections Towards a Better Understanding of the Swedish Character. London: Secker and Warburg, 1968.

Brodin, Katarina, Christian Lange, and Kjell Goldmann. "The Policy of Neutrality: Official Doctrines of Finland and Sweden." Cooperation and Conflict, 1968, No. 1, pp. 18-51.

Brox, Ottar. Hva skjer i Nord-Norge? En studie i norsk utkantspolitikk. Oslo: Pax Forlag, 1966.

Brundtland, Arne Olav. "Hvorfor ikke skandinavisk forsvarsforbund?" Internasjonal Politikk 1964, No. 3, pp. 132-150.

Brundtland, Arne Olav. "Nordic Balance". Cooperation and Conflict, 1966, No. 2, pp. 30-63.

Buchanan, James M. Cost and Choice. An Inquiry in Economic Theory. Chicago: Markham, 1970.

Bull, Edvard. Arbeiderklassen i Norsk Historie. Oslo: Tiden Norsk Forlag, 1948.

Bull, Edvard. "The Labor Movement in Scandinavia." in Scandinavia Past and Present, Vol. II. Odense, Denmark: 1959, pp. 853-863.

Bull, Trygve. Mot Dag og Erling Falk. Oslo: Cappelen, 3rd revised edition, 1968.

Burgess, Philip M. Elite Images and Foreign Policy Outcomes. A Study of Norway. Columbus, Ohio: The Ohio State University Press, 1968.

Carlson, Bo. Trade Unions in Sweden. Stockholm: Tiden, 1969.

Christensen, Chr.A.R. "Norge i 1945". Nordisk Tidskrift, 1946, pp. 60-74.

Christophersen, Jens A. "The Making of Foreign Policy in Norway." Cooperation and Conflict, 1968, pp. 52-74. (Translated from "Avgjørelsesprosessen i norsk utenrikspolitikk," Internasjonal politikk, 1968, No. 7, pp. 662-700.)

Clark, P.B. and J.Q. Wilson. "'Incentive Systems': A Theory of Organization". Administrative Science Quarterly 6, (1961) pp. 129-166.

Claude, Inis L. Power and International Relations.New York: Random House, 1962.

Connery, Donald S. The Scandinavians. New York: Simon and Schuster, 1966.

Coplin, William D. Introduction to International Politics. A Theoretical Overview. Chicago: Markham, 1971, second edition 1974.

"Dagens namn" [Rolf Edberg]. Dagens Nyheter, 6 September 1966.

Dahlgaard, Bertel. Kamp og Samarbejde. Copenhagen: 1968.

Danielsen, Rolf. "Samlingspartiet og Unionen." Historisk tidskrift, Vol. 41, No. 4 (1962) (with English summary).

Dau, Mary. Danmark og Sovjetunionen 1944-1949 (Dansk udenrigspolitisk institutets skrifter 2), Århus, Munksgaard, 1969.

Den Danske Historiske Forening ved Henry Brunn. Dansk Historisk Bibliografi, 1913-1942. vol. 1. Copenhagen: Rosenkilde og Bagger, 1966.

Derry, T.K. A History of Modern Norway 1814-1972. Oxford, Clarendon Press, 1973.

Det Norske Studentersamfund gjennom 150 år, 1813-2. oktober 1963. Oslo: Aschehoug, 1963.

Deutsch, Karl W. Nationalism and Social Communication: An Inquiry into the Foundations of Nationality (1st edition), Cambridge, Mass.: MIT Press, New York, John Wiley, 1953.

Deutsch, Karl W. "Communication Theory and Political Integration". The Integration of Political Communities, Philip E. Jacob and James V. Toscano (eds.), Philadelphia: Lippincott, 1964.

Dexter, Lewis A. "Analogies for Interpreting and Studying Congress." The Sociology and Politics of Congress. Chicago: Rand McNally, 1969.

Diebold, William Jr. Trade and Payments in Western Europe. A Study in Economic Cooperation 1947-1951. New York: Harper & Row, 1952.

"Doubts about free travel." The Norseman, May-June 1953.

Dörfer, Ingemar. "Stalin's nordiska balans." Internasjonal Politikk, 1965, No. 2, pp. 132-150.

Dörfer, Ingemar. "System 37 Viggen: Science, Technology and the Domestication of Glory." Public Policy, XVII (1968).

Dörfer, Ingemar. System 37 Viggen: Arms, Technology, and the Domestication of Glory. Oslo: Universitetsforlaget, 1973.

Eckstein, Harry. Division and Cohesion in Democracy: a Study of Norway. Princeton, N.J.: Princeton University Press, 1966.

Edberg, Rolf. I morgon, Norden. Stockholm: 1944.

Edberg, Rolf. Öppna grindarna! Stockholm: KF:s forlag, 1952.

Edberg, Rolf. Den öppna nordisk arbetsmarknaden. Stockholm: Foreningen Norden, 1954.

Edberg, Rolf. "Osynliga gränser i Norden." Nordisk tidskrift, (1954), pp. 197-207.

Edberg, Rolf. "Folkliga kontakter i Norden." Norden i världen. (Speeches at Foreningen Norden's second congress, Stockholm (1959). Stockholm, Rabén & Sjögren, 1960, pp. 72-89.

Einhorn, Eric S. "The Reluctant Ally: Danish Security Policy 1945-49", Journal of Contemporary History, 10:3 (July 1975) pp. 493-512.

Einhorn, Eric S. National Security and Domestic Politics in Post-War Denmark. Some Principal Issues, 1945-1961. Odense (Denmark): Odense University Press, 1975.

Elster, Torolf. "Norges utenrikspolitiske stilling." Økonomi og Politik (Copenhagen), XXV, Nos. 2-3 (1951), pp. 120-143.

Elvander, Nils. "Fran liberal skandivanism till konservativ nationalism i Sverige." Scandia, XXVII, No. 2 (1961) pp. 366-386.

Elvander, Nils. Intresseorganisationerna i dagens Sverige, Lund, Sweden: C.W.K. Gleerup Bokförlag, 2nd revised edition, 1972.

Enckell, R. "Nordic Cooperation at the United Nations". Nordisk udredningsserie, 1965, No. 9, pp. 40-47.

Eriksen, Knut. "Debatten om sikkerhetspolitikken i DNA 1948 og 1949." Utdrag. Norge og Bevinplanen. in Etterkrigshistorie 2. Et alliert Norge. Emner fra norsk historie etter 1945. Oslo: Universitetsforlaget, 1971, pp. 114-120.

Eriksen, Knut. DNA og NATO. En redegjørelse for debatten og vedtakene i Det norske Arbeiderparti 1948-49. Oslo: Gyldendal Norsk Forlag, 1972.

Eriksen, Knut Einar and Geir Lundestad (eds.). Norsk utenrikspolitikk, (Kilder til moderne historie: I). Oslo: Universitetsforlaget, 1972.

Erlander, Tage. "Muligheder og Begraensninger i Nordisk Politik." Idé og Arbejde. En bog til Hans Hedtoft på 50-årsdagen, Copenhagen: Forlaget Fremad, 1953, pp. 11-15.

Erlander, Tage. 1940-1949. Stockholm: Tidens forlag, 1973.

Etzioni, Amitai. "European Unification. A Strategy of Change." In International Political Communities: An Anthology. Garden City, N.Y.: Anchor Books. 1966. (Reprinted from World Politics, XVI (October 1963)), pp. 32-61.

Etzioni, Amitai. Political Unification: A Comparative Study of Leaders and Forces. New York: Holt, Rinehart and Winston, 1965.

Faaland, Just. "Economic Policy in Norway, 1949-1961", in Economic Policy in Our Time. Edited by E.H. Kirschen, II. New York: Rand McNally, 1964, pp. 155-224.

Feis, Herbert. From Trust to Terror. The Onset of the Cold War, 1945-1950. New York: W.W. Norton, 1970.

Fink, Troels. Otte foredrag om Danmarks krise 1863-64. Århus: Universitetsforlaget i Århus, 1964.

Forsmann, Lennart. "Norges hållning 1949." Dagens Nyheter. 28 Oktober 1966.

Fox, William T.R. "American Foreign Policy and the Western European Rimlands." American Academy of Political Science. XXII, No. 4 (1948), pp. 431-438.

Frankel, Charles. "Being In and Being Out." The Public Interest, No. 17 (Fall 1969), pp. 44-59.

Froelich, N., J.A. Oppenheimer, and Oran R. Young. Political Leadership and Collective Goods. Princeton: Princeton University Press, 1971.

Fulcher, James. "Class Conflict in Sweden", Sociology 7:1 (January 1973).

Gabrielsen, Bjørn. "Einar Gerhardsen 70 år." Socialistisk Perspektiv (utgitt av Det norske arbeiderparti.) IV, No. 2 (1967).

Gabrielsen, Bjørn. "Harding i Hovedstaden." [Interview with Professor Magne Skodvin]. Arbeiderbladet, 25 April 1970.

Gerhardsen, Einar. Fellesskap i krig og fred, Erindringer 1940-45. Oslo: Tiden Norsk Forlag, 1970.

Gerhardsen, Einar. Samarbeid og strid, Erindringer 1945-55. Oslo: Tiden Norsk Forlag, 1971.

Gerhardsen, Rolf. Einar Gerhardsen som en bror ser ham. Oslo: Tiden Norsk Forlag, 1969.

Getz-World, Knut. "Økonomisk samarbeid i Norden." Samtiden, Vol. 64, No. 2 (1956), pp. 88-102.

Goldmann, Kjell and Christian Lange. "Nordisk Sakerhetspolitik i 1949-1965-197?." Strategisk Bulletin No. 2-3 (April 1966).

Greve, Tim. Norway and Nato. Oslo: Oslo University Press, 1959.

Groennings, Sven. Scandinavia in Social Science Literature. An English Language Bibliography. Bloomington and London: Indiana University Press (for the International Affairs Center), 1970.

Gruchy, Allan E. Comparative Economic Systems. Competing Ways to Stability and Growth. Boston: Houghton Mifflin, 1966.

Haagerup, Niels Jørgen. De Forenede Nationer og Danmarks Sikkerhed. Aarhus: Universitetsforlaget, 1956.

Haas, Ernst B. "The Balance of Power: Prescription, Concept, or Propaganda?" World Politics, V, No. 4 (July 1953), pp. 442-477.

Haas, Ernst B. The Uniting of Europe: Political, Social, and Economic Forces 1950-1957. Stanford, California: Stanford University Press, 1958.

Haas, Ernst B. Consensus Formation in the Council of Europe. London: Stevens and Sons Ltd., 1960.

Haas, Ernst B. "Internation Integration: The European and the Universal Process ..." International Organization, XV (Summer 1961), pp. 361-392.

Haas, Ernst B. "Technocracy, Pluralism, and the New Europe." A New Europe? Edited by Stephen R. Graubard. Boston: Beacon Press, 1963, pp. 62-88.

Haas, Ernst B. Beyond the Nation-State. Functionalism and International Organization. Stanford, California: Stanford University Press, 1964.

Haas, Ernst B. "The Uniting of Europe and the Uniting of Lation America." The Journal of Common Market Studies, V (June 1967), pp. 315-343.

Haas, Ernst B. "Regional Integration." International Encyclopedia of the Social Sciences, VII, pp. 522-528.

Haas, Ernst B., and Philippe Schmitter. "Economics and Differential Patterns of Political Integration: Projections about Unity in Latin America." International Organization, XVIII (Autumn 1965), pp. 870-884.

Hadenius, Stig, Björn Molin, and Hans Weislander. Sverige efter 1900. En modern politisk historia. Stockholm: Aldus/Bonniers, 1969.

Haekkerup, Per. "Scandinavia's Peace-Keeping Forces for the United Nations," Foreign Affairs, Vol. 42 (July 1964), pp. 675-681.

Hammar, Thomas. Sverige åt svenskarna. Invandringspolitikk, utlänningskontroll och asylrätt 1900-1932. Stockholm: 1964.

Hammar, Thomas. "Den svenska utlänningspolitiken." Svenska minoriteter. Edited by David Schwartz. Stockholm: Aldus/Bonniers, 1968.

Hancock, M. Donald. Sweden: The Politics of Postindustrial Change. Hinsdale, Illinois: The Dreyden Press, 1972.

Hansen, H.C. "Socialdemokratiets formaend." Idé og Arbejde. En bog til Hans Hedtoft på 50-årsdågen. Copenhagen: Forlaget Fremad, 1953, pp. 24-32 [on Hedtoft, pp. 29-32].

Hansen, Roger D. "Regional Integration. Reflections on a Decade of Theoretical Efforts." World Politics, XXI, No. 2 (January 1969), pp. 242-271.

Hanssen, Halle Jørn. "Tilbakeblikk på debatten om nordisk tollunion i Nordisk Råd 1953-54." Internasjonal Politikk, 1968, pp. 57-72.

"Han ville fred, men han ville også frihet," [Eulogies at H. Lange's funeral]. Arbeiderbladet, 29 May 1970.

Harkjaer, Ole. Foreningen Norden. Organisation og virksomhed. Copenhagen: Foreningen Norden, 1966.

Harsanyi, John C. "Measurement of Social Power, Opportunity Costs, and the Theory of Two-Person Bargaining Games." Behavioral Science, VII (1962), pp. 67-80.

Harsanyi, John C. "Models for the Analysis of Balance of Power in Society." Logic, Methodology, and Philosophy of Science. Edited by Ernest Nagel et al. Stanford: Stanford University Press, 1962, pp. 442-462.

Harsanyi, John C. "Rational-Choice Models of Political Behavior vs. Functionalist and Conformist Theories." World Politics, XXI (July 1969), pp. 513-538.

Hartz, Louis. The Liberal Tradition in America: An Interpretation of American Political Thought Since the Revolution. New York: Harcourt, Brace and Co., 1955.

Hartz, Louis (ed.). The Founding of New Societies. Studies in the History of the United States, Latin America, South Africa, Canada, and Australia with contributions of Kenneth D. McRae, Richard M. Morse, Richard, N. Rosecrance, Leonard M. Thompson. New York: Harcourt, Brace and World, Inc., 1964.

Haskel, Barbara G. "Is there an Unseen Spider? A Note on 'Nordic Integration'. Cooperation and Conflict, (Stockholm) 1967, Nos. 3-4, pp. 229-234.

Haskel, Barbara G. "Regionalism without Politics?" Cooperation and Conflict 1968, No. 3, pp. 195-198. (A review of Anderson, The Nordic Council ...).

Haskel, Barbara G. "A Mirror for Princes? Elite Images." Cooperation and Conflict, 1968, No. 4, pp. 240-246.

Haskel, Barbara G. "External Events and Internal Appraisals. A Note on the Proposed Nordic Common Market." International Organization, XXIII, No. 4 (1969), pp. 960-964.

Haskel, Barbara G. "What is Innovation? Sweden's Liberals, Social Democrats, and Political Creativity." Political Studies, Vol. XX, No. 3, (September 1972), pp. 306-310.

Haskel, Barbara G. "The Scandinavian Option: Opportunities and Opportunity Costs in Postwar Scandinavian Foreign Policies." Harvard University, Ph.D. dissertation, 1972.

Haskel, Barbara G. "Disparities, Strategies and Opportunity Costs. The Example of Scandinavian Economic Market Negotiations." International Studies Quarterly, vol. 18, No. 1 (March 1974), pp. 3-30.

Haugen, Einar. Language Conflict and Language Planning: the Case of Modern Norwegian. Cambridge, Mass.: Harvard University Press, 1966.

Haugen, Einar (Editor-in-chief). "Historical Background of Norwegian," Norwegian-English Dictionary, Second American Printing with Addendum and Corrections. Oslo: Universitetsforlaget, and Madison, Wisconsin: The University of Wisconsin Press, 1967, pp. 20-34.

Heckscher, Gunnar. "Interest Groups in Sweden: Their Political Role." Interest Groups on Four Continents. Edited by Henry W. Ehrmann for the International Political Science Association. Pittsburgh: The University of Pittsburgh Press, 1958, pp. 154-172.

Heclo, Hugh. Modern Social Politics in Britain and Sweden. From Relief to Income Maintenance. New Haven and London: Yale University Press, 1974.

Helle, Egil. "Historikerne har vanskelig for å akseptere en enkel forklaring." [Interview with Einar Gerhardsen]. Arbeiderbladet, 28 June 1969.

Henningsen, Sven. "The Foreign Policy of Denmark." Foreign Policies in a World of Change. Edited by Joseph E. Black and Kenneth W. Thompson. New York: Harper and Row, 1963, pp. 89-114.

Herlitz, Nils. "Nordiskt samarbete inom offentlig rätt?" Festskrift tillägnad Hans Excellens Riksmarskalken Birger Ekeberg den 10 augusti 1950. Stockholm: Norstedt, 1950, pp. 267-279.

Herlitz, Nils. "Publicity of Documents in Sweden." Public Law. London: Stevens and Sons, 1958.

Herlitz, Nils. Elements of Nordic Public Law. Stockholm: Institutet for rättsvetenskaplig forskning, LIV, 1969.

Hirschfeldt, Lennart. Skandinavien och Atlantpakten. De skandinaviska alliansforhandlingarna. 1948-1949. (Världspolitikens dagsfrågor. Nos. 4-5), Stockholm: Utrikespolitiska Institutet, 1949.

Hirschman, Albert O. "The Principle of the Hiding Hand." The Public Interest, No. 6 (Winter 1967), pp. 10-23.

Hirschman, Albert O. Exit, Voice, and Loyalty. Cambridge, Mass.: Harvard University Press, 1970.

Hoffman, Paul. "Trade Restrictions-- and Peace." Proceedings of the Academy of Political Science, XXIII, No. 4 (January 1950), pp. 459-466.

Hoffmann, Stanley. Gulliver's Troubles. The Setting of American Foreign Policy. New York: McGraw Hill, 1968.

Hoffmann, Stanley. "The European Process at Atlantic Cross-purposes." Journal of Common Market Studies, II, No. 2 (February 1965), pp. 85-101.

Hoffmann, Stanley. "Obstinate or Obsolete? The Fate of the Nation-State and the Case of Western Europe." in International Regionalism. Edited by Joseph S. Nye Jr. Boston: Little, Brown, 1968, pp. 177-230.

Holst, Johan Jørgen. "Surprise, Signals and Reaction. The Attack on Norway, April 9, 1940." Cooperation and Conflict, 1966, No. 1, pp. 29-45.

Holst, Johan Jørgen. "Norwegian Security Policy." Cooperation and Conflict, 1966, No. 2, pp. 64-79.

Holst, Johan Jørgen. Norsk sikkerhetspolitikk i strategisk perspektiv. 2 vols. Oslo: Norsk Utenrikspolitisk Institutt, 1967. [Includes public opinion polls on security questions.]

Holsti, Ole. "The Belief System and National Images: A Case Study." Journal of Conflict Resolution, VI (September 1962) pp. 245-252.

Holsti, Ole. "The 'Operational Code' Approach to the Study of Political Leaders: John Foster Dulles' Philosphical and Instrumental Beliefs." Canadian Journal of Political Science, III (March 1970), pp. 123-157.

Hope, Francis. "To Young Scandinavians, EEC is Old Stuff." The New Statesman, November 17, 1967.

Horney, Nils. "Sa föddes SAS." Industria (Stockholm), 1966, pp. 68-112.

Hveem, Helge. International Relations and World Images. A Study of Norwegian Foreign Policy Elites. Oslo: Universitetsforlaget, 1972.

Håstad, Elis. Sveriges historia under 1900-talet. Stockholm: Aldus/Bonniers, 1958.

International Political Communities. An Anthology. Garden City, N.Y.: Anchor Books, 1966.

Internasjonal Politikk (Issue on "Nordisk balans") 1966, No. 5.

Internasjonal Politikk, 1968, No. 1. "En nordisk økonomisk alternativ?" (whole issue.)

Internasjonal Politikk (Oslo). (Articles commenting on J. Christophersen), 1968, No. 7, pp. 701-763; 1969, No. 6, pp. 664-760.

Internasjonal Politikk (Oslo). "Scandinavia i EEC uten Storbrittania?" (Articles replying to V. Angell) 1969, No. 6, pp. 761-776.

Jacobsen, Knut. "Voting Behavior of the Nordic Countries in the General Assembly." Cooperation and Conflict, 1967, Nos. 3-4, pp. 139-157.

Jenkins, David. Sweden: The Progress Machine, London: R. Hale, 1968.

Jervis, Robert. "Hypotheses on Misperception." World Politics, XX, No. 3 (April 1968), pp. 454-479.

Jervis, Robert. "The Costs of the Quantitative Study of International Relations," in Contending Approaches to International Politics. Edited by Klaus Knorr and James Rosenau. Princeton: Princeton University Press, 1969, pp. 177-242.

Jervis, Robert. "Consistency in Foreign Policy Views" in Richard Merritt (ed.) Communications in International Politics, Urbana, Illinois: The University of Illinois Press, 1972, pp. 272-294.

Jones, Joseph M. The Fifteen Weeks (February 21-June 5, 1947). New York: Viking Press, 1955.

Kaiser, Karl. "The Interaction of Regional Subsystems: Some Preliminary Notes on Recurrent Patterns and the Role of the Superpowers." World Politics, XXI, No. 1 (October 1968), pp. 84-101.

Kalela, Jaakko. "The Nordic Group in the General Assembly." Cooperation and Conflict, 1967, Nos. 3-4, pp. 158-170.

Kellgren, Nils. "Nordiskt ekonomiskt samarbete." Fackföreningsrörelse, 1951, No. 47, pp. 468-473.

Kelman, Steven. "Letter from Stockholm." The New Yorker, December 26, 1970, pp. 36-48.

Kennan, George F. Memoirs 1925-1950. Boston: Little, Brown, 1967.

Koblick, Steven. "Wartime Diplomacy and the Democratization of Sweden in September-October 1917." Journal of Modern History, Vol. 41, (1969), pp. 29-45.

Koblick, Steven (ed.), Sweden's Development from Poverty to Affluence 1750-1970 (translated by Joanne Johnson), Minneapolis: University of Minnesota Press, 1975. (Swedish edition, Stockholm: Wahlström and Widstrand, 1973.)

Kogan, Nathan, and Michael A. Wallach. Risk Taking. A Study in Cognition and Personality. New York: Holt, Rinehart, and Winston, 1964.

"Kontaktmandsseminar." Nordisk udredningsserie, 1966, No. 6.

Kristensen, Thorkil. "Danish Economy." Scandinavia Past and Present, III, pp. 465-476.

Kurth, James, R. "A Widening Gyre: The Logic of American Weapons Procurement", Public Policy XIX No. 3 (Summer 1971), pp. 373-404.

Kvavik, Robert B. Interest Groups in Norwegian Politics, Oslo: Universitetsforlaget, 1976.

Lafferty, William M. Economic Development and the Response of Labor in Scandinavia. A Multi-Level Analysis. (Oslo: Universitetsforlaget, 1971.)

Lange, Christian. "Nordisk offentlig samarbeid--en regional integrasjonsprosess?" Internasjonal Politikk (Oslo) 1965, No. 2, pp. 151-164.

Lange, Halvard. "Internasjonale Innslag i Norsk Arbeiderbevegelse i 90-årene." Festskrift til Halvdan Koht på sekstiårsdagen 7de juli 1933 i Oslo. Oslo: Aschehoug, 1933, pp. 321-329.

Lange, Halvard. "European Union: False Hopes and Realities." Foreign Affairs, XXIII (April 1950), pp. 441-450.

Lange, Halvard. Norsk utenrikspolitikk siden 1945. (Foredrag og debattinnlegg.) Oslo: Johan Grundt Tanum, 1952.

Lange, Halvard. "Scandinavian Cooperation in International Affairs." International Affairs (London), July 1954, pp. 285-293.

Lange, Halvard. Norges vei til Nato. Oslo: Pax Forlag, 1966.

Langfeldt, Knut. Moskva-tesene i norsk politikk. Oslo: Universitetsforlaget, 1961.

Larsen, David L. "Marshall-planen og Norge", Internasjonal politikk 1972, vol. 2, pp. 251-275.

Larssen, Olav. Sti gjennom ulendt terreng. Laeretid, partistrid, ny vekst. Oslo: Aschehoug, 1969.

Larssen, Olav. Den langsomme revolusjonen. Oslo: Aschehoug, 1973.

Lauwerys, Joseph A. (ed.) Development of Democratic Thought and Institutions in Denmark, Norway, and Sweden. New York and Copenhagen, 1959.

Lehmann, Johannes, (ed.). Nordisk Samarbejde. Tre taler i idraetshuset 5 december 1934 af Per Albin Hansson, Johan Nygaardsvold, Thorvald Stauning. Copenhagen, Poul Branner, 1943.

Leiserson, Mark W. "A Brief Interpretive Survey of Wage-Price Problems in Europe." Study Paper No. 11, Joint Economic Committee, Congress of the United States, 86th Congress, 1st Session, Washington, D.C., pp. 33-60.

Lewin, Leif. Planhushållningsdebatten. (Skrifter utgivna av Statsvetenskapliga föreningen i Uppsala, XLVI.) Stockholm: Almqvist & Wiksell, 1967.

Lindström, Jan-Erik, and Claes Wiklund. "The Nordic Countries in the General Assembly and its two Political Committees." Cooperation and Conflict, 1967, Nos. 3-4, pp. 171-187.

Lie, Trygve. Hjemover. Oslo: Tiden, 1968.

Lieber, Robert J. British Politics and European Unity: Parties, Elites, and Pressure Groups. Berkeley: The University of California Press, 1970.

Lieberman, Sara. The Industrialization of Norway 1800-1920. Oslo: Universitetsforlaget, 1970.

Lijphart, Arend. The Politics of Accommodation: Pluralism and Democracy in the Netherlands. Berkeley, California: The University of California Press, 1968.

Lindberg, Leon N. and Stuart A. Scheingold. Europe's Would-Be Policy, Patterns of Change in the European Community. Englewood Cliffs, N.J.: Prentice-Hall, 1970.

Lindgren, Raymond E. Norway-Sweden, Union, Disunion, and Scandinavian Integration. Princeton, N.J.: Princeton University Press, 1959.

Lippmann, Walter. U.S. Foreign Policy. Shield of the Republic. New York: Pocket Books, 1943.

Lorenz, Einhart (ed.). Norsk sosialisme. En dokumentasjon. Oslo: Pax Forlag, 1970.

Lowi, Theodore J. "American Business, Public Policy, Case Studies, and Political Theory." World Politics, XVI (July 1964), pp. 677-715.

Lowi, Theodore J. "Making Democracy Safe for the World: National Politics and Foreign Policy." Domestic Sources of Foreign Policy. Edited by James Rosenau. New York: The Free Press, 1967, pp. 314-323.

Lundström, Hans O. Capital Movements and Economic Integration. Leyden: A.W. Sijthoff, 1967.

Lüning, Nils. "Police Systems in the Scandinavian Countries." Scandinavia Past and Present, 1959, Vol. III, pp. 122-124.

Löchen, Einar. "Mål och medel i nordiskt samarbete." Nordisk kontakt, 1967, No. 1, pp. 3-4.

Mackay, Donald M. "The Informational Analysis of Questions and Comments", in Modern Systems Research for the Behavioral Scientist: A Source-book. Chicago: Aldine Publishing Co., 1968.

Malmström, Vincent II. "The Norwegian State Railroads--1854-1954." The American Scandinavian Review, XLII, No. 3 (September 1954.)

Meissner, Frank. "Scandinavian Customs Union." The Norseman, July-August 1954, pp. 246-254.

Mellom nøytrale og allierte. Norge og den 2. verdenskrig. Studier i norsk samtidshistorie. Oslo: Universitetsforlaget, 1968.

Miller, Kenneth E. Government and Politics in Denmark. Boston: Houghton Mifflin, 1968.

MM. "En ambassadør vender hjem" [about Rolf Edberg]. Dagbladet, 28 October 1967.

Moberg, Erik. "The 'Nordic Balance' Concept." Cooperation and Conflict, 1968, No. 3, pp. 210-213.

Montgomery, Arthur. "From a Northern Customs Union to EFTA." The Scandinavian Economic History Review, VIII, Nos. 1-2 (1960), pp. 45-70.

Morgenstierne, Wilhelm M. "The Atlantic Pact: A Norwegian Point of View." Proceedings of the Academy of Political Science (XXIII, No. 3 (1949), pp. 325-330.

Nelson, Robert A. "Scandinavian Airlines System: Cooperation in the Air." Journal of Air Law and Commerce, XX (1963), pp. 178-196.

Neustadt, Richard E. Alliance Politics. New York: Columbia University Press, 1970.

"New Paths for Sweden. A Special Survey." The Economist (London), 28 October-3 November 1967.

Nielsson, Gunnar P. "The Nordic and Continental European Dimensions in Scandinavian Integration: Nordek as a Case Study." Cooperation and Conflict, 1971, Nos. 3-4, pp. 173-181.

Nilson, Sten Sparre. "Valuation: The Basis of Foreign Policy Decision-Making." Cooperation and Conflict, 1969, No. 2, pp. 99-118.

Nilstein, Arne H. "Sweden." White Collar Trade Unions. Edited by A. Sturmthal. Urbana, Illinois, and London: The University of Illinois Press, 1966, pp. 261-304.

Nordahl, Konrad. Minner og meninger. Oslo: Tiden norsk forlag, 1967.

Nordahl, Konrad. Med Lo i friheten. Oslo: Tiden norsk forlag, 1969.

"Norden og Vestblokken." Fremtiden (Copenhagen) III, No. 7 (July 1948), (Whole issue); III, No. 10 (October 1948), pp. 27-34.

"Nordic Cooperation." Conference Organised by the Nordic Council for International Organisations in Europe. Hässelby 2-4 June 1965. Stockholm: 1965. Nordisk udredningsserie, 1965, No. 9.

"Nordic Economic and Social Cooperation." Second Conference Organized by the Nordic Council for International Organizations in Europe. Imatra 28-30 September, 1967. Nordisk udredningsserie, 1968, No. 9.

Nordisk udredningsserie. "Nordiska rådets verksamhet 1952-1961", 1962, No. 8.

Nordisk udredningsserie. "Översikt över lagar tillkomna genom nordiskt samarbete", 1965, No. 2.

Nordisk udredningsserie. "Nordic Cooperation", 1965, No. 9.

Nordisk udredningsserie. "Kontaktmandsseminar", 1966, No. 6.

Nordisk udredningsserie. "Nordic Economic and Social Cooperation", 1968, No. 9.

Nordiske Muligheder, Afhandlinger udgivet af Foreningen Norden, Dansk Forening for Nordisk Samarbejde. Copenhagen: 1943.

North, Robert. "Research Pluralism and the International Elephant." Contending Approaches to International Politics. Edited by Klaus Knorr and James Rosenau. Princeton: Princeton University Press, 1969, pp. 218-242.

Nye, Joseph S. Jr. "Corruption and Political Development: A Cost-Benefit Analysis". The American Political Science Review, LXI, No. 2 (1967), pp. 417-427.

Nye, Joseph S. Jr. "Patterns and Catalysts in Regional Integration." International Regionalism. Edited by Joseph S. Nye Jr. Boston: Little, Brown, 1968.

Nye, Joseph S. Jr. "Comparative Regional Integration." International Organization, XXII, No. 4 (Autumn 1968), pp. 855-880.

Nye, Joseph S. Jr. Peace in Parts. Integration and Conflict in Regional Organization. Boston: Little, Brown and Co., 1971.

Olson, Mancur Jr. The Logic of Collective Action. Public Goods and the Theory of Groups. Cambridge, Mass.: Harvard University Press, 1965.

Olson, Mancur Jr. "Economics, Sociology, and the Best of All Possible Worlds." The Public Interest, No. 12 (Summer 1968), pp. 96-118.

Olson, Mancur Jr. and Richard Zeckhauser. "An Economic Theory of Alliances". Review of Economics and Statistics, 48 (1966), pp. 266-279.

Ording, Arne. "Norwegian Foreign Policy." (A review of Halvard Lange, Norsk utenrikspolitikk siden 1945). The Norseman. XI (1953), pp. 73-76.

Ortmark, Åke. Maktspelet i Sverige. Ett samhällsreportage. Stockholm: Widstrand, 1967.

Padelford, Norman J. "Regional Cooperation in Scandinavia." International Organization, XI (1957), pp. 597-614.

Puchala, Donald J. "International Transactions and Regional Integration". International Organization, Vol. XXIV, No. 4 (Autumn 1970), pp. 732-763.

Rapoport, Anatole. Fights, Games, and Debates. Ann Arbor: The University of Michigan Press, 1960.

Reske Nielsen, Erik, and Erik Kragh. Atlantpagten og Danmark 1949-1962. Copenhagen: 1962.

Riker, W.H. The Theory of Political Coalitions. New Haven, Conn.: Yale University Press, 1962.

Riste, Olav. "Alliansepolitikk og brubyggning". (Review of Udgaard, Great Power Politics) Historisk tidskrift, September 1973.

Riste, Olav. London-Regjeringa. Norge i krigsalliansen 1940-1945. Vol. I, Oslo: Det norske samlaget, (Forsvarets krigshistoriske avdeling) 1973.

Robertson, A.H. The Council of Europe. Its Structure, Functions, and Achievements. London: Stevens & Sons, Ltd., 1961.

Rokkan, Stein. "Numerical Democracy and Corporate Pluralism." Political Oppositions in Western Democracies. Edited by Robert A. Dahl. New Haven and London: Yale University Press, 1966, pp. 70-115.

Rokkan, Stein. "Geography, Religion, and Social Class: Cross-cutting Cleavages in Norwegian Politics." Party Systems and Voter Alignments, Cross-National Perspectives. Edited by Stein Rokkan and Seymour M. Lipset. London: Collier-Macmillan Limited, New York: The Free Press, 1967, pp. 415-425.

Rokkan, Stein. "Electoral Systems." International Encyclopedia of the Social Sciences. David L. Sills (ed.), XII. New York: The Macmillan Company and The Free Press, 17 vols., 1968.

Rokkan, Stein, and Henry Valen. "Regional Contrasts in Norwegian Politics." Cleavages, Ideologies, and Party Systems. Edited by Erik Allardt and Yrjo Littunen. Helsinki: Westermarck Society, 1964, pp. 162-238.

Ross, Arthur M. Trade Union Wage Policy. Berkeley and Los Angeles: The University of California Press, 1950.

Russett, Bruce. Economic Theories of International Politics. Chicago: Markham, 1968.

Rustow, Dankwart A. The Politics of Compromise: A Study of Parties, and Cabinet Government in Sweden. Princeton, N.J.: Princeton University Press, 1955.

Ryding, Göran. "Nordisk ekonomisk samverkan." Nordisk Kontakt, 1967, No. 1, pp. 63-67.

Sainsbury, Diane. "A Critique of Leif Lewin's Planhushållningsdebatten." Statsvetenskaplig tidskrift (Stockholm) 1968, No. 2, pp. 109-125.

Sanness, John. "Huvuddragen av Norges historia." Norge ockuperat och fritt. Stockholm: Kooperative Forbundet, 1943.

Sanness, John. "Norge uten komplekser." [on Lange's significance for Norway]. Arbeiderbladet, 20 May 1970.

Scandinavia Past and Present. 3 vols. Odense, Denmark: 1959.

Scandinavian Political Studies. Universitetsforlaget and New York: Columbia University Press, Vol. 1, 1966 and Vol. 8, 1973.

Schelling, Thomas. The Strategy of Conflict. Cambridge, Mass.: Harvard University Press, 1960.

Schelling, Thomas. Arms and Influence. New Haven: Yale University Press, 1966.

Schelling, Thomas. "The Ecology of Micromotives". The Public Interest, No. 25 (Fall 1971).

Schmidt, Folke, and Stig Strömholm. Legal Values in Modern Sweden. Stockholm: 1964: Totowa, N.J.: Bedminister Press, 1965.

Schwartz, David (ed.). Svenska minoriteter. En handbok som kartlägger invandringspolitiken och befolkningsminoriteternas ställning inom det svenska samhället. Stockholm: Aldus/Bonniers, 1966.

Seip, Helge. "Social and Economic Problems in Connection with the Nordic Labour Market." Nordisk udredningsserie, 1968, No. 9, pp. 45-56. (Issue "Nordic Economic and Social Cooperation").

Seip, Jens Arup. Et regime foran undergangen. Oslo: (Johan Grundt Tanum Forlag, 1945) Gyldendal Norsk Forlag, 1965.

Selznick, Philip. Leadership in Administration. A Sociological Interpretation. New York: Harper & Row, 1957.

Sharkansky, Ira. "Regional Pattern in the Expenditures of American States." Western Political Quarterly, Vol. 20 (December 1967).

Shonfield, Andrew. Modern Capitalism. The Changing Balance of Public and Private Power. New York and London: Oxford University Press, 1965.

Singer, J. David. "Inter-Nation Influence: A Formal Model." The American Political Science Review, LVII (1963), pp. 420-430.

Siotis, Jean. "The Secretariat of the United Nations Economic Commission for Europe and European Integration: The First Ten Years." International Organization XIX, No. 2 (1969), pp. 177-202.

Sjøqvist, Viggo. Danmarks udenrigspolitik 1933-1940. (Udgiverselskab for Danmarks nyeste historie) Copenhagen: Gyldendal, 1966.

Skodvin, Magne. "Norge" ("De nordiska ländernas utrikespolitik 1939-41"). Finska Historiska Samfundet, Nordiska Historiker Mötet. Helsingfors: 1967, pp. 139-169.

Skodvin, Magne. Norden eller Nato? Utenriksdepartementet og alliansespørsmalet 1947-1949. Oslo: Universitetsforlaget, 1971.

Sletten, Vegard. Five Northern Countries Pull Together. Published by The Nordic Council and under the auspices of the Ministries of Foreign Affairs of the five Nordic countries.

Snyder, Glenn H. Deterrence and Defense. Toward a Throry of National Security. Princeton: Princeton University Press, 1961.

Spiro, Herbert J. Government by Constitution: The Political Systems of Democracy. New York: Random House, 1959.

Sproule-Jones, Mark. "Strategic Tensions in the Scale of Political Analysis: An Essay for Philomphalasceptics". British Journal of Political Science, I, pp. 173-191.

Stahl, Ivar. "Scandinavian Cooperation in the Field of Legislation". Scandinavia Past and Present, Vol. III, pp. 113-117.

Stahl, Ivar. "The Scandinavian Jurists' Congresses," Scandinavia Past and Present, Vol. III, pp. 118-121.

Stehower, Jan. "Long Term Ecological Analysis of Electoral Statistics in Denmark." Scandinavian Political Studies, II (1967), pp. 94-116.

Stein, Janice Gross. "L'Analyse de la politique étrangère: à la recherche de groupes de variable dépendentes et indépendentes." Études Internationales. III, No. 3 (September 1971), pp. 371-394.

Steinbruner, John D. The Cybernetic Theory of Decision. New Dimensions of Political Analysis. Princeton, N.J.: Princeton University Press,1974.

Stenstadvold, K. "Langtidsplan for Nordforsk." Nordisk udredningsserie, 1968, No. 11.

Stjernqvist, Nils. "Sweden: Stability or Deadlock?" Political Oppositions in Western Democracies. Edited by Robert A. Dahl. New Haven and London: Yale University Press, 1966, pp. 116-146.

Stonehill, Arthur. Foreign Ownership in Norwegian Enterprises. Oslo: Statistisk Sentralbyrå (Samfunnsøkonomiske studier nr. 14), 1965.

Storing, James A. Norwegian Democracy. Oslo: Universitetsforlaget, 1963.

Sundelius, Bengt. "Nordic Cooperation: Dead or Alive?", Scandinavian Review 64:2 (June 1976) pp. 46-50

Särlvik, Bo. "Political Stability and Change in the Swedish Electorate." Scandinavian Political Studies. A Yearbook Published by the Political Science Associations in Denmark, Finland, Norway, and Sweden, I (1966), pp. 188-224.

Söderpalm, Sven Anders, "The Crisis Agreement and the Social Democratic Road to Power" in Steven Koblick, (ed.), Sweden's Development from Poverty to Affluence 1750-1970, (translated by Joanne Johnson), Minneapolis: University of Minnesota Press, 1975, pp. 258-278. (Swedish edition: Stockholm: Wahlström and Widstrand, 1973, pp. 235-257.)

Sømme, Axel. A Geography of Norden: Denmark, Finland, Iceland, Norway, Sweden. Oslo: 1960, London: 1961.

Tingsten, Herbert. The Swedish Social Democrats. Totowa, N.J.: Bedminister Press, 1974. (Den svenska socialdemokratiens idéutveckling. Stockholm: Tidens Forlag, 2 vols. 1941).

Tingsten, Herbert. Mitt liv 1946-52. Stockholm: Bonniers, 1963.

Tingsten, Herbert. Tredje Standpunkten--en Orimlighet. Stockholm: Bonniers, 1951.

Tomasson, Richard F. Sweden: Prototype of Modern Society. New York: Random House, 1970.

Torgersen, Ulf. "Borgerkrigen som ble vekk." Tidskrift for samfunnsforskning, 1967, Nos. 2-3, pp. 247-255.

Torgersen, Ulf. "Political Institutions" in Norwegian Society. Edited by Natalie Rogoff Ramsøy. Oslo: Universitetsforlaget, London: C. Hurst and Co.., New York: Humanities Press, 1974, pp. 194-225. (Det Norske Samfunn, Oslo: Gyldendal Norsk Forlag, 1968).

Torsvik, Tomas. "Politisk vinter i Finnland." Samtiden, Vol. 71, Nos. 2 (1962), pp. 63-73.

Torsvik, Tomas. 15 års i Nato. Oslo: Forsvarets Presstjenste. 1964.

Truman, Harry S. Memoirs, Vol. II ("Years of Trial and Hope, 1946-1952"), (1956), Signet, 1965.

Udgaard, Nils Morten. "Utenrikspolitikk og Forestillingsverden." [A review of Burgess.] Aftenposten (Oslo), January 7, 1969.

Udgaard, Nils Morten. "Ingen krigspanikk da Norge gikk inn i NATO. Skodvin om Langes Washington-møter." Aftenposten, 3 December 1969.

Udgaard, Nils Morten. Great Power Politics and Norwegian Foreign Policy. A Study of Norway's Foreign Relations November 1940-February 1948. Oslo: Universitetsforlaget, 1973.

Ulsaker, Berger. "Det Nordiske Arbeidsmarkedsutvalg." Arbeidsmarkedet, Utgitt av Arbeidsdirektoratet, September 1960, pp. 3-5.

Undén, Östen. "Pressdebatt om utrikespolitiken." Tiden (Stockholm) May 1948, pp. 268-271.

Undén, Östen. Sveriges utrikespolitik. Printed speech. (Tal i Riksdagen den 4 februar 1948), Stockholm: Tidens forlag, 1948.

Undén, Östen. Minnesanteckningar. Stockholm: Bonniers, 1966.

Valen, Henry and Daniel Katz. Political Parties in Norway. A Community Study. Oslo: Universitetsforlaget, 1964.

Valen, Henry and Willy Martinussen, in cooperation with Philip E. Converse and Daniel Katz. Velgere og politiske frontlinjer, Stemmegivning og stridsspørsmal 1957-1969. Oslo, Norway: Gyldendal norsk forlag, 1972.

Verney, Douglas, "The Foundations of Modern Sweden: The Swift Rise and Fall of Swedish Liberalism", Political Studies March 1972, pp. 42-59.

Vickers, Sir Geoffrey. The Art of Judgement. New York: Basic Books, 1965.

Wahlbäck, Krister. Norden och blockuppdelningen 1948-49. Stockholm: Utrikespolitiska institutet, [Internationalla studier,] 1973.

Waldemarsson, Axel. "Norden och de yttre sju." Svenska Dagbladets årsbok 1959, Stockholm: 1960, pp. 73-76.

Walker, Jack L. "The Diffusion of Innovations Among the American States." The American Political Science Review, LXIII (September 1969), pp. 880-899.

Wallmén, Olof. Nordiska rådet och nordiskt samarbete. Stockholm: Norstedt, 1966.

Walton, Richard E., and Robert B. McKersie. A Behavioral Theory of Labor Negotiations. An Analysis of a Social Interaction System. New York: McGraw Hill, 1965.

Weinwurm, Ernest H. "Measuring Uncertainty in Managerial Decision-Making." Management International, III, No. 4 (1963), pp. 114-122.

Wendt, Frantz. "The Norden Association," in Scandinavia Past and Present, Vol. III, pp. 49-54.

Wendt, Frantz. The Nordic Council and Cooperation in Scandinavia. Copenhagen: Munksgaard, 1959.

Wendt, Frantz. Danmarks historia. Edited by John Danstrup and Hal Koch. Vol. XIV. ("Besaettelse og Atomtid 1939-1965"). Copenhagen: Politikens forlag, 1966.

Westergård Andersen, Harald. Dansk Politik i Går og i Dag 1920-66. Copenhagen: Fremads Focusbøger, 1966.

Wigforss, Harald. "Sweden and the Atlantic Pact." International Organization, III (August 1949), pp. 434-443.

Wiklund, Claes. "The Zig-Zag Course of the Nordek Negotiations." Scandinavian Political Studies, 1970, No. 5, pp. 307-335.

Wilson, James Q. "The Bureaucracy Problem", The Public Interest No. 6 (1967), pp. 3-9.

Wilson, James Q. Political Organizations. New York: Basic Books, 1973.

Wuorinen, John H. "Scandinavia and the Rise of Modern National Consciousness." Nationalism and Internationalism, Essays inscribed to Carlton J.H. Hayes. Edited by Eric M. Earle.

Wyller, Thomas Chr. Frigjøringspolitikk. Regeringsskiftet sommeren 1945. Oslo: Universitetsforlaget, 1963.

Wyller, Thomas Chr. Nyordning og Motstand. En framstilling og en analyse av organisasjonenes politiske funksjon under den tyske okkupasjonene 25.9.40--25.9.42. (English summary) Oslo: Universitetsforlaget, 1958.

Zachariassen, Aksel. Fra Marcus Thrane til Martin Trammael. Oslo: Arbeidernes Opplysningsforbund, 1962.

Zeckhauser, Richard and Elmer Schaefer. "Public Policy and Normative Economic Theory". The Study of Policy Formation, (Raymond A. Bauer & Kenneth J. Gergen, eds.) New York: Free Press, 1968, pp. 27-101.

Ørvik, Nils. The Decline of Neutrality, 1914-1941. Oslo: Johan Grundt Tanum Forlag, 1953.

Ørvik, Nils. Trends in Norwegian Foreign Policy. Oslo: Institute of International Affairs, 1962.

Ørvik, Nils. "Integration for Whom, against Whom?" Cooperation and Conflict, 1967, No. 1, pp. 54-59.

Ørvik, Nils. "Base Policy--Theory and Practice". Cooperation and Conflict, 1967, Nos. 3-4, pp. 198-204.

Ørvik, Nils (ed.). Fears and Expectations. Norwegian Attitudes toward European Integration. Oslo: Universitetsforlaget, 1972.

Ørvik, Nils. "Nordic Cooperation and High Politics". International Organization 28:1 (Winter 1974) pp. 61-88.